Social Control

Social Control

An Introduction

JAMES J. CHRISS

polity

First published in 2007 by Polity Press

Reprinted in 2008

Polity Press
65 Bridge Street
Cambridge CB2 1UR, UK

Polity Press
350 Main Street
Malden, MA 02148, USA

ISBN-10: 0-7456-3857-0
ISBN-13: 978-07456-3857-7
ISBN-10: 0-7456-3858-9 (pb)
ISBN-13: 978-07456-3858-4 (pb)

A catalogue record for this book is available from the British
Library.

Typeset in 9.5 on 12pt Utopia
by Servis Filmsetting Ltd, Longsight, Manchester
Printed and bound in the United States of America by Maple-Vail

The publisher has used its best endeavours to ensure that
the URLs for external websites referred to in this book are
correct and active at the time of going to press. However, the
publisher has no responsibility for the websites and can
make no guarantee that a site will remain live or that the
content is or will remain appropriate.

Every effort has been made to trace all copyright holders,
but if any have been inadvertently overlooked the publisher
will be pleased to include any necessary credits in any
subsequent reprint or edition.

For further information on Polity, visit our website:
www.polity.co.uk

Contents

Acknowledgments

There are a number of persons I wish to thank for contributing to the production of this book.

First off, I would like to thank the Department of Sociology at Cleveland State University for granting me a sabbatical during the fall semester of 2005. This time off from teaching and administrative duties allowed for substantial progress to be made on the writing of the manuscript.

Second, I would like to thank various friends and colleagues, both near and far, who provided stimulation and feedback concerning the major themes and issues of social control with which I was grappling. In the Cleveland State Department of Sociology these persons include Phil Manning, Dana Hubbard, Teresa LaGrange, and Wendy Regoeczi. And, from outside the department, a list of individuals who provided feedback in some form includes Peter Conrad, Elianne Riska, Donald Black, and Steve Herbert.

Third, I would like to thank Emma Longstaff at Polity Press, whose editorial work on the book was both tenacious and effective. Although at times I was not happy with her and reviewers' suggestions for revisions, once I worked through them – but not all of them, mind you – they actually made the book better. So she apparently did her job, and did it quite well.

Last but certainly not least, I would like to thank my family, Mandana, Ariana, and Johnny, for providing a constant source of love, support, and inspiration.

Introduction

What are we to make of Stanley Cohen's assertion that social control has become a "Mickey Mouse" concept in sociology and the broader social sciences?[1] What Cohen meant by this is that, because it is used so extensively to cover so many things, the concept "social control" has no clear meaning at all. It is simply a catch-all phrase for explaining all the ways conformity is induced in human beings.

That there is a vast array of mechanisms and procedures in place for attempting to do just that – to extract compliance of individuals or groups to some ideal standard of conduct, whether this takes place at home, in the factory, in school, within personal relations, at the doctor's office, while driving a car, or at the stadium watching a ballgame – is undeniable. Indeed, as anthropologist Siegfried Nadel argued, "In this sense control is simply coterminous with society, and in examining the former we simply describe the latter."[2] The study of social control is the study of how society patterns and regulates individual behavior.[3] So, in response to Cohen, why should the extensiveness of a procedure, practice, or process render the study of that procedure, practice, or process somehow problematic or even futile?

I would argue that, even given its vastness and ubiquity, social control is very much a viable concept for sociology and other social and behavioral sciences. The study of social control can be managed by keeping in sight its basic forms. In this book, I lay out a typology of social control consisting of three main forms: legal, medical, and informal. The explanation of the derivation of this typology will be provided in chapter 2, but it should be acknowledged here that over the years a number of thinkers have developed alternative strategies for explaining social control. Two of the four strategies discussed below, by Beniger and Gibbs, are good examples of general theories of control which deal with social control as merely one type of control. The other two strategies are more micro-oriented theories which were created to deal specifically with *social* control as opposed to other kinds of control.

Four alternative approaches to control

Let us begin with the two micro- or middle-range theories of social control. In chapter 6 I examine in detail the control theory of Travis Hirschi. In fact, an earlier version of control theory was developed by F. Ivan Nye.[4] Nye's theory is similar to my own to the extent that he envisions three main types of control. It is quite different, however, in its substantive details, conceptualizing the three categories as direct, internal, and indirect control.

By *direct control,* Nye is referring to all the actual or possible restraints that can be marshaled against deviance. The category of direct control renders irrelevant the distinction I am making between formal (legal and medical) and informal control, because direct control includes such things as legal punishments, informal sanctions such as shaming and ridicule, or even parental supervision of youth. *Internal control* refers to internalization, namely, a system of socialization by which individuals are inculcated with a set of norms, values, beliefs, and rules which in effect keeps them from deviating. Finally, *indirect control* refers to the warm and secure bonds of attachment that persons feel toward conventional others. The paradigmatic example of indirect control is children's attachment to parents, and hence the family is the major source of indirect control in society.

Nye seems to be suggesting that social control boils down to sanctions (direct control), culture and socialization (internal control), and relationships (indirect control). But many sanctions are indirect, and some are meted out within the context of relationships. Also, the boundaries, if they exist at all, between internal and indirect control appear blurred and porous. For example, within the context of the family, both socialization and relationship formation occur simultaneously (ideally). Wouldn't it be more profitable to understand this nexus of activities or processes as amounting to the same kind of control, namely informal control?

The second micro-oriented theory of social control to be discussed is that of Michael Katovich. Although the connotation of control is that it is "evil" – especially in the hands of Marxists or conflict theorists, who argue that the more powerful groups in society take advantage of less powerful groups through race, class, gender, or other forms of oppression – Katovich points out that there are cooperative as well as coercive bases of control.[5] As discussed more fully in chapter 3, everyday life is held together by systems of informal control which are largely cooperative, such as those based in family life, peer and interpersonal relations, and face-to-face interaction more generally.

Katovich argues that within the micro-realm of face-to-face interaction informal control takes four basic forms: instrumental, ceremonial, interpersonal, and categorical control. *Instrumental control* refers to the fact that persons often come into contact with other persons over long periods of time to get various collective endeavors accomplished. In other words, instrumental control refers to the mutual give and take that actors exert on one another within relatively stable and persistent relationships. The kinds of cooperative arrangements indicative of instrumental control include marriages, partnerships, and organizational associations. *Ceremonial control* represents a special kind of cooperation or mutuality between actors which tends to be more fleeting and episodic than instrumental control. For example, persons who aren't closely acquainted will nevertheless provide to one another a smile, eye contact, and even a "Hi" when crossing each other's paths in public. This is done merely for the sake of establishing mutual identification and availability should the need arise. Katovich's ceremonial control is very close to Erving Goffman's notion of interaction ritual, the latter of which will be explored in more detail in chapter 3.

Interpersonal control, according to Katovich, refers to two or more persons who share a focus on some immediate social objective. They are not merely bystanders who happen to be at the same place at the same time observing some event. They invest their *selves* in the mutual project at hand. Control occurs when identities are identified, committed to, and mutually available to all participants in the project as needed. If mutual establishment of identities is not available in a particular strip of shared activity, the interpersonal control necessary to bring it to completion or fruition would be absent. Interpersonal control means that everyone is "on the same page" and understands their roles in the accomplishment of the activity or event.

Finally, *categorical control* refers to the binding together of participants on the basis of structural or categorical identities, rather than on the basis of personal identities as was the case in interpersonal control. Categorical identities refer to designations of persons on the basis of widely acknowledged social categories such as a person's age, occupation, or income level. For example, if I want to sell my home I will not do business with a person until I know that he or she is a reputable real-estate agent.

The main problem with Katovich's theory of the cooperative bases of control is that it does not get us much beyond the category of informal control, which we will be examining in much more detail in chapters 3 and 6. In other words, there is nothing particularly wrong with Katovich's four categories of control, but everything that he claims to accomplish by way of distinguishing between the four basic types of cooperative control is already covered in the much simpler and parsimonious notion of informal control.

We now turn briefly to the two grand or general theories of control. The first one to be discussed is a very broad conceptualization of control developed by James Beniger.[6] Beniger suggests that, from the beginning of life on earth (more than one billion years ago), there have developed four levels of control. The *first level* represents the emergence of organic matter and the appearance of protoplasm, namely, organisms moving about in space and time in a physical environment. All life is a struggle for existence, and organisms that are best able to adjust to their environments – that is, that are able to control themselves and any available resources – are the fittest for purposes of survival of their species.

Level two, which appeared on the scene about 100 million years ago, is the emergence of patterned behavior through imitation. Most sentient beings, above the level of the insects, engage in some form of imitation. Over the millennia, however, rote imitation was supplemented by learning by teaching, and with the rapid increase in brain size after the divergence of hominids and apes (which occurred some ten million years ago), humans developed linguistic systems which in turn increased teaching, learning, memory, and hence control exponentially. The creation of culture, characteristic of *Homo sapiens*, is an important step forward toward greater control of the environment and fellow beings at this level.

Level three, which occurred with the Neolithic or agricultural revolution (beginning about 5,000 years ago but accelerating with the rise of philosophy and science in Greece around 300 BC), vastly increased the need to organize activities associated with the production of food. Greater food productivity leads to larger populations, as well as greater stratification, to the extent that some persons are now in positions to reap the benefits of the economic surplus created by this mode of production. The rise of the formal organization, or the bureaucracy, begins here as well but increases rapidly with the take-off point, which is the Commercial Revolution (about 450 years ago).

Finally, *level four* represents the transition from agriculture to industry as the major mode of production (beginning about 175 years ago). The Industrial Revolution leads to an acceleration of technological innovations (such as the railroads, the telegraph, and the harnessing of steam power and electricity), all of which lead to greater control of the natural and built environment. With the emergence of computers in the 1950s and the rapid acceleration of related information technologies since then (culminating in such things as the Internet as well as medical and genetic programming technologies), information itself becomes the basis of the new Control Revolution.

Within this developmental timeline, human social control is understood as merely one species of control which sentient beings have always produced and which they continue to produce in new forms over time. As one can see, however, this broad panoramic sweep of the whole of earth history leaves the case of human control somewhat on the back doorstep. There is no doubt that the sketching out of this grand backdrop can be useful for understanding how we got from there to here, but it cannot be the focal point for explaining what social control is and how it operates in the here and now.

A second grand theory of control has been developed by Jack Gibbs, but it is somewhat more manageable than the all-encompassing perspective of Beniger, and parts of it are directly related to issues of social control.[7] At the grandest, most abstract level of his theoretical system, Gibbs argues there are three basic forms of control: inanimate, biotic, and human. *Inanimate control* is the human attempt to control, modify, or affect an inanimate object or its characteristics. Examples include throwing a rock to ward off a predator, as well as many forms of technology, the development and creation of which, after all, are attempts by humans to gain greater control over their environment (as Beniger similarly argued).

Biotic control is the human attempt to alter, affect, or change the characteristics of plant or animal organisms. Examples include food quests, the creation and maintenance of monoculture forests, and the use of animals for various purposes, including transportation, as beasts of burden, in medical research, or even in warfare. This means, for example, that genetic engineering would fall under biotic control.

The third category, *human control*, amounts to the diverse ways humans attempt to control human behavior. Within human control there are two subcategories: internal and external control. *Internal* human control equates simply to self-control. Going on a diet to lose weight, changing jobs to reduce depression or increase salary, or even trying to stop smoking are all examples of self-control, according to Gibbs.[8]

External human control refers to the human attempt to control the behavior of human beings, excluding self-control (which is covered under internal control). External control consists of three subcategories, which are proximate, sequential, and social control. *Proximate control* refers to attempts at direct or unmediated control of other human beings. Examples include coming into physical contact with another person (a pat on the back, a kiss, or an assault) or acts that do not require direct contact, such as inviting someone over for dinner, saying hello, or hailing a cab.

The category of *sequential control* is necessitated because not all social life is conducted in face-to-face settings with co-present others. That is, often persons try to control others when there is spatial distance between the parties. Examples of sequential control include the chain of command in the military, use of communications technologies such as the telephone or the Internet, or person-to-person communications dispersed across social networks.

With regard to the category of *social control*, Gibbs breaks from the traditional understanding of the term, which typically emphasizes norms and conceptualizes control as the counteraction of deviance. In contrast, Gibbs believes defining deviance and social control with reference to norms is overly narrow, primarily because such an approach cannot account for large-scale attempts at social control such as mass media advertising or state terrorism. Gibbs attempts to overcome the deficiencies of traditional approaches by defining attempted social control as

> overt behavior by a human, the first party, in the belief that (1) the overt behavior increases or decreases the probability of a change in the behavior of another human or humans, the second party in either case; (2) the overt behavior involves a third party but not in the way of sequential control; and (3) the increase or decrease is desirable.[9]

The main thing to note about Gibbs's theory of control is that the typology is generated on the basis of the *objects* of control. To summarize, control efforts aimed at inanimate objects is inanimate control, control efforts aimed at biological organisms (other than human) is biotic control, while control efforts aimed at human beings is human control. Within human control, control efforts aimed at oneself is internal control, while control efforts aimed at other humans is external control. Finally, external human control may be in the form of proximate control, sequential control, or social control. Notice also that, according to Gibbs's definition, social control must always involve at least three parties (but not in the way of sequential control). This leads to some complexity in that there are five different types of social control, namely referential, allegative, vicarious, modulative, and prelusive control.

In order to better understand Gibbs's theory of social control, some concrete examples of referential social control are provided here. In referential social control, the first party makes reference to a third party in order to influence the behavior of a second party. So, for example, a little boy might tell his brother, "Give me back my candy or I'll tell mother!"[10] Not all referential social control occurs at the small-group or micro-level, however. For example, law is a type of referential control according to Gibbs. In the courtroom lawyers direct their arguments to a third party (the judge, the jury, and a mass public if the trial is being televised) in an effort to win a conviction against the defendant, the second party.

Creating a general theory of control on the basis of the objects of control is ingenious, but Gibbs's system may also be too radical for purposes of social control specifically. One source of radicalism is Gibbs's rejection of the traditional emphasis on norms, which we have already discussed. Another, perhaps even more important aspect of this radicalism is that the complexity of social control itself, with its five types, may discourage any attempt to utilize or test the theory within the research setting. Finally, the notion that social control occurs only in situations involving three or more parties appears to exclude from consideration or treatment a vast array of dyadic, or two-party, control situations. Gibbs's solution is simply to treat such dyadic situations as proximate control, a move which makes sense only with a full-blown commitment to his theory of control.

A brief overview of the book

As a broad introduction to social control, with emphasis placed on the development and utilization of the concept as it has appeared within both classical and contemporary sociology, in this book it is impossible to get into the detail needed to fully explore Nye's, Katovich's, Beniger's, or Gibbs's theories. Nevertheless, exposure to the basic outlines of their approaches by way of this preface is useful for any student of social control.

This book may profitably be used at the undergraduate or beginning graduate level, in a wide variety of courses including of course social control, but also deviance, juvenile delinquency, criminology, criminal justice, sociology of law, corrections or the sociology of prisons, the sociology of policing, and the administration of justice. It should also be noted that the topic of social control brings together literatures from a number of fields, including history, social psychology, medical sociology, sociological and criminological theory, law, criminal justice, and sociology more generally. As a consequence, the bibliography is quite large, and should be a useful reference to scholars in many of the disciplines and fields of study listed above.

Part I of the book lays out the groundwork for understanding the concept of social control, including its history and usages. As discussed in chapter 1, the early American sociologist Edward A. Ross was the first person to investigate, in sustained fashion, something called "social control," beginning with a series of articles written on the subject in 1896. It should be pointed out that, unlike Ross, most of the authors we will be investigating in this book did not set out to study social control per se. That is, a number of philosophers, political theorists, and social scientists from the 1600s onward have written about the relationship between the individual and society, and in most of these instances, although the term "social control" may never have been explicitly invoked, there nevertheless was a concern with how the individual is held in check by wider social arrangement or structures, whether in the form of the state, the family, the community, the economic system (the explicit focus of Marx's political philosophy, for example), the group or tribe, or some other regulative mechanism.

After the threefold typology of social control is established in chapter 2, separate chapters are devoted to issues and controversies associated with informal control (chapter 3), medical control (chapter 4), and legal control (chapter 5). These five chapters will provide the student with a rigorous understanding of social control as it is typically used and applied in sociological analysis.

Part II is dedicated to critical case studies in social control. Chapters 6, 7, and 8 build upon the basic groundwork established in chapters 3, 4, and 5 respectively. For example, while chapter 3 lays the foundation for an understanding of informal control, chapter 6 provides critical case studies of informal control. Because they continue to play a prominent role in modern society, race and race relations form the theme connecting the three case studies of chapter 6, as well as those of chapter 8 (on legal control). The case studies of medical control in chapter 7 focus on the control of youth and adolescence.

Chapter 9 focuses exclusively on terrorism, since it is the most pressing concern of Western democracies today. Finally, chapter 10 ponders what the future of social control may hold in light of the distortions to the social fabric which global terrorism has wrought. It also examines broad cultural, political, and social trends which, in concert with the specter of terrorism, have produced a blending of medical and legal controls, all for the avowed purpose of shoring up what is presumed to be a weakening of informal control.

Finally, at the end of each chapter I have provided suggestions for further reading consisting of five books and/or articles which are strongly recommended to readers seeking more in-depth information about the topics and issues treated therein.

PART I

UNDERSTANDING SOCIAL CONTROL

1 What is Social Control?

Introduction

Thursday July 7, 2005, started out like any other day in London, England. Large numbers of daily commuters, many of whom were using the buses and underground trains of the public transit system, were sent into a state of shock, panic, and chaos as four simultaneous bomb blasts ripped through the hustle and bustle of the early morning rush hour.[1] As of July 18, fifty-two persons were confirmed dead and some 700 injured as a result of the blasts. Although early speculation was that the bombs were set off by remote control – perhaps by using cell phones as detonation devices, as was the case in the bombings a year earlier in Madrid, Spain – it was later discovered that it had been the work of four suicide bombers. Subsequent investigations revealed that the four men were homegrown terrorists who, although not officially linked to al-Qaeda, nevertheless identified with the organization's major aims and ambitions.[2]

Two weeks later, on July 21, London was hit by yet another mass transit incident, when four explosions occurred around midday, three on underground trains and one on a bus. Since only the detonators went off, however, none of the bombs exploded and thankfully no one was killed. Nevertheless, there had been a palpable sense among Londoners over those two weeks that something in society had changed, and that was that the stability of the environment could no longer be taken for granted. Indeed, after the second incident an unprecedented number of Londoners began riding bicycles to work.

It was also likely that governmental commitment to routine camera surveillance of public places would expand even further, and that most citizens would go along with these measures in the name of public safety. In England and Wales, for example, the numbers of closed-circuit television (CCTV) surveillance cameras in use increased from only 100 in 1990 to 40,000 in 2002.[3] Although the use of CCTV systems may contribute to a decline in vehicle crime, there is no firm evidence that such systems deter violence.[4]

Nevertheless, it appeared that routine surveillance already in place had been helpful in subduing at least one of the suspects connected with the July 21 failed bombing attempt. Plainclothes officers observed a man fleeing from a residence located in an area that was already under general CCTV surveillance, and with the officers in hot pursuit the suspect ran into the Stockwell Tube train station in South London.

With shoot-to-kill orders, and in front of horrified commuters, the man was shot eight times at point-blank range. Immediately after the shooting Metropolitan Police commissioner Ian Blair announced that the slain man had been directly linked to the terrorism investigation, and for a while at least London residents were able to breathe a collective sigh of relief.

But this reassurance of the effectiveness of surveillance and police responses to the terrorist attacks did not last long. A day later it was discovered that the suspect killed in the train station was not connected to the terrorist plot after all. The man was identified as Jean Charles de Menezes, a 27-year-old Brazilian citizen, an innocent victim killed at the hands of police specially trained in identifying and responding to terrorist threats. A few days after the shooting, Brazilian protestors marched in the streets of Gonzaga – Menezes' hometown – demanding the arrest of the British officers who fired the shots. Some of the protestors held up signs denouncing British police as the "real terrorists." British officials vowed to deal "sympathetically and quickly" with a claim for compensation from the victim's family back in Brazil.[5]

Terrorism and how to combat it forms one of the most pressing issues law enforcement has ever had to face, and we will examine this in more detail in chapter 9. Not only is terrorism an extremely serious threat, the split-second decisions that law-enforcement officers have to make regarding the use of deadly force against such threats may lead to a number of high-profile mistakes, such as the one in London just discussed. This in turn leads inexorably to rounds of discussion among law-enforcement officers, legislators, scholars, policy analysts, news organizations, and the lay public over how best to deal with terrorism, as well as questions concerning whether current policies, strategies, and approaches are effective or perhaps even harmful in some respects. Indeed, since the passage of the USA PATRIOT Act in 2001 and the creation of the Department of Homeland Security, there has been much talk of the erosion of privacy, civil liberties, and the circumventing of due process in the name of assuring the security and public safety of American citizens.

Terrorism and ideas about how best to combat it illustrate in vivid detail the central preoccupation with social control in modern society. The study of *social control* – namely, all those mechanisms and resources by which members of society attempt to assure the norm-conforming behavior of others – is almost as old as the discipline of sociology itself. If we mark the beginning of scientific sociology with the publication of Lester Ward's *Dynamic Sociology* in 1883, social control did not appear as a specific and sustained focus for sociological analysis until about thirteen years later, in 1896. In that year, Edward A. Ross published the first of many articles on the topic of social control in the *American Journal of Sociology*. Although Ross is credited as being the innovator of the study of social control within sociology, by no means did he create this subfield out of whole cloth. Rather, like the great majority of intellectual innovators, Ross drew on the extant literature, deftly synthesizing pertinent aspects that dealt with the relation between the individual and society, as well as with the problem of social order more broadly.

Before we get to the more familiar treatment of social control as it has appeared in the sociological literature over the last forty years, we must first tell the story of how and under what circumstances the study of social control appeared, beginning with Ross's seminal writings in the late 1800s. Ross provided a justification for a sociological agenda which placed the study of social control at or near the top of the list of substantive sociological phenomena. In order to understand the justification for Ross's agenda, it is important to understand the context within which his work was appearing. The context, in short, is the founding of sociology as a scientific discipline in America in the last three decades of the nineteenth century.

After establishing the social context within which the study of social control emerged in American sociology, we will then be in a position to analyze similar movements of thought among classical European sociologists, two of the most prominent being Emile Durkheim and Max Weber. Although this overview of the thought of Ross, Durkheim, and Weber will provide a solid foundation for conceptualizing social control, in later chapters additional theoretical background will be presented as particular substantive phenomena are introduced, including norms, sanctions, socialization, groups, culture, the professions (especially medicine), and the criminal justice system (police, courts, and corrections).

The Gilded Age, the Progressive Era, and the establishment of American sociology

The fifty or so years leading up to the Progressive Era was a time of immense social change and shifting cultural and political landscapes in America. First of course there was the Civil War, which ended in 1865. Then a period of economic prosperity known as the Gilded Age arose, especially for those businesses such as oil, steel, and transportation which reaped the benefits of the massive efforts of social reconstruction. This was also a period in which the theory of evolution came to prominence, and social thinkers such as Herbert Spencer applied notions of survival of the fittest to human society and championed both rugged individualism (supported as well by the Protestant work ethic) and *laissez-faire* or "hands off" government policies. Finally, by the 1890s a Progressive Era had emerged which in effect attempted to ameliorate the dislocations experienced by working- and lower-class Americans who were left behind during the Gilded Age, as well as a large group of immigrants arriving to America during the great "second wave" of immigration running from 1880 to 1920. The impetus toward progressivism in America was also the operational logic for the establishment and institutionalization of sociology. In effect, sociology was turned to for "scientific" understandings of the bewildering social changes unleashed over the course of the century since America had gained its independence from Britain.

1st
1st course

The stirrings of professional sociology in America can be traced back to the early 1870s. Indeed, the founding of American sociology can be said to have occurred during the twenty-year period stretching from 1875 to 1894. The first notable event was William Graham Sumner's offering of the first course in sociology taught in any university. The course was offered at Yale University, and Sumner used Herbert Spencer's *Study of Sociology*, published in 1873, as the primary textbook.

2nd
1st Book synthesis

The second event in the establishment of American sociology was the publication, in 1883, of Lester Ward's two-volume *Dynamic Sociology*. Ward, who fought and was injured in the Civil War, went into government work as a botanist and paleontologist shortly after he was discharged from military service in 1864. By 1869, he had begun work on *Dynamic Sociology*, writing and conducting research for the book throughout the decade of the 1870s while in government service in Washington, DC. *Dynamic Sociology* was the first general theoretical synthesis of sociology in America.

3rd
1st Dept of Soc
+ 1st Journal

The third event was the establishment in 1892 of the sociology department at the University of Chicago. Albion W. Small was named to head the department, which at the time was the first full-fledged department of sociology to be established in any university in the world. Three years later, Small would also be named editor of the *American Journal of Sociology*, sociology's first academic journal.

4th
Columbia

The fourth event in the establishment of sociology in America occurred in 1894. Franklin H. Giddings was appointed professor of sociology at Columbia University, although for many years he was affiliated with the economics department since a sociology department had yet to be established. Up through at least the 1930s the University of Chicago and Columbia University were the twin pillars of scientific sociology in America, being led both intellectually and organizationally by Small and Giddings respectively.

The founding of the *American Journal of Sociology* at Chicago in 1895 was a pivotal moment in the establishment of professional sociology in America, for it provided a forum for the latest theorizing, research, and discussion in the newly established discipline. Small commissioned some of the prominent names in the field to write series of articles on selected topics. For example, surveying the whole of sociology (which at the time was dubbed 'general sociology') in a series of articles between 1895 and 1902 was Lester Ward, Charles Ellwood wrote a series of articles on social psychology (or "psychological sociology" as he often called it), as well as on methodology and social problems. And, of course, Edward Ross was commissioned to write a long series of articles on social control. We now turn to a discussion of these writings.

Ross and social control

Edward Ross's first article on the topic of social control appeared in the *American Journal of Sociology* in 1896 and was titled, appropriately enough, "Social Control."[6] Ross began by stating that, although society is certainly not some magical "super-organism" or "social mind" – as suggested by Herbert Spencer – neither is it a mere assemblage of human beings. Following the position of Lester Ward,[7] Ross argued that the true constitution of human society is to be found somewhere between the lone individual and the social group or collectivity. How do we make sense of this twin reality, that is, the reality of the individual and society? For Ross, there is good evidence of the existence of sources of influence whereby individuals are transformed into social beings. These distinct sources or social forces create patterns of association between members of society.

What were these social forces? Ross, whose theory of the development and growth of human society was informed not only by Lester Ward, but also by French sociologist Gabriel Tarde and German biologist and philosopher Ernst Haeckel, and even before them by the tradition of utilitarianism beginning with Thomas Hobbes, argued that in the original state of nature human beings were solitary and brutish, and only much later in their evolution did they become social creatures. This was an abiding issue for Ross and other early American sociologists, because, even as human beings over the eons had been transformed from solitary, selfish, and brutish to thoughtful, rational, and social, there were new challenges to the social order and the spirit of progressivism in early twentieth-century America. As historian Gillis Harp explains,

> In effect, [Ross's] examination of how social control functioned in human society represented a new way to reconcile the competing claims of order and progress. Ross was chiefly worried that the potentially anarchic individual would undermine the kind of social order without which there could be no authentic social progress.[8]

Ross's concern with shoring up the foundations of social order and control in the face of the appearance of rampant individualism had much to do with some key historical and cultural changes. For much of the early history of human civilization, human beings were held in check by the powerful forces of kinship and small, tight-knit communities where everybody knew everybody else and shared the same experiences, beliefs, values, and aspirations. In essence, for eons the group reigned supreme over the individual. But somewhere along the way this changed. Certainly the breakdown of feudalism contributed to the demise of group control, as persons were now free – as individuals – to offer their services to anyone who would hire them in newly burgeoning capitalist markets.

Additionally, the Enlightenment affected the way social thinkers began talking about human society. For example, beginning in the mid- to late-1700s, utilitarian thinkers such as Cesare Beccaria and Jeremy Bentham conceptualized human beings as rational actors who seek to maximize pleasure and minimize pain on an individual basis. Here, the individual is released from the constraining pressures of the group or the collectivity, and this loss of informal social control is one of the factors that explains rising rates of criminality and deviant behavior, especially beginning in the 1800s across Europe and in the United States. Indeed, these observations and concerns contributed as much as anything to the beginnings of criminology as a field of study.[9]

The forces of industrialization, migration, urbanization, and secularization were in effect releasing the individual from group control, and by the late 1800s criminologists and sociologists were theorizing how such changes were affecting the relationship between the individual and society. For Ross specifically, the question was "What is the nature of social control in today's society, and how does it differ from the past?" Following Ward, the major social forces impelling human beings to act are feelings, desires, or passion. But, with the advance of human society, actions based on raw passion give way to "reasoned" or "rational" actions coinciding with the evolution of the human brain and the upgrading of the intellectual faculty.[10] The growth of reason also coincides with the growth of human population and the simple fact that, with more anonymous others around with whom one must interact on a routine basis, more care, restraint, and calculation is needed in dealing with them.[11] Hence, in answer to the question posed above, Ross suggested that the feelings and desires of individuals are continually and in innumerable ways being shaped by the community of fellow human beings with whom they live and associate.

Here Ross distinguished between social coordination and social control. Social coordination consists of the rules and procedures for ordering a society's activities so as to avoid mutual interference between its various parts. An example of social coordination would be traffic regulations. Since everyone is on the road for ostensibly the same reason – to get from point A to point B – the ends that actors pursue in this case are harmonious. Rather than controlling, traffic regulations merely coordinate the combined activities of the multitude of individuals using public thoroughfares. Social control, on the other hand, seeks to harmonize potentially clashing activities by checking some and stimulating others. According to Ross, social coordination adjusts the essentially harmonious actions of society, while social control regulates incompatible aims and actions.[12]

The distinction Ross made between social coordination and social control is no longer prevalent in the social sciences. Since the 1920s or so, social control has been used as a general concept for describing all manner of activities involving the coordination, integration, regulation, or adjustment of individuals or groups to some ideal standard of conduct.[13] Indeed, social control has almost become synonymous with regulation, whether in terms of regulating persons in their interpersonal

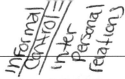

relations with others (informal control); regulating or defining human behavior more broadly irrespective of the nature of one's relationships, especially in terms of health, wellness, or public safety (medical or psychological control); or enforcing laws and punishing those who have been convicted of violating such laws (legal control).[14]

Although French classical sociologist Emile Durkheim did not focus as explicitly as Ross did on social control per se, his observations on the changing nature of society nevertheless continue to inform contemporary understandings of and research on social control. Let us examine the ideas of Durkheim in somewhat more detail.

Durkheim: from mechanical to organic solidarity[15]

In his *Division of Labor in Society* (first published in 1893), Durkheim argued that earlier forms of human society (e.g., hunter-gathering, horticultural, pastoral) are characterized by a mechanical solidarity where everyone is held in check through likeness and day-to-day familiarity with everyone else in the community. Hence, in primitive, preliterate, or preindustrial societies, the basis of social solidarity is cultural homogeneity, to the extent that all members share a common set of understandings, beliefs, symbols, and life experiences.

Since folk societies tend to be small, attachments between members are deep and abiding, grounded in large part along kinship lines and secured via a shared understanding of the sacred. In this *mechanical solidarity*, group cohesion is strong; indeed, the group takes precedence over the individual in virtually all social settings. Because of this, individuals are held in check because violations of the normative order are interpreted as an assault on the collective conscience of the community, and hence punishments against violators tend to be harsh, public, and focused on the body.

With the advent of industrialization and the democratic revolutions occurring across Western society beginning in the late 1700s, central cities experienced increases in population density as productivity increased and as more and more persons migrated to these cities in hopes of finding work in the newly burgeoning industrial economy. As populations grow denser, the social solidarity previously ensured through likeness, familiarity, and face-to-face contact is imperiled as the urban metropolis now becomes characterized by anonymity as well as temporal, spatial, and social distancing between its members.

Durkheim was worried that, in this new associational society, the quality and quantity of attachments would become increasingly superficial and impoverished as persons are set adrift in a sea of faceless and anonymous others. Especially as exhibited in his book *Suicide*, published in 1897, Durkheim's pessimism about modern society was fueled by data, already well documented by the late 1800s, which indicated that social pathologies (suicide, divorce, poverty, homelessness, mental illness, crime, violence, and drug use and abuse) were occurring

City = Disfunctional

at higher rates, per capita, in these urban, metropolitan communities. The assumption was that the city was a dysfunctional place that threatened the socialization process, the unity of the family, the routine commitment to civic participation, and the development of secure and stable attachments to others.

In this new situation of heightened individualism and aggrandizement of the self, what would be the basis of social solidarity? Durkheim argued that it is the division of labor, as well as the increasingly prominent role law would play in adjudicating conflict between an increasingly disparate citizenry.[16] Hence, the nature of social solidarity changes from mechanical to organic. Instead of by likeness and cultural homogeneity, the modern society is characterized by anonymity, cultural heterogeneity, and a vastly expanded division of labor where tasks become increasingly specialized. Because of this increased task specialization, persons are no longer self-reliant. They must turn to others for their day-to-day necessities, whether it is figuring out taxes, getting a medical checkup, buying a house, or even attending to one's mental wellness. In this new *organic solidarity*, social integration is assured as a result of the heightened interdependence between citizens of the community.

Concomitantly, whereas in earlier times the group was everything while the individual was nothing, in modernity the individual attains prominence over the group. Indeed, because of the increasingly divergent characteristics of inhabitants of the modern metropolis, the last remaining thing we all share is our humanity. This abstract ideal becomes further embodied in the activities of the democratic welfare state, which remains further and further committed, through the creation of welfare legislation and other provisions, to protecting its citizens against accident, injury, illness, and death.

Table 1.1 provides a summary of Durkheim's distinction between mechanical and organic solidarity. It should be noted that since Durkheim's time a number of social scientists have gone beyond the two-era classification – that is, an earlier primitive era of humanity (coinciding with mechanical solidarity) contrasted with a later modern era (coinciding with organic solidarity) – and have begun speaking of a third, so-called postmodern era.[17]

Where modernity emphasized centralized authority and operations, postmodernity emphasizes decentralization (for example, the use of police mini-stations under community policing, as well as the rise of community corrections). In modernity, there were sovereign nations with well-defined borders, while under postmodernity there is a collapse of such distinctions, with the new realities of deindustrialization, globalization, and shifting or disappearing national borders. And whereas in modernity there was trust in the grand narrative of science and Enlightenment reason, in postmodernity there is a fragmentation into a number of discourses (scientific and otherwise) that compete for attention. This idea of a "postmodern" condition, and how social

Conflict

Society turns to ↓ Organic anonymity + division of labor + specialization = non self reliant

Diversity = non human shared

Modernity vs Post-Modernity

Table 1.1 *Mechanical vs. organic solidarity*

Area of application	Forms of social solidarity	
	Mechanical	Organic
Type of society	Small, rural, agricultural, culturally homogeneous (familiarity and similarity)	Large, urban, industrial, culturally heterogeneous (anonymity)
Basis of evaluation	Ascription (who you are)	Achievement (what you do)
Basis of recognition	Family (primary groups)	Work (secondary groups)
Prevalence of law	Low (disputes handled informally)	High (needed to adjudicate conflict between increasingly disparate citizenry and to enforce contracts)
Punishment	Harsh, focused on the body (public)	Rehabilitative and restitutive, focused on the mind (private)
Division of labor	Not a great deal of task specialization	High task specialization
Education	Informal (family and church)	Formal (esoteric knowledge and the rise of professions)
Nature of social bonds	Strong and abiding	Weak and shallow
Source of social solidarity	Collective conscience	Division of labor and law
Societal focus	The group	The individual
Sense of self	Weak or non-existent	Strong (flowering of personality with multiple cross-cutting affiliations)

control is conceptualized and operates today, will be returned to in the last several chapters.

Social control as regulation

The work of both Ross and Durkheim places emphasis on the idea of social control as regulation. This amounts to the idea that, within society,

norms /
   rules

starting
   point
~~Socialization~~
= learning of
   a culture

guidelines
   morals
= cultural

Reward
   vs
Punishment

Held in check
by sanctions
     +
Internalization
= standards
     of fair,
          just
          etc

(over) *Freud*
Id = raw
          passion
(under)
Superego = moral

a system is in place to deal specifically with the sanctioning or punishment of individuals who do not comply with the rules, that is, with social norms. The starting point for any system of control is *socialization,* which can be defined as the learning of a culture. Because human infants are helpless at birth, ideally there should be competent adults – usually their parents – available to supervise children's activities and provide them with their physical and emotional needs as they mature. Beyond food, warmth, clothing, shelter, and emotional nurturing and support, agents of primary socialization also provide the growing child with a set of guidelines for proper conduct. These guidelines can be thought of as a moral template, the contents of which are drawn from the prevailing cultural traditions of a society.

According to Sigmund Freud, Talcott Parsons, and others, the ultimate goal of socialization is the production of self-controlled individuals.[18] Children will typically be rewarded by parents and other agents of socialization – teachers, priests, friends, and other family members to name a few – for good behavior and punished for bad behavior, thereby compelling individuals to comport their behavior to the expectations of the group.[19] That is to say, if socialization works properly, individuals will choose to act in norm-conforming ways because the costs and pains associated with deviance or nonconformity are simply too great. Equally important, however, is that, once individuals take the position that deviance is too costly to engage in, they have in effect internalized society's standards of what is fair, proper, just, appropriate, normal, ethical, or lawful. In this way, socialization assures the production of self-controlled individuals, insofar as persons are held in check by the threat of external sanctions as well as by internal feelings of blameworthiness, guilt, disgust, shame, embarrassment, chagrin, sorrow, self-loathing, or regret whenever they do something that does not meet the approval of significant others in society. No society can properly be maintained merely by way of external constraints such as those embodied in the legal system and its means of sanctioning.[20] The internalization of the moral code of a group by way of socialization is typically a far better mechanism for ensuring social control (as we shall see in chapter 3).

Although this point cannot be discussed in detail in this chapter, it should be noted that a seemingly growing number of persons believe that today's youth are not being raised properly and lack a conscience, that is, an internal voice that tells them right from wrong. This again is reflected in Freud's notion that stunted or incomplete socialization is likely to produce individuals whose personality is characterized by an overdeveloped id (where raw passions hold sway) or an underdeveloped superego (where moral conscience is not fully formed). News accounts profiling cases of children acting badly and for inexplicable reasons – such as the famous "wilding" incident in 1989 where six boys attacked a woman jogging in Central Park just for the "fun" of it, or the string of school shootings that have occurred sporadically across America since 1996 – are especially likely to prompt observers to suggest that the socialization process is in decline and perhaps irreparably damaged.[21] This then leads to talk that not only are children in crisis, but so are families, schools, neighborhoods, and civic participation, the traditional sites and activities of informal control. If mechanisms of informal control can no longer be trusted to assure the production of self-controlled individuals, then formal mechanisms of control are turned to with growing frequency. This growth of formalism, especially the increasing reliance on law in modern or postmodern society, is one of the key elements in any overview of social control. On this topic, the thought of Max Weber is especially helpful.

Weber on power, domination, and the rise of the state

Oftentimes within social relationships actors will be guided to act based upon the belief of the existence of a *legitimate* order.[22] For example, a member of a firing squad aims and fires at the person sentenced to death because he or she believes in the legitimate authority of the state to impose death sentences in certain cases.

The concept of legitimacy is closely connected with two other concepts: power and domination. *Power* is defined by Weber as "the probability that one actor within a social relationship will be in a position to carry out his own will despite resistance." And *domination* is "the probability that a command with a given specific content will be obeyed by a given group of persons."[23] For all practical purposes Weber understood "domination" to mean "authority," and he employed an ideal-type methodology to specify the types of legitimate domination (or authority).

There are, according to Weber, three ideal types of authority.[24] *Legal authority* rests on the belief in the legality of rules and the right of those in positions of authority to issue commands. In the case of legal authority, the validity of the claims to legitimacy is based upon rational grounds. The member of the firing squad mentioned above is acting on the basis of the perceived legal authority of the squad leader to give the order to fire.

Traditional authority rests on an established belief in the sanctity of long-standing traditions and the legitimacy of those exercising authority under them. Traditional authority is often vested in the eldest members of a group because of their intimate and longtime familiarity with the sacred traditions of a culture. It may also be vested as a result of inheritance, as for example in patriarchalism, where males are designated as heads of households. Members of societies in which such systems of traditional authority operate give their obedience to the masters (elder tribal leaders and fathers in patriarchal society), not to any enacted regulation.[25]

Finally, *charismatic authority* rests on devotion to the exceptional qualities or exemplary character of an individual person. A charismatic person is said to be endowed with supernatural, superhuman,

(Margin notes: informal in decline turn to formal more; legitamate order; Power = will over resistance; Domination = command obeyed = Authority; Legal Auth = belief in the legality of command; Traditional Auth = experience, longtime familiarity; Charismatic Auth = quality of person)

or exceptional powers or qualities that distinguish him or her from ordinary persons. Oftentimes these special powers or characteristics are understood as being magical or of divine origin. As Weber explains, "In primitive circumstances this peculiar kind of quality is thought of as resting on magical powers, whether of prophets, persons with a reputation for therapeutic or legal wisdom, leaders in the hunt, or heroes in war."[26]

Notice that, although a head of household exercises domination over other members of the household, he or she does so more or less as a solitary individual in that under normal circumstances there is no executive staff assisting the head. Domination and authority can be extended, however, beyond the situation of individuals or small groups, especially in the case of a political authoritarian association. The rise of the modern state is one such political authoritarian association. Weber defines the *state* as "an institutional enterprise of a political character, when and insofar as its executive staff successfully claims a monopoly of the legitimate use of physical force in order to impose its regulations."[27] A state, then, seeks to maintain the integrity and viability of its regulations over a specified geographical area by the use, or the threat, of physical force by its executive staff. This view is consistent with the earlier work of Franklin Giddings, who argued that the primary purpose of the state is to perfect social integration by way of the maintenance of armies to protect against external threats and tribunals and police to enforce peace within its own borders.[28]

States may vary with regard to the distribution of power in society. Some states are autocratic or totalitarian, meaning that power is concentrated in the hands of a single ruling elite (such as a king) or a small ruling class (such as the mullahs of Iran), while other states, such as constitutional democracies, disperse power more evenly across the citizenry, guaranteed (ideally) by a Bill of Rights, including the right to vote.

Beyond the case of complete and utter domination of the citizenry at the hands of a dictator, most states maintain regulations within a sovereign territory via a combination of what Jürgen Habermas calls facticity and validity.[29] *Facticity* reflects the reality of laws as a "social fact," in Durkheim's words, to the extent that laws are codified in writing and are backed by the state's monopoly on legitimate force to compel citizens to align their conduct to its prescriptions and proscriptions. *Validity*, on the other hand, refers to the state's concern with legitimating its rules and regulations in the eyes of the citizenry.[30] Ruling is made easier if those being ruled assent to the system of regulations being imposed. Ideally, then, states seek to administer a citizenry which obeys the law not only because of the threat of punishment, but because it is the "right thing to do."

Socialization is the single most important and efficient mechanism by which moral and legal rules are inculcated in and internalized by citizens. These rules are first those of the family, but then continue to expand outward as children encounter other spheres and activities of social life as they mature, such as same-age peers, education, the church, the public sphere, business, and so forth. The sum total of these activities adds up to the state's efforts to maintain both moral and legal regulation over a specific political territory, utilizing both facticity and validity in the ways described above.[31]

Rationalization

In many of his writings, Weber is concerned with the historical trend toward greater rationality in modern societies, and away from the sort of traditionalism that characterized folk or village society. Rationality became especially prominent in the *Occident*, that part of the world located to the west of Asia, specifically Europe and the Americas. Consistent with this idea of the rise of occidental rationalism was the emergence of the Enlightenment beginning in the eighteenth century in Europe. Massive changes in Western society before and up to Weber's time signaled to him the continuing march of the Enlightenment ethos of rationality, especially with regard to measurement, systematic observation, and calculation in human affairs. For example, the Industrial Revolution gave rise to formal organizations such as the factory, where "scientific" knowledge of human beings was being utilized to coordinate and manage the activities of large numbers of workers, but also to gather data on the output of products coming off the assembly line. An important activity within industrial capitalism is calculating what price to put on these products, based upon the cost of labor and materials, so as to maximize profit. This meant that an extensive system of accounting and bookkeeping had to be in place to keep track of both personnel and the production process.

Yet, rationalization is not restricted to the economic sphere alone. Beginning in the 1920s the American legal system began to expand enormously, thus setting the stage for a new form of statecraft the effects of which would be felt in all corners of society. New York State alone passed almost 1,600 new laws during 1928 and 1929. In 1870 there were an estimated 39,000 lawyers in America, but by 1930 that number had risen to 161,000. (Today the United States has over one million lawyers.) This growth in law and litigation points to the prominent role law has played, and continues to play, in progressive socio-economic lawmaking, culminating of course in the creation of the modern welfare state. Beginning in the 1920s and continuing to this day, the American nation-state has been characterized by the centralization of power, the individualization of rights, and the constitutionalization of law.[32] Although America has been in the forefront among constitutional democracies in assuring liberty and maximizing the life chances of its citizens through public law and welfare provision, both public and private, the threat of terrorism has convinced at least some observers that democratic constitutional states (in America and elsewhere) are imperiled.[33] In other words, in times of real or perceived threat the

Ethos

centralization of power trumps both the notion of liberal rights and the constitutionalization of law.

The creation of surnames

As discussed above, Weber's main task with respect to the issue of rationalization was to examine those aspects of economy and society that gave rise to and were characteristic of occidental rationalism. For early colonial powers especially, the centralization of power was not only a crucial consideration, but a manifest strategy in attempts to expand political control over wider and wider territories. A good example of rationalization has to do with the general projects of standardization and legibility carried out by state governments. In some instances, states have engaged in the enforcement of naming practices on its citizenry. As James Scott argues, the invention of permanent, inherited patronyms (taking the last name of the father) was the last step in establishing the necessary preconditions of modern statecraft.[34] With the rise of the state, administrators felt the need to identify citizens unambiguously, whether for purposes of taxation, tithing, census-taking, the maintenance of property rolls, or conscription lists. In earlier human societies it was not uncommon simply to use first names for purposes of identification. In such informal settings, this simple system of naming could be used and understood by members of kinship groups and the local community.

In England in the fifteenth century only wealthy aristocratic families had surnames. These were often designated according to their places of origin in Normandy (e.g., Beaumont, Percy, Disney). For the rest of the population, naming was limited to linking fathers and sons (but not daughters). For example, William Robertson's son Thomas might be called Thomas Williamson (son of William), while Thomas's son Henry in turn might be called Henry Thompson (Thomas's son). Such naming practices based upon local logic and practices worked for the immediate needs and understandings of members of the community, but it made more formal tracing of descent by outside observers difficult.

As populations grew denser, it was less likely that the government would know or be able to identify individuals by sight or kinship affiliation. The development of the personal surname (the last name, usually a family name) went hand in hand with the development of written official documents such as birth, marriage, and death certificates, censuses, tax and land records, and travel documents such as passports. Such official records were necessary to the conduct of any administrative exercise involving large numbers of people who had to be identified for various state purposes.[35]

States that oversee colonial populations are especially concerned with legibility. When the Philippines were a Spanish possession (from 1565 to 1898), Filipinos were instructed by the decree of November 21, 1849, to take on permanent Hispanic surnames. Up to that time they generally lacked individual surnames, as the local naming custom involved drawing from a small group of saints' names. This caused Spanish administrators "great confusion." The remedy was the *catalogo*, a compendium of personal names as well as "nouns and adjectives drawn from flora, fauna, minerals, geography, and the arts."[36] The authorities used these to assign permanent, inherited surnames. These names were divvied up by alphabetical order to populations in particular areas of the Philippines.

The "confusion" was of course from the perspective of administrators and tax collectors. The colonial subjects had a perfectly workable naming system in place, internal to the particular logic and way of life of the people. Western ideas and practices of rationalization were especially well represented in the use of universal last names, which facilitates the administration of justice, finance, and public order. The ultimate goal of these state builders was a complete and legible list of its subjects.

We see, then, that universal last names are a fairly recent historical phenomenon, beginning near the end of the eighteenth century with the expansion of the Western European colonial powers (especially England, Spain, and France). The surname was the critical first step in making individual citizens officially "legible."

Conclusion

Although the theoretical work of Ward, Ross, Durkheim, and Weber greatly contributed to the establishment of social control as a distinct object of study within sociology, in actuality this classical phase of the project represents merely a beginning. In the next few chapters other prominent thinkers, both classical and more contemporary, will be brought into the discussion to help flesh out and bring to life the tripartite classification of social control (to be presented in the next chapter) which will serve as the conceptual guide for the remainder of the book.

Suggestions for further reading

Durkheim, Emile. 1984 [1893]. *The Division of Labor in Society,* **trans. W. D. Halls. New York: Free Press.**
This book, which evolved from Durkheim's doctoral dissertation, contains a complete elaboration of the transition from mechanical to organic solidarity, as well as the rise of restitutive (or civil) law within modern society.

Ross, Edward A. 1901. *Social Control: A Survey of the Foundations of Order.* **New York: Macmillan.**
The definitive early statement on social control, which established an agenda for its study within sociology and other social sciences for decades to come.

Scott, James C. 1998. *Seeing Like a State: How Certain Schemes to Improve the Human Condition Have Failed.* **New Haven, CT: Yale University Press.**

A magisterial overview of the grand schemes – many of which have failed – that modern nation-states have devised for better predicting and controlling both human populations and the physical environments within which they reside.

Ward, Lester F. 1883. *Dynamic Sociology,* **2 vols. New York: Appleton.**

This book was the first systematic formulation of scientific sociology in America. Covering some 1,400 pages in two volumes, Ward introduced ideas such as telesis, synergy, meliorism, and sociocracy, which set the agenda for American sociology into the early twentieth century. Ward was also an important influence on Edward Ross's early formulation of social control.

Weber, Max. 1968. *Economy and Society,* **trans. and ed. by Guenther Roth and Claus Wittich. New York: Bedminster Press.**

Perhaps the leading classical statement on the nature of the state and associated concepts such as power, authority, and domination.

2 A Typology of Social Control

Introduction

As we saw in the previous chapter's discussion of terrorism, the idea of social control is often associated with the physical or coercive powers of the police. It is certainly true that police force is an important and prominent example of social control, which as defined in the previous chapter consists of all those resources – both material and non-material – available for ensuring the norm-conforming behavior of members of society.

Yet social control is much more than police control. In everyday life, for example, individuals you know exert pressures on you to conform to their wishes and expectations. Some of these methods are subtle, while others are flagrant and meant to be noticed by all present. For example, when a wife slams the phone down on her husband without a goodbye because he just called to say that he will be late from work and will miss his son's cello recital, that is a form of informal control. Or when a professor is scolded in front of the entire faculty for not having the minutes ready from the last department meeting, that again is a form of informal control. And when a complete stranger glares at you because she is offended by the slogan on your t-shirt, that too is an example of informal social control.

In addition to police (or more broadly legal) control and the types of informal control exerted in everyday life, there is also a form of control that arises in those cases where someone has done something that, although not necessarily illegal, is nevertheless seen as threatening, scary, weird, strange, bizarre, or just downright senseless. Medical or psychiatric control, then, is a catch-all category that straddles the borders between informal or everyday control on the one hand, and legal control on the other.

The main goal of this chapter is to introduce a typology of social control consisting of three main types: informal, medical, and legal control. The three forms of control amount to a range of normative prescriptions and proscriptions covering the areas of interpersonal relations and group living (*informal control*), behavior more generally irrespective of the nature of the ties between persons in interaction (*medical control*), and the law and legal systems (*legal control*). These three areas of the human experience – relationships, behavior, and the law – have associated with them the three respective systems of control that comprise our typology.

[Handwritten margin notes: Types — Prescriptive = told to do; Proscriptive = told not to do]

We will also examine a number of concepts closely linked to social control, including norms, sanctions, and the nature of social order, and how key thinkers, both classical and contemporary, have used these concepts to explain the ways in which order is maintained in society, but also under what circumstances this order may break down. In addition, we will briefly consider how social control is typically conceptualized within social scientific research. For example, some researchers seek to explain how various factors lead to or produce social control (that is, social control as a dependent variable), while other researchers seek to explain how social control itself, in its various guises, gives rise to various social outcomes or processes (that is, social control as an independent variable). Finally, the definition of social control is reconsidered in light of these research issues.

Conceptualizing social control: an example

As we begin our discussion of social control and its three major forms – informal, medical, and legal – the category of medical control needs to be dealt with somewhat carefully. It is important to understand, for example, that in our routine, everyday lives we are quick to use phrases such as "You're crazy!" or "How weird!" or even "What have you been smoking?" when someone does or says something that is seen as unexpected or somewhat out of the ordinary. But just so long as the societal reaction to the act in question remains at the level of comments of this sort, without further formal actions being taken, then this counts as a form of informal control. In other words, any disturbance that is handled within the context and boundaries of everyday life, where no official or quasi-official representatives of the government or medical community are brought in to assist those witness to the bizarre or odd act, remains at the level of informal social control.

An example may help to clarify the boundaries of the three basic forms of control. Suppose you are eating in a fast food restaurant and someone a few tables away is staring at you, perhaps grinning wildly but saying nothing. You could simply ignore him, or move to another table, or even hurry up your meal and get out of there as quickly as possible. If any of these options is taken, the disturbance remains in the realm of informal control. In this case informal sanctions – specifically, avoidance – were applied against the person for his perceived deviance. What if, on your way out the door, you tell the manager about the "weird" guy disturbing the customers? Here's where things can get interesting. If the manager decides to go over and ask the guy to leave, as far as our categories of social control go, there still is "no harm no foul." In other words, at this point the manager has decided that the disturbance can best be handled informally, and by politely asking the fellow to leave he is attempting to avoid a scene. His hope is that the person will get up from the table and walk out voluntarily. The condition of informal control still applies.

But what if the confrontation between the manager and the guy at the table does not go this smoothly? What if the person starts complaining loudly, perhaps cursing at the manager, showing signs of being prepared to make a very big scene? At this point, although the manager could take it upon himself to lay his hands on the individual and forcibly wrestle him out the door, he probably will not do it. He has probably already decided that the guy is just too dangerous, too out of control; at the very least the manager simply has no idea where he is coming from. If this scenario unfolds, very likely the next course of action is for the manager to threaten to call the police. This may in fact do the trick, in that the mere threat that the police will be summoned may be enough to convince the fellow to vacate the premises. Although the disturbance has certainly escalated, if it ends here it is still resolved by means of informal social control. The guy goes away and everyone gets back to their normal activities as best they can.

But what if the threat to call the police does not work? What if the guy remains at the table, daring the manager to make the call? Very likely the next step is for the manager to make good on his threat, and he calls the police. At this point, when a police report is made and a squad car is dispatched to the scene, we have now entered the realm of legal control. Indeed, in most jurisdictions when a manager of a business establishment asks a patron to leave and he or she refuses to do so, a criminal trespass has occurred.

Being now convinced that a call has been made, perhaps the fellow bolts the premises in hopes of avoiding a confrontation with the police. But even if he gets away safely, the manager will have a description of the man to give to the police once they arrive, and it will be up to the discretion of the responding officers either to pursue or not pursue the case further. If for example they find out that police headquarters has received similar complaints from other restaurants in the area about a guy matching the suspect's description, they may indeed continue to pursue the case.

If on the other hand the fellow decides to stay even as the police officers are arriving at the restaurant, we have a full-blown legal control situation. It is very likely that once at the scene and face to face with the suspect, the officers will not mince words. They will ORDER the suspect to come along with them, telling him that "we can do this the easy way or the hard way." The easy way is simply escorting him out of the restaurant, with the suspect providing little or no resistance. The hard way would amount to yet another, even more severe, escalation of the confrontation, should the man decide not to go along peacefully and forces the officers to handcuff him and drag him away.

In any event, the legal control scenario may well end with the arrest of the suspect, who could get cited for anything from disturbing the peace, trespassing, criminal menacing, or resisting arrest, to a whole slew of even more serious charges, depending on what happens between the suspect and the police. It is hard to say how this case would eventually be disposed of, owing to the myriad of possibilities with regard to the suspect's past record, the nature of the police report, the suspect's own demeanor while in police custody, and so forth. But one thing that could happen touches upon the third realm of social control, namely medical control. Somewhere along the way, the judge may request that the suspect be given a psychological examination, based upon the somewhat bizarre nature of his actions in the restaurant. For example, if it is discovered that the man has a history of being angry and confrontational with others, the judge may order him to attend anger management counseling as a condition of his probation, assuming he is not incarcerated.

Legal → medical
In many situations, then, medical social control occurs only after legal control has been brought to bear against a suspect. Here we may think about the social conditions necessary to call forth medical personnel as the primary agents of control, rather than legal officials. First, disturbances involving those who are known to one another are more likely to call forth medical forms of control than disturbances involving strangers. In other words, the more intimate the gathering, the more likely a breach of propriety will be viewed as a medical issue rather than as a legal issue (assuming it has already progressed beyond the level of informal control). Second, the social class of the participants involved in the disturbance often affects the nature of control responses. Higher status offenders and victims will tend to seek medical or therapeutic remedies for their problems, while lower status offenders are more likely to be dealt with by representatives of legal control.[1]

Let us return to our example of the person in the fast food restaurant staring at fellow patrons. Imagine this exact same behavior occurring in an exclusive dues-paying dinner club. Because of its exclusivity and high cost, member rosters are likely to be relatively small, and there is a very good chance that on any given night patrons of the club will know most everyone in attendance. A person engaging in this sort of behavior will probably first get the attention of the maitre d', who most likely will recognize the individual. If the person is unresponsive upon further discussion with the maitre d', he or she will likely have a phone number of a wife or an acquaintance who could be summoned to come and pick up the offender. Having arrived at the club, the friend or family member may whisk the person away, saying something to the effect that "Dr Long is not feeling well." Here, instead of a police officer, we have a friend, family member, or perhaps even a family physician or psychiatrist intervening as a therapeutic agent.

The idea of intervention, whether by a sworn law-enforcement officer or a therapeutic agent, is the key to distinguishing between informal and formal control. In informal control, disturbances are dealt with by persons acting only in their capacity as fellow human beings or citizens. This means that rarely are external third parties brought in to ameliorate this class of disturbances.[2] Formal control on the other

hand, whether of the legal or medical variety, always involves the intervention of a third party.

Sometimes agents of medical control intervene before agents of legal
control are brought to bear on a disturbance or dispute. Again, just as in
the example above, social class is often a factor whenever this happens.
In April, 2005, Jennifer Wilbanks of Duluth, Georgia, disappeared from
her home. After not hearing from her for several days, frantic relatives
reported her missing, and Duluth law-enforcement officials initiated
a search for her. Shortly thereafter Wilbanks called police from
Albuquerque, New Mexico, claiming to have been kidnapped and sexually assaulted.

As it turns out, Wilbanks made the whole thing up. She left her home
in Duluth on April 26 and took a bus to Las Vegas and then to
Albuquerque, all because she was soon to be married and simply got
cold feet. The wedding, scheduled for April 30th, was to be lavish
indeed, with some 600 guests and twenty-eight attendants. By this time
Wilbanks was widely known as the notorious Runaway Bride. After her
return to Georgia on April 30th family spokespersons claimed that she
was "ill," and she voluntarily checked herself into a psychiatric clinic for
"treatment."

The looming threat of legal sanctions, including charges of making a
false statement, making a false police report, and possibly being held
responsible for the money spent on her search, obviously played a part
in her decision to seek therapy.[3] Those of middle-class or higher standing, such as Wilbanks, are often afforded the luxury of bringing in
medical personnel as an expedient for possibly avoiding the more serious legal sanctions that could follow. Voluntary commitment to treatment is often seen by law enforcement as a "good faith" gesture on the
part of the offender. And the legal establishment will often play along
with this game. Gwinnett County District Attorney Danny Porter, for
example, stated that he would wait until Wilbanks completed treatment before asking her to turn herself in to local law enforcement.

Eventually, Wilbanks agreed to pay the city of Duluth $13,250 of the
estimated $50,000 cost of the search. And in early June she pled no
contest to a felony charge of making a false police report. This was part of
a plea deal whereby the lesser charge of making a false statement was
dropped. She could have faced up to six years in prison and fines of
$11,000 if convicted on both charges. She was sentenced to two years'
probation and 120 hours of community service, and was also required to
continue her mental-health treatment as well as pay the sheriff's office
$2,550. In a statement to the court Wilbanks said, "I'm truly sorry for my
actions and I just want to thank Gwinnett County and the city of Duluth."[4]

The derivation of the three primary forms of control

The three primary forms of control – informal, legal, and medical – are
derived from Egon Bittner's discussion of the functions of the police in

modern society.[5] Drawing from Max Weber and other sources, Bittner argues that the capacity to use force is the essential characteristic of the police role. Yet, as was pointed out above, police use of force does not exhaust the management and organization of responsive force in modern society. In most types of human societies, three distinctive forms of responsive force are viewed as legitimate given the right set of circumstances.

First, societies authorize the use of force in cases of *self-defense*. Self-defense, or self-help, is synonymous with informal social control. Over the course of human history, self-help, based originally in kinship or clan systems, has been the predominant mode of organizing responsive force and settling disputes. But with the rise of modern legal systems, it is no longer acceptable to "take the law into your hands," so to speak. Indeed, except in those cases where self-defense is recognized as a legitimate action by the courts, vigilantism is itself a crime. Those who claim to be victims of a crime are legally prohibited from meting out justice on their own. Rather than victims pursuing justice against offenders, it is the state that steps in to prosecute cases against criminal defendants. All forms of informal social control are examples of self-help, and only the small percentage of cases which raise the issue of the legality of self-defense ever come to the attention of the courts.

Second, there is a form of coercive response which authorizes certain agents to enter specifically named persons into a *custodial* arrangement, for example, the involuntary or voluntary admittance of a person to a mental hospital for tests, observation, or simply for his or her "own good." The nature of such custodial arrangements runs the gamut from extremely formal (e.g., a judge involuntarily committing a defendant sentenced for the first time for driving under the influence into a drug or alcohol rehabilitation program), to less formal (e.g., a disruptive student in school being diagnosed with Attention Deficit Disorder or Attention Deficit Hyperactivity Disorder by a school physician and placed on a drug regimen, typically Ritalin), to nearly informal (e.g., a married couple seeking counseling for various problems in their marriage). Custodial arrangements, where a third person (a therapeutic agent) is brought in either voluntarily or as a result of some prior or impending legal action, are synonymous with medical social control.

Third, legitimate responsive force can take the form of military (in the case of a sovereign nation) or *police* (in the case of a state or municipality, or an administrative or governance body) actions. This represents the realm of legal social control. As Bittner explains, "Contrary to the case of self-defense and the limited authorization of custodial functionaries, the police authorization is essentially unrestricted."[6] Police and military personnel are authorized to use whatever force is necessary to enforce laws or pursue combat objectives, up to and including the use of deadly force. Police coercive powers are *essentially* but not completely unrestricted, however. There are three limitations on police use of force.

- In most jurisdictions the *use of deadly force* is authorized in only a limited number of cases (e.g., against an armed suspect or a fleeing felony suspect).
- Police may use force only in the *performance of their duties*, and not for personal reasons or as private citizens.
- Police may not use force in a *malicious or frivolous* manner (the problem of police brutality).[7]

The police and other agents of formal control are entrusted with enforcing legal norms (or laws), while the norms of everyday life are enforced by private citizens. It is important, however, to explain how norms arise in the first place, and how they are sustained and enforced in various contexts. On the topic of the emergence of norms, we shall first examine the early writings of William Graham Sumner. After that, we will look at a more contemporary view of the issue as developed by sociologist James S. Coleman.

[margin note: Police enforce legal norms]

[margin note: Citizens enforce norms of ev-day. life]

The emergence of norms

If it is not apparent by now, our discussion of social control relies heavily on the concept of norms. It is now time to define this concept more explicitly. A *norm* is a rule for behavior, a guide to conduct. In essence, norms are statements that regulate behavior.[8] This is the epitome of social control as regulation, as discussed in the last chapter. Even so, norms need not be explicitly stated or codified. Indeed, many norms, especially those operating in the realm of everyday life, are not manifest or overt or committed to paper. Rather, many norms are part of a group's tacit understandings of the proper way to act given certain conditions or situations, and these norms are passed on more or less informally through socialization and other means available to group members.

[margin note: norms reg. behavior passed through Socialization]

Where do norms come from? How do they arise in society, and why do different societies, and even different groups or subcultures within the same society, have different norms? An important theory of the emergence of social norms was developed by the early American sociologist William Graham Sumner in his book *Folkways*, published in 1906. Let us briefly examine this work.

Sumner and Folkways

The subtitle of Sumner's book is "a study of the sociological importance of usages, manners, customs, mores, and morals." Sumner ranges far and wide in this book, on topics as varied as cannibalism, abortion, infanticide, incest, slavery, prostitution, and sports, all with an eye toward ascertaining why in certain times and places these and other acts have been either tolerated or condemned.

Sumner argues that early human beings lived a brutish existence where the instinctual urge for survival guided them in their quest for all the things needed to sustain life, be it food, clothing, shelter, warmth, and so forth. The brutal realities of a harsh physical environment mean that, in this primitive stage of existence, human beings have little more to go on than clumsy trial and error in the fight for survival. But each time a fellow human being succumbs to the elements, there are others around to learn, even in very rudimentary and awkward terms, about what seemed to work and what didn't, thereby gaining incremental advantages over their fallen brethren over the long stretch of human history. Pleasure and pain are the rudimentary "psychical powers" that guide men and women in this ongoing quest, and from this vantage point we can see why Sumner found Darwinism and Spencerian evolutionism useful.

Since human beings live in groups, first very small in size, such as in the very primitive hunter-gatherer societies, then growing larger as food technologies and production increase, members of groups learn from one another the best approach – for the time being anyway and within the context of that group's or society's storehouse of experiences – for coping with their situation. As Sumner explains,

> Thus ways of doing were selected, which were expedient. They answered the purpose better than other ways, or with less toil and pain. Along the course on which efforts were compelled to go, habit, routine, and skill were developed. The struggle to maintain existence was carried on, not individually, but in groups. Each profited by the other's experience; hence there was concurrence towards that which proved to be most expedient.[9]

In any given human group, then, all members adopt the same way to do things for the purposes at hand. Over time these ways turn into customs, and these customary ways of doing things get passed on to the young through tradition, imitation, and authority. The sum total of these informal ways of doing things, these customs, which provide for all the needs of members of the group, Sumner calls *folkways*. Folkways are a societal force to the extent that the frequent repetition of acts by all members of the group produces habits, and these habitual ways of acting produce a strain on everyone else to conform to them (the folkways). The folkways are "one of the chief forces by which a society is made to be what it is."[10] And because folkways arise only after a long period of trial and error, out of the efforts of those who came before, appearing in the present as the traditional ways of doing and knowing, they are unconsciously set into operation. Indeed, persons may have only a dim perception or understanding of why things are done the way they are. Members of folk communities or primitive tribes, when asked by a visiting anthropologist why they have this or that custom, often respond by saying, "That's the way it's always been."

It is not difficult to see, then, why in such human groups it is the older and more experienced members that accrue the greatest authority and respect. Almost without exception traditional, folk, or primitive societies deem the oldest members of the group – the elders – as the wisest and the most deserving of authority and deference. Because primitive societies have not yet developed technologies for the mass production of food, their populations tend to be small, and differences within the group (tribes, sects, etc.) tend to break along kinship or family lines. In such a society there are strong and abiding attachments developed within each distinct family or tribe, and a concomitant lack of trust or even open hostility toward all those who are not members of the immediate family. Deftly summarizing empirical findings from the anthropological literature, Sumner clearly shows how the folkways tend also to produce strong in-group sympathies as well as strong out-group hostilities.

It is here that Sumner introduces another concept that has become a staple in sociology and across the social sciences.[11] *Ethnocentrism* is the tendency for groups to judge other groups by their own standards. Stated differently, ethnocentrism is the process by which members of one group use their own folkways to judge other groups. There is also a tendency to assume that one's own folkways are the best ways of doing things, thereby characterizing the ways, means, attitudes, and behaviors of members of other groups as somehow deficient, strange, or even threatening. Ethnocentrism, then, contributes to the heightening of tensions between distinct sects or factions within a society.

Over time, the informal ways of knowing and acting, informed and guided by the folkways, start becoming formalized or codified as "truths," raising the folkways to a new plane which Sumner calls the *mores* (pronounced "mor-ays").[12] Although folkways provide guides for behavior, because they are tacit or unstated, their violation brings only mild punishment or sanctions. For example, in many families a folkway exists which suggests one ought to address one's parents as "mom" and "dad." If one starts calling one's parents by their first names, although it may cause a mild disturbance within the family system, it is unlikely to be seen as a major issue or a violation which requires a serious negative sanction. For the most part, then, the violation of a folkway is not seen as a major threat to the well-being of the community.

Violations of the mores, on the other hand, are seen as serious and tend to illicit harsh punishments. A large class of mores consists of *taboos*, namely, things which ought *not* to be done. Anything seen as injurious to the group can become taboo, whether it is eating the wrong types of food, carrying out war, having sex with the wrong persons (incest, for example), making the gods or ghosts angry, or what have you. As societies advance even further, for example, moving away from a reliance on self-help in settling disputes to the development of formal agents of control specializing in order maintenance and crime control, some of the mores become codified and institutionalized even further, and these become *laws*.[13] Laws are norms that are considered to be so vital to the well-being of the group that their violation is to be addressed by whatever collective resources are available, and ought to be addressed in a systematic,

[handwritten margin notes:]
groups small → family vs outsiders → Ethnocentrism = Judge oth. groups by their standards

Folkways (over time) → Mores (over time) → Law

Taboos = things not to be done

Statue
= Legal
*   document*

Folkways
= main importance

standard way. This means that the norm or prohibition ought to be codified, that is, committed to paper and embodied in a legal document
(statute), stating explicitly what the illegal act is and what sort of punishment will be meted out if persons are found guilty of the violation.

Sumner argues forcefully that the folkways are the most important
operation by which the interests of the members of society are served.
He suggests further that sociology ought to take folkways as its core
concept or primary object of study. As Sumner states, "The life of society consists in making folkways and applying them. The science of society might be construed as the study of them."[14]

Coleman on the demand for effective norms

Norms emerge

1) Demand for
*   effective norm*
*   +*
2) Right of
*   control*

In many ways sociologist James Coleman's view on the emergence of
norms owes much to Sumner, with some updating and modifications.[15]
Coleman argues that "a norm concerning a specific action exists when
the socially defined right to control the action is held not by the actor
but by others."[16] This reflects the assumption that a consensus among
persons potentially affected by the norm has been formed concerning
the legitimacy of others to sanction (punish or reward) persons for their
conduct.

According to Coleman, norms emerge when two social-structural
conditions are present. The first is a condition under which a *demand
for effective norms* will arise. Interests in or demands for a norm arise
wherever an action or set of actions has consequences (Coleman calls
these "externalities") for a group of others. For example, at baseball
games there is a tacit norm that when eating peanuts persons should
deposit their shells neatly at their feet rather than spreading them
around haphazardly. This ensures that everyone's messes will be their
own and will be dealt with on that basis. The collective or social-
structural aspect of this norm can be illustrated by the following princi-
ple: "I will deal with my mess, but I don't want to deal with yours." The
second is a condition under which such a demand for a norm will be
satisfied. Stated differently, there is more to the emergence of norms
than a mere desire that a particular norm should exist (that is, the first
condition). The second condition takes us from interest to the actual
conditions under which a norm can be created which is backed by the
sanctioning power of the collectivity.

The key to the second condition is the establishment of a social-
structural arrangement in which all persons potentially affected by the
norm have the right to exercise control over those who violate the
norm. In the realm of legal control, this *right of control* falls squarely
only on a relatively small group of persons designated as formal agents
of control (police and so forth). Within the realm of everyday life, on
the other hand, the right of control is informal and diffuse, extending to
virtually all persons deemed to be competent social actors. With regard
to the baseball example, anyone sitting close enough to a person

violating the peanut shell norm who may be affected by the person's actions would be in a position to apply negative sanctions against the violator, whether in the form of a glare or dirty look, moving to another seat if one is available, a verbal request to cease and desist, or possibly even more drastic measures.[17]

Perspectives on social order

Both Sumner's and Coleman's theories of the rise of norms, laws, and values are reflective of a consensus theory of society. The *consensus theory* originated with utilitarianism and the classical contract theories, beginning in the seventeenth century, of Hobbes, Locke, and later Rousseau. In short, the theory states that the unity of social life is a matter of agreement and understanding between individuals.[18] With the rise of evolutionary theory in the nineteenth century, the contract theory was merged with the so-called organismic theory – the idea that society is or is like an organism – whose various parts were held together as functional elements in the broader social system.[19] This newer consensus theory was initiated by Herbert Spencer in sociology and picked up by both Sumner and Emile Durkheim, and even later by functionalist sociologists such as Talcott Parsons, all of whom argued that shared norms and values are the key element in the maintenance of a stable and orderly society.

Conflict theory, influenced by the writings of Karl Marx, suggests on the other hand that, rather than being maintained by a voluntary consensus of the citizenry, social order is just as likely to be maintained by advantaged groups whose members use their privileged positions in society to dominate and oppress members of less powerful (often minority) groups. In this sense, laws do not reflect the general will; instead, they reflect and protect the vested interests of the powerful, who through the law systematically cast the powerless into the class of the criminal, the deviant, the deranged, and the unfit.

A third perspective on social order is represented by *interpretive theory*. The main goal of interpretive theory (examples include symbolic interactionism, phenomenology, dramaturgy, and ethnomethodology) is to learn how persons make the social world meaningful. Interpretive theorists assume social phenomena are fundamentally different than natural phenomena, and as a result sociology requires distinct methodological and explanatory approaches from those found in the natural sciences. Rather than seeking to discover the timeless laws of the social universe, interpretive theorists emphasize the importance of meaning and the subjective orientations of persons as they do things together. Additionally, the interpretive approach "does not seek an objective truth so much as to unravel patterns of subjective understanding."[20]

Whereas consensus theorists assume that social order arises from the fact that persons will seek agreement and understanding between one another in order to avoid what Hobbes called the "war of all against

[Handwritten margin notes:]
Shared norms and values = maintenance of stable and orderly society

Rich classify poor as deviant, unfit, etc

Interpretive = unravel patterns of subjective understanding

Consensus = understanding between one another

all," interpretive theorists make no such assumptions regarding the basis of social order. Instead, following George H. Mead, social order and hence social control is explained as a result of persons taking the attitudes of others with whom they interact in everyday life.[21] Social control is not imposed from above, but instead negotiated between real flesh-and-blood human beings who develop selves through everyday social interaction and shared activities. From the interpretive perspective, social control is not a timeless "social fact" but rather a phenomenon to be explained on a case by case basis, taking into account the peculiar set of circumstances and conditions facing members of a society in any given situation.

The nature of sanctions

As we have seen, norms are rules for conduct. Norms aim to guide behavior via a system of *sanctions*: those who comply with norms are rewarded (positive sanctions) while those who violate them are punished (negative sanctions). When we talk about norms and sanctions we generally assume that it is individuals who are either rewarded or punished for complying with or violating norms. But there is also the possibility of *collective sanctions*, namely, a situation in which a group is punished (or rewarded) for the actions of one or several of its members. In boot camp, for example, if a recruit is caught using a light to read after lights out, the whole unit may receive a punishment, for example, lights out an hour earlier for the next week. Systems of collective sanctions create especially intense pressures for members to conform to group norms.

In reality, however, sanctions are rarely purely individual or collective. This is because individuals are not isolated units, but are members of groups and thereby interdependent. For example, if a man who is married with children is sent to prison for embezzlement, not only is he being punished, but so are his wife and children, who now must find other sources of material, social, and emotional support.[22] Another point to consider is that, contrary to utilitarian perspectives which assume that human beings rationally calculate the costs and benefits of any line of action and adjust their behavior accordingly (a forward-looking version of social control), in reality actors often have no (or merely partial) knowledge of the long- or even short-term consequences of their actions. Rather than being forward-looking and possessing complete (or nearly so) information about the gains and losses associated with any possible course of action, actors rely more on past experiences to judge to what extent negative or positive sanctions may apply to current situations. This means that the system of norms and sanctions operating in most human societies aptly may be characterized as *backward-looking social control*.[23]

Sanctions may also be either centralized or diffuse. The most obvious and important form of *centralized sanctions* is the legal system of a nation-state supported by formal agents of control (police, courts, corrections, and so forth). Social order may be seen, then, as a problem of collective action, and the classic dilemma is how to motivate enough people to contribute to the production of this shared or public good (in this case, social order). In the collective action "game" of human society, centralized sanctions must be available to apply against "free riders," namely those who do not contribute to the public good, either through their overt violation of the social order (*meat eaters* who directly engage in criminal or deviant behavior) or through their failure to sanction other violators (*grass eaters*).[24] On the other hand, *diffuse sanctions* are rewards or punishments meted out by individuals or organizations on a local, informal basis against violators (either individuals or collectivities). By "local" is meant the more or less informal realm of face-to-face behavior, including small groups, neighborhoods, and communities. In this sense, we see how the concepts of centralized and diffuse sanctions are compatible with Coleman's notion of the right of control.

So far we have covered the distinctions between positive and negative sanctions, collective and individual sanctions, and centralized and diffuse sanctions. Travis Hirschi and Michael Gottfredson have incorporated these various distinctions into a general theory of sanctions consisting of four basic types: natural, social, legal, and supernatural.[25]

Natural sanctions are negative, harmful, or painful consequences of operating within a natural environment, such as the dangers associated with heat or fire, animals, diseases and similar factors affecting human health and well-being, or even other human beings. The idea of natural sanctions places great emphasis on evolutionary learning, and stresses for example that the most important thing parents and other competent adults do is protect children from such sanctions. *Social sanctions* are a product of human society, such as the pains associated with a friend's withdrawal of friendship, being expelled or isolated from a group, or the expression of disappointment or anger from a parent. Whereas natural sanctions are automatic and direct, social sanctions require the presence and participation of other human beings.

Legal sanctions are the penalties provided by the state for violations of the criminal, administrative, or civil law. Today legal sanctions are confined to fines, imprisonment, and a range of intermediate sanctions, but in earlier times they included flogging, transportation, bodily mutilation, and various forms of torture (see chapters 5 and 8). Finally, *supernatural sanctions* are rewards or punishments individuals receive upon their death. These supernatural sanctions, such as the belief that one will go to Hell for breaking a religious commandment, are ostensibly geared toward shaping the behavior of individuals in this world, in the here and now.

Hirschi and Gottfredson further argue that the four sanctions can be ranked according to the time that elapses between behavior and the receipt of sanctions.[26] Natural sanctions are the most direct and certain, followed by social sanctions, legal sanctions, and finally supernatural sanctions (the consequences of the last can never be known for certain and must remain an article of faith). According to these authors, the history of human society has been a slow and inexorable adding on of the secondary sanctions (supernatural, social, and legal) to augment those natural sanctions which are primordial and most immediate.

Social control as a dependant or independent variable

Scientific explanation typically involves stating the relationship between two or more variables or concepts of interest. For example, a researcher studying juvenile delinquency might argue that religiosity – namely, the intensity of one's relation to the sacred – is related to rates of juvenile delinquency. Further, the nature of the relationship would be assumed to be causal, meaning that changes in religiosity are associated with changes in delinquency, and that, because religiosity occurs in time before delinquency, changes in the former "cause" changes in the latter. (Indeed, it would not make much sense to say that one's delinquency causes one's religiosity.) Simply stating that "as x changes, y changes" says nothing about the direction of the relationship, however. It simply states that changes in x (the independent variable) are somehow related to changes in y (the dependent variable). In order to bring more precision into scientific explanation, it is usually desirable to state the direction of the relationship as well. A better hypothesis, then, might state, "As religiosity increases, delinquency decreases." In plain language, this hypothesis asserts that, as the intensity of one's orientation toward the sacred increases, the likelihood of being juvenile delinquent decreases.

Traditionally social scientific explanations have tended to view social control as a *dependent variable*. This is because traditional conceptualizations of social control are reactive: a person is robbed at gunpoint and calls the police; a woman is mad at her husband and gives him the silent treatment; a person seeks counseling for a gambling problem. In other words, various forms of deviance or criminality are conceived as igniting social control responses. This relationship may be stated in the form "as deviance increases social control increases."

The labeling perspective

Treating social control as a dependent variable certainly does not exhaust the possibilities for its conceptualization, however. The labeling perspective – a theory within the interpretive paradigm – suggests that social control leads to deviance, or at least certain types of deviance. In this sense, social control is conceptualized as an *independent variable*. Beginning with the work of Frank Tannenbaum in 1938 and continued by David Matza, Howard S. Becker, and Edwin Lemert during the 1950s and 1960s, the *labeling* perspective takes the position that societal reaction to deviance can produce further deviance because of the difficulties and strains persons encounter as a result of being labeled criminal, delinquent, mentally ill, strange or weird, or by any other negative characterizations.[27]

Consider the example of a person (call him Bob) who has spent seven years in federal penitentiary for armed robbery, and is being released upon completion of his sentence. Even as he leaves the prison a free man, the label of "ex-con" will follow Bob around wherever he goes. Labeling theorists argue that once applied such labels are "sticky" and difficult to shake. With whatever money he had before his incarceration or accumulated during his stay in prison, Bob would likely try to rent an apartment, apply for a job, and meet new people. But it is equally likely that he will be rebuffed at every turn: employers are unlikely to hire him because of his felony conviction; the apartment complex will reject his application either because his credit rating is too low or because of the negative information contained in the background check; and most persons are simply leery about befriending someone fresh out of prison.

The stickiness of the label makes it difficult for Bob, or anyone for that matter – save for high-profile celebrities such as Martha Stewart – to reintegrate into conventional society. Left with few alternatives, Bob may end up engaging in petty theft or other street crimes to make ends meet, or at the very least going back to old haunts and acquaintances, thereby falling back in with the very same crowd that helped get him into trouble in the first place. Labeling theorists are not so much interested in *primary deviance* – Bob's original criminal act which brought the attention of law enforcement – but in *secondary deviance*, namely, the deviant behavior that occurs as a result of the affixing of a stigmatizing label. According to labeling theorists, the high *recidivism* (or repeat-offending) rate that afflicts the correctional systems of the United States and Western Europe is indicative of this labeling process and the incidents of secondary deviance.

Labeling theorists such as Jason Ditton have gone so far as to suggest that, rather than focusing on crime, which is of course the traditional approach in sociology and criminology, what should be the focus instead are the control attempts embodied in societal reactions to perceived deviance. This approach Ditton has aptly called *controlology*, or the study of control.[28] Individual intentions and acts are irrelevant (or at least unworthy of scientific scrutiny) without societal reactions to those acts. Indeed, a "crime" is never committed in and for itself. For something to be labeled a crime, it must be reported or detected, and the person alleged to have committed the act must be tried in a court of law and found guilty. This shifts the focus from individual *responsibility* to societal *response ability*.[29]

Reconsidering the definition of social control

So far we have defined social control as all those resources available by which members of society attempt to assure the norm-conforming behavior of others. It is assumed in this definition that the norms to which people are being compelled to conform are in some sense "legitimate" or "conventional," and that the sanctions imposed against deviants are accepted as appropriate by the wider collectivity, whether embodied in law (formal control), group sentiment (informal control), or general behavioral guidelines (medical control).

Hence acts that are criminal, that violate group sentiments, or that are simply weird, strange, or threatening, are the kinds of things that are conceptualized by social scientists as prompting social control efforts. What are we to make, then, of Donald Black's argument that crime itself can be considered a form of social control?[30] Black points out that many acts defined as criminal are acts of self-help: a group of men beat up a man who was allegedly peeping in a young girl's bedroom window; another man damages the paintwork of the car of someone who stole a parking spot from him at a busy mall; a woman threatens another woman whom she suspects is cheating with her boyfriend. Black is able to argue that crime is a form of social control because of the way he defines social control, namely "any process by which people define or respond to deviant behavior."[31] By defining social control in this way, what is emphasized is the reaction to perceived or real deviance, but it does not specify what the nature of the reaction is. In other words, the reaction to acts of deviance can take myriad forms, ranging from accepted, appropriate, or legal responses on the one hand, all the way to deviant and criminal responses on the other.

This idea of Black's – that self-help crimes are a form of social control – has been influential across the social sciences as well as in legal and policy studies, yet on first blush it appears to be inconsistent with the threefold typology of social control developed here. If deviant and criminal responses were included in the types of resources available by which members of society attempt to ensure the norm-conforming behavior of others, then perhaps a fourth category of social control (for example, deviant or illegal control) would have to be developed to supplement informal, medical, and legal control. Obviously, this would introduce further complications into an already complex and multifaceted phenomenon. Yet, the seeming incompatibility between Black's definition of social control and the one presented in this book can be resolved by collapsing deviant, criminal, or illegal types of control efforts into the category of informal control.[32] How this may be accomplished will be illustrated in chapter 6 (on the topics of linguistic profiling and the informal code of the street of the urban inner city) and again in chapter 9, where Black's general theory of social control will be applied to the problem of terrorism.

Suggestions for further reading

Bittner, Egon. 1970. *The Functions of the Police in Modern Society.* Chevy Chase, MD: National Institute of Mental Health.

Bittner's sophisticated analyses of police operations and organizations contributed immensely to scholarship in the field of police studies. His argument that the core of the police role is the distribution of non-negotiably coercive force in modern society is still very much on the mark.

Black, Donald. 1998. *The Social Structure of Right and Wrong,* **rev. edn. San Diego, CA: Academic Press.**

Black's general theory of social control is one of the most inventive and influential in legal studies and the social sciences.

Heckathorn, Douglas D. 1990. "Collective Sanctions and Compliance Norms: A Formal Theory of Group-Mediated Social Control." *American Sociological Review* **55: 366–84.**

In this paper, Heckathorn establishes the conditions under which collective sanctions (rather than simply individual sanctions) are likely to be enforced. Additionally, Heckathorn makes the important point that timeframes are typically different in formal versus informal control. That is, where everyday deviance is often responded to instantaneously (e.g., saying something to your wife that she doesn't like may elicit a frown from her), under formal control the time elapsed between discovery of a crime and its eventual sanction may take years or perhaps decades (in the case of the death penalty, for example).

Macy, Michael W. 1993. "Backward-Looking Social Control." *American Sociological Review* **58: 819–36.**

The rational choice perspective argues that human beings act in a forward-looking fashion, to the extent that they anticipate the future costs and benefits (or sanctions) of any lines of action. However, this endows actors with an unrealistically high level of knowledge about the future. Emphasizing an evolutionary approach (consistent with Sumner), Macy views social control as more backward-looking: actors base their current choices of actions on the way they were sanctioned (positively or negatively) in the past.

Sumner, William Graham. 1906. *Folkways.* **Boston: Ginn.**

Sumner, an early American sociologist, provided one of the first systematic treatments of the evolution of norms and values in society. Even today, 100 years later, the book is still an engrossing read.

3 Informal Control

Introduction

When we are born, we arrive at a time and place, in a particular society, that is not of our own making. For most of us, most of the time, there is hardly any thought of problematizing or questioning this "natural surrounding world" which we have come to know and within which we operate.[1] It just *is*. It is a stubborn reality. It is the pre-given social reality that we come to know and accept, the taken-for-granted background for virtually everything we do. It is the world of everyday life.[2]

As a *social* world, as distinct from a physical world or the subjective world of our own thoughts and reflections, it is populated by other human beings, some of whom are very close to us – our mothers, aunts and uncles, brothers and sisters, good friends – while others we know only in passing or not at all. The human condition is the condition of association, of living among fellow human beings, however distant or near they may be relationally. Indeed, it is very rare to find a truly isolated person or group.

Although human beings are carbon-based life forms operating and moving about in a physical world, and thereby subject to the same physical laws as are other objects whether animate or inanimate, it is quite limiting to think of the human condition in only this physicalist or objectivist sense. This is because, with the rise of human society, something has been added to the physical conditions of existence that characterize the situation of all lower life forms. Because of the superior intellect of the human being, the continuity of human groups is predominantly cultural and historical. Since the dawn of the human species knowledge and ideas have grown slowly but surely, and the most useful of these have been maintained and transmitted across human groups. As Charles Ellwood explains,

> In this way man gradually builds himself up out of the perceptual world, the world of objects, with which he began, into an ideational world, the world of culture. As the social tradition grows in bulk it increases in influence. Men now come to live, not so much in a world of objects, as in a world of ideas – of pattern ideas – which immediately control their adjustments both to the objects of nature and to their fellows.[3]

Informal social control consists of all those mechanisms and practices of ordinary, everyday life whereby group pressures to conform are brought to bear against the individual. Beginning in the 1930s, concepts such as group "culture" and "climate" were being developed and tested by various researchers. These studies documented the ways in which groups regulate, modify, and sometimes distort the judgment and actions of individuals.

Before examining these studies, however, we will first summarize and reiterate the importance of socialization for the understanding of informal social control. Any understanding of informal control and the role of socialization in assuring social order must be squarely grounded in the social psychological literature on the nature of groups and group living. This will require an introduction to and brief discussion of such concepts as primary groups, secondary groups, and reference groups, as well as identifying the various agents of socialization. Finally, a somewhat extended overview and discussion will be provided of the dramaturgical theory of Erving Goffman, whose ideas regarding the nature of face-to-face interaction amount to a general theory of informal control.

Back to socialization

In everyday life individuals may conform to the pressures of a strong group consensus, to perceived authority figures, or to some combination of these. As discussed in the previous chapters, the starting point of informal social control is the process of socialization. In a sense, individuals in their everyday lives are continually held in check – even as there also exist pressures and incentives to deviate given the right set of circumstances – by the mere presence of fellow human beings living and operating within shared lifeworlds. If informal control is to work in any meaningful way, then, the individual must be conceptualized as being formed by the group, if not wholly then in some large measure. The assumption of the dominance of the group over the individual typically is held by a number of sociologists both classical and contemporary, but is represented especially forcefully in the writings of Ludwig Gumplowicz, who in 1899 stated that:

> The individual simply plays the part of the prism which receives the rays, dissolves them according to fixed laws, and lets them pass out again in a predetermined direction and with a predetermined color.[4]

The most direct forms of informal social control come by way of our closest associates, these being our families and friends. These act more or less as the important authority figures in informal control and, following the terminology of Charles Horton Cooley, are known as *primary groups*. The behavior of primary groups is characterized as *expressive*, meaning that members interact with one another for the sake of each other's company, or simply because it is the right thing to do (such as the bonds of loyalty and commitment typical of consanguineous, or family, relations). For example, when a child asks his father why he has to do something, the father may respond by saying,

"Because I'm your father." Following Weber's notion of traditional authority, the father in this case is invoking the tacit authority that is vested in him by the patriarchal family system, a system which, as we shall see later, is in decline.

Individuals are also influenced to conform by so-called *reference groups*, namely, groups that individuals identify with or look up to.[5] Close identification with the values of the reference group means that individuals so bonded to these groups will emulate their actions and ideas, that is, will conform to what they perceive to be the normative expectations of the group. These reference groups may be actual groups (such as a motorcycle gang or members of a university chess club) but they need not be. For example, a young girl who acts and dresses up like Mariah Carey, Shakira, Fergie, or Christina Aguilera is holding as a reference group currently fashionable pop star divas.

Behavior in *secondary groups* (such as work groups, casual acquaintances, and service encounters), on the other hand, is characterized as *instrumental*, meaning that group activities are engaged in for the sake of pursuing a collective goal, not necessarily for the sake of simply being together. For example, students in a university classroom taking courses together are there for instrumental reasons, namely, to fulfill the requirements of their degree program. Although along the way friendships may be struck and primary groups may be formed within the secondary group, the original orientation of students coming together to take courses is instrumental. And again following Weber, the types of authority figures found here are most likely to be of the legal-rational kind. A large part of informal control, then, flowing from the socialization process itself, is the ways in which group pressures to conform hold individuals in check.

Agents of socialization

Socialization, or the learning of a culture, begins at birth and ends only with death. A person learns the rules and cultural traditions of a society through routine contact with various other persons and groups throughout his or her life. There are eight basic *agents of socialization* that help steer persons toward norm-conforming and away from deviant behavior. Seven of these basic sources of socialization, to be covered below, are the family, the community, peers, school, work, religion, and the mass media.[6] (The legal system will be covered in much more detail in later chapters.)

The family

In the earliest stages in the development of the human species, men did not take on traditional fatherly roles, but were more concerned with gaining access to females for purposes of sexual consummation. This meant that it was mothers, along with other women of the clan, who had to band together to raise children. This meant also that the earliest human societies were likely matriarchal, with descent being traced through the mother's line, since biological fathers were invariably absent and could not be relied upon for support.[7] Somewhere along the way, however, fathers started becoming more or less permanent fixtures within kinship systems, as human populations increased and group norms began developing with regard to greater accountability in the areas of sexual and procreative behavior. Moving beyond the original primitive stage of human existence, then, the collective wisdom has been that children ought to be raised in the most stable environment possible. This stable environment was (and still is) the family, a supportive infrastructure consisting of a mother, a father or close male relative, and extended kin (aunts, uncles, grandparents, and so forth).

Parents, biological or otherwise, have traditionally taken on the societal responsibility of caring for young children as well as instructing them about the rules of their society. As George Hillery has pointed out, "primary responsibility for imparting the tradition of the village to its new 'recruits' rested with the family."[8] Hillery notes further that, although families are the primary agents of socialization of children, in no known society do parents perform this task alone. Families are typically located within broader social settings known as communities.

The community

In 1995 Hillary Clinton published a book entitled *It Takes a Village*.[9] The main thesis of the book is that, although parents are important in imparting societal norms and values to their children, socialization is complete only when parental oversight is supplemented by a supportive community – the "village" – consisting of safe schools and neighborhoods, caring teachers and neighbors, churches, civic organizations, and other private and public institutions. In smaller, tight-knit communities characterized by mechanical solidarity, it is indeed the case that many community members beyond those of the immediate kinship group are actively involved in the instruction and guidance of youth.[10]

With increasing modernization and the advent of organic solidarity, however, community standards of behavior play a less direct role in assuring the conformity of youth. Because of this loss of informal oversight and regulation with advancing modernity, on the parts of both families and communities, more emphasis is placed on the work of formal agencies and agents of control, including the criminal justice system and medical oversight of youth in the guise of social service and public health agencies, as well as medical and therapeutic personnel employed in the schools. This is why the recent trend in municipal governance has been the systematic attempt to bring the community back in, whether in the form of community policing, family and community preservation, alternatives to traditional punishment which include heavy doses of community sanctions, and a concern with

shoring up "social capital," namely, the collective resources arising from close and sustained social relations between members of a community. (We will return to these issues in chapter 6.)

Peers

Because schooling is emphasized in advanced industrial societies, and because they are being placed into formal education at younger and younger ages, children are spending much of their time in the presence of same-age peers. Although schools provide the primary context for peer socialization, the influence of peers can also be felt in the community, in homes with siblings, and in more general social settings. Conventional peers and the youth cultures arising from shared activities and orientations exert strong pressures to conform, but deviant peers and deviant youth subcultures may produce equally strong inducements toward deviance and delinquency.[11]

Although it has long been felt that parents are the single most influential agents of informal control for assuring the norm-conforming behavior of youth, a growing number of observers believe that other agents of control, especially same-age peers, exert as much as or even more influence than parents. Indeed, psychologist Judith Harris argues that the nurture assumption – that parents and especially mothers have the most direct bearing on how their children turn out – is wrong.[12] According to this line of thinking, because children are now spending more time than ever before in the presence of other children, whether at school, in daycare, or in other settings, parents have been dethroned as the frontline agents of socialization.

School

The primary function of schooling is to impart the knowledge that children will need to take on adult roles, especially in the areas of work, citizenship, family, and community relations. In school they are confronted with an array of rules and regulations, and this early exposure to authority figures beyond those of the household is considered to play a crucial role in the moral development of youth. The major agents of socialization in school are of course teachers, while other agents include school administrators, school medical personnel, and of course fellow students.

Because the trend in modern society is to place children into formal education at younger and younger ages, a battleground of sorts has developed as families are increasingly pitted against schools for the souls and minds of children. From the perspective of schools, parents are mainly to blame for the underachievement and/or misconduct of their children, both within and outside of school settings. As schools attempt to take more complete control of the lives of youth – because of the assumption that parents are failing in their roles as agents of socialization – parents demand more accountability from schools, thereby producing more strains and antagonisms on all sides.

One important manifestation of this conflict between schools and families is that traditional parental authority is diminished, to the extent that the local culture and knowledge of the family (as in "family values") are replaced by the more cosmopolitan and "modern" values of the school system. The authority of the school system is presumably based not on status (for example, the father as the unquestioned head of the patriarchal household), but on impersonal and universal knowledge which transcends local knowledge and circumstances.[13]

Work

Although schooling prepares individuals to join the adult labor force with the hopes of their becoming relatively self-sufficient and productive members of society, persons must still "learn the ropes" once they become members of a work organization. In other words, whether entering the workforce for the first time, changing jobs, or reentering the workforce after a period of idleness, persons must learn the particular norms, values, rules, and history of the place of their employment. This learning process, often referred to as *organizational socialization*, consists of several domains.[14]

First, there is *performance proficiency*, which simply refers to the learning and mastery of tasks associated with one's position within a work organization. Second, there are other *people* within the organization to whom workers must learn to adjust in order to do their jobs effectively. In the modern workplace, this ability to deal with others – often referred to as *soft skills* – is considered to be nearly as important as traditional performance proficiency. Third, there are *political* considerations, in terms of being aware of various aspects of the organization, specifically (1) who the politically powerful actors are (on the formal side), but also (2) the nature of the informal networks which are vital for general information and as sources of social solidarity. Fourth, workers must learn the special *language* (or argot) that is used within their particular line of work. Fifth, workers must be familiar with the organization's *goals and values*, represented in the rules and principles – both formal and informal – which (ideally) help to maintain the integrity of the organization. Finally, persons are expected to be familiar with the *history* of the organization within which they work. In this sense, organizational history includes the traditions, customs, myths, and rituals used to transmit cultural knowledge to organizational members.[15]

Religion

Throughout the course of human history religion has served as an effective means of assuring the conformity of its members to the system of beliefs embodied in its teachings. *Religious socialization* is the process by which important principles of a religious belief system are transmitted to new members across generations.[16] Religious socialization is especially concerned with the collective solidarity and identity of a group of true believers, otherwise known as the church or the congregation. Elements of the collective memory forged through religious teachings include:

- an *origin myth*, a story of how the world was created and humanity's place within it;
- a set of *rituals* through which true believers partake of the religious life and forge a sense of solidarity and collective identity;
- an understanding of the *soul*, which is believed to survive the physical death of the body; and
- a set of *rules for living* in this world which, if devoutly followed, may lead to the attainment of grace or salvation in the afterlife for chosen believers of the faith.

Mass media

In modern society entertainment and news media – television, film, radio, music, newspapers, magazines, the Internet, and mass-marketed video games – provide a tremendous range of information and images which are consumed by the mass public with varying results. Some observers believe the effects of the mass media on the public are generally bad, while others believe that various types of media can have a positive impact on society.

For example, because television news is in the business of maximizing viewership and ratings, the crime stories they choose to cover tend to be more sensational, bizarre, and violent than the typical crime. This then distorts the picture of crime that the average citizen receives, thereby also fueling higher levels of fear of crime among the citizenry than is warranted. Additionally, many observers believe that the generally high levels of sex, violence, and depiction of deviant behavior in films, cable television, and video games leads to a host of behavioral problems among younger members of viewing audiences. For example, a recent study concluded that adolescents who are exposed to high levels of sexual content in television, movies, magazines, and music are more sexually promiscuous than youths who are not exposed to such content.[17] On the other hand, in countries that provide citizens with only a narrow range of media (such as China or Iran), the Internet is considered to be an important source of democratization, to the extent that totalitarian states are less able to control access to, as well as the content of, this particular communications medium.[18] (Table 3.1 provides a summary of agents of socialization and the nature of social control associated with these domains.)

An understanding of the nature and function of agents of socialization allows us to connect back to classical theorists such as Lester Ward,

Examples of
+ and –
impact

Table 3.1 *Agents of socialization and types of control exerted*

Domains of socialization	Agents of control		
	Informal	Legal	Medical
Family	Mother, father, siblings, and extended kin	Social workers	Family physician, health visitors (UK)
Community	Neighbors, local businesses, community organizations	Municipal planning, social and welfare services	Public health initiatives, community nurses
Schools	Students, teachers, PTAs, and other school personnel		School nurses and others school health professionals
Peers	Friends in schools, communities, daycare, etc.		
Work	Co-workers, managers, and supervisors	Administrative rules and regulations, e.g., legal department staff	Employee Assistance Programs (EAPs) and related organizational health professionals
Religion	Priests, members of the congregation		
Mass media	Music, film, television, and sports celebrities, as well as expert 'talking heads' who form reference groups for some viewers		
Legal system		Police, judges, lawyers	

Franklin Giddings, Emile Durkheim, and Georg Simmel, all of whom documented the fact that society exists to the extent that people are aggregated together and associate with one another across space and time. Because they do things together in groups, persons are allowed to do certain things and are constrained from doing others. By the 1930s

this insight began being formalized by a number of thinkers in psychology, sociology, and social psychology. For example, Kurt Lewin asserted the existence of a group "climate" which was a key factor in shaping and directing group outcomes. In his Robber's Cave study, Muzafer Sherif also posited the importance of group culture in the creation and resolution of intergroup conflict. And a few years later sociologist William Foote Whyte showed how status hierarchies in groups are formed, and how in turn such structuring impacts not only the group's culture but also the personal identities of its members.[19]

Solomon Asch: how groups shape individual conformity

The groundwork laid by Lewin, Sherif, and Whyte among others paved the way for even more sophisticated studies of the ways in which groups shape, modify, and sometimes distort the judgments of individual members. Solomon E. Asch published a paper in 1951 which reported on a series of experiments investigating the effects of group pressure upon the judgments of individuals.[20] Research subjects were asked to look at two cards. One card contained a single line, and the other card contained three lines of varying lengths. The subject's task was to judge which of the three lines (A, B, or C) on the second card was closest to the length of the line on the first card, and to proclaim his or her judgment publicly (see Figure 3.1). Unbeknown to the subject, however, all the other persons in the room who were given the same task were confederates of the experimenter. In this particular version of the experiment each of seven bogus subjects gave an obviously wrong answer when it was their turn to judge the length of the lines. The research subject, who was always called on last, faced the difficulty of having to decide whether or not to go along with a group of people whose judgments were obviously in error.

Fig. 3.1 The Asch experiment

Note: Research subjects were given Card 1 and asked to judge which line in Card 2 matched the line in Card 1. Here, B is clearly the correct answer. However, confederates in the experiment were instructed to always give the wrong answer, either A or C. The experiment examined the effects of the erroneous majority on the subject's judgements. (Adopted with modifications from Asch [1952, p. 52].)

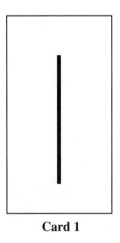

Card 1

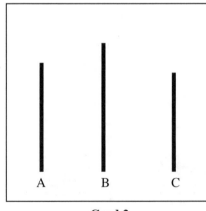

Card 2

Even though the errors made by the bogus subjects were large (ranging from ½" to 1¾" differences in the lengths of lines which they declared to be equivalent), 32 percent of the naïve subjects still went along with the majority. What Asch demonstrated in this experiment is that a surprisingly large number of persons will go along with the majority even when they are clearly wrong. In variations of this experiment, Asch reduced the number of bogus subjects from seven to three. The question was: Would a majority of three persons offering erroneous judgments be as effective as a majority of seven? The answer was yes. The probability that a naïve subject will go along with the judgments of a mistaken majority is not increased significantly as the size of the majority is increased beyond three members. Indeed, a majority of three is much more powerful and persuasive than a majority of seven with one dissenting vote. This finding supports Georg Simmel's theory that the effects of group size are not altered appreciably beyond the level of the triad or the three-person group. In other words, the crucial effect of group size is found in the transition from the dyad to the triad. All things being equal, then, not much changes when a group grows from three to four, five, or more members.

Another point illustrated in Asch's experiments is the importance of *social support*. A lone dissenting voice against a majority of three or more is not very effective. However, add just one person who supports the lone dissenter, and the effects can be profound, even against a much larger majority. When a person acts or thinks in ways that go against group consensus, the dissenting person is seen as, and often labeled, strange, weird, odd, sick, or deviant. Persons generally conform to group expectations, then, simply to avoid being labeled as defective or deficient by others. Nevertheless, persons who are able to find others who act or think like them can mitigate somewhat the negative sanctions imposed by a group against non-conformers.

Later research on conformity and obedience

In documenting the ways in which groups structure conformity in individuals, and how in turn individuals may resist social control measures, especially when various forms of social support are available, Asch's work paved the way for more sophisticated research and theorizing in the social psychology of conformity, deviance, and social control. For example, a few years after Asch's conformity experiments began appearing, Stanley Milgram, a student of Asch, began his own series of experiments on the nature of obedience.[21]

Milgram's obedience experiments

In a series of famous experiments, Milgram told research subjects that they would be participating in a learning experiment in which they would be instructed to give an electric shock to other subjects whenever they did not provide the correct answer in a paired word test. The cover story was that the experiment was designed to examine the effects of punishment on memory and learning. The true aim of the experiment, however, was to see how far research subjects would go in delivering shocks to other research subjects. The research subjects who were receiving the shocks were not true research subjects, however, but confederates of the researcher. And the "shocks" being delivered by the naïve subjects were not shocks at all, only elaborate-looking devices that made it appear as if other research subjects were receiving sometimes high voltage shocks whenever a button was pushed or a lever was pulled.

The naïve subjects were the ones delivering the shocks at the prod-dings and promptings of the experimenter. Milgram varied a few things in the experiment to ascertain under what conditions subjects would deliver the maximum voltage shocks, even as those receiving the shocks were sometimes screaming in pain or begging the research subject to stop. For example, Milgram discovered that subjects were more likely to deliver the maximum voltage shock when he was stand-ing next to them in the room, rather than giving orders from another room. In the 1963 experiment, twenty-six of forty test subjects (or 65 percent) did indeed deliver the highest shocks on the generator, which was a complete surprise both to Milgram and to outside observers after the results of the experiments began being published.

The issue of obedience to authority became a pressing issue espe-cially after World War II and the discovery of the Nazi atrocities at Auschwitz in which some 6 million Jews were exterminated between 1933 and 1945. Many persons asked how it was possible that Nazi soldiers and other functionaries of Hitler's regime could follow orders to kill on such a widespread and grotesque level. Beyond trying to explain how a genocide of this magnitude could occur, however, Milgram also faced the realization that, with the rise of the professions in modern society, more and more persons routinely were turning to a variety of "experts" in various fields, including medicine, law, business and finance, and education, but also in the burgeoning "helping professions" such as social work, marriage and family therapy, mental health counseling, public health, and so forth. The proliferation of experts across growing expanses of everyday life pointed to something like a willing acquiescence on the part of citizens to this growing legion of perceived authority figures, a cultural trend that seemed to be veri-fied in the Milgram experiments.

The Emperor's Dilemma

One way this sort of acquiescence to perceived authority or the will of the group appears is by way of the phenomenon of the popular enforce-ment of unpopular norms. Sociologists Damon Centola, Robb Willer, and Michael Macy refer to this as "the Emperor's Dilemma."[22] The Emperor's Dilemma is derived from Hans Christian Andersen's fairy tale about a vain king who believed the story of two swindlers who claimed the ability to fashion a suit of clothes that was invisible to anyone incompetent or stupid.[23] The swindlers brought the "robe" to the king and all members of his court to see, but of course they saw nothing because the swindlers hadn't really fashioned a suit of clothing at all. The king and his aides acted as if they did see the elegant robe, for admitting not being able to see it would cast them into the category of incompetent or stupid. The king went to the people, leading a procession through the heart of the kingdom, for all to see his new regal gown. And all the townspeople acted as if they could see the king's clothes as well, fawning over and admiring them, when in fact he had nothing on at all. A small child in the crowd, however, proclaimed, "But he doesn't have anything on!" This then spread to the rest of the people assembled there, who also started openly asserting that the emperor had no clothes. Even so, the emperor carried on as if his new clothes were real.

Using network theory as well as agent-based computational models, Centola, Willer, and Macy sought to explain under what conditions an unpopular norm or a mistaken idea would be enforced or allowed to continue by a group of people. Certainly one reason why people comply with unpopular norms is that they fear whatever social sanctions may accrue to them for non-compliance. But, as the authors ask further, "Why would people publicly enforce a norm that they secretly wish would go away?"[24]

One reason this happens is that most people seek not only to go along with the crowd to avoid social sanctions, but also to look sincere in their belief in the rightness or propriety of the norm. One way of showing sincerity, then, is by enforcing the norm publicly. As more and more people act in this way, it produces a cascading effect whereby large numbers of persons are enforcing a norm that they secretly do not support.

Cascades of enforcement of unpopular norms arise and are sustained primarily through local misrepresentations perpetrated, at least initially, by potentially only a handful of true believers (or persons posing as true believers). The enforcement of the unpopular norm in an area may be enough to coax disbelievers into enforcing the norm as well, and the cascade rolls across the social network. How far it goes depends on the nature of the ties (or relationships) between members of the network. For example, the swindlers in the Hans Christian Andersen story started the cascade, as they influenced the most powerful person in the kingdom, the emperor, to buy into the story of the invisible clothes. From there the norm spread rapidly throughout the kingdom. The nature of social influence is not global, however, but local and hence fragile, as a variety of factors may potentially disrupt enforcement of the norm. These include the presence of persons who have an accurate estimate of the actual public support for the norm, or the presence of a person who is immune to any negative sanctions imposed for failure to comply with or enforce the norm, such as the young child in the fairy tale who saw that the emperor indeed had no clothes and was not afraid – or simply knew no better – to proclaim it publicly .

The authors of the Emperor's Dilemma article also point out the limitations of traditional (namely, consensus or functionalist) theories which argue that norms arise because they are useful to society or because they protect important social values. More in line with insights from conflict or critical theory, the authors make the case that, rather than solving social dilemmas, some norms create them, thereby serving to undermine social welfare.[25] The Emperor's Dilemma, and all such examples of the enforcement of unpopular norms (be it in the guise of witch hunts, repressive state regimes, or even college drinking), are testament to this.

The importance of small groups

Much of the work of informal control, then, is done within the context of small groups on a local level. Georg Simmel is the classical theorist most directly identified with the work of mapping human groups and providing a taxonomy for the various dimensions of group life and how these social structures impact members' group relations. Rather than placing emphasis on the substance or content of group relations (that is, analyzing what sort of things persons are trying to achieve through social exchange and interaction, and the motivations for their actions), Simmel's formal sociology emphasizes the *form* of such relationships. For example, Simmel noted the structural characteristics of *dyads* (two-person groups) and *triads* (three-person groups), and how they differ regardless of the aims or ambitions of group members. These early observations of the social structure of small groups led to the research tradition of social network theory, to which we will return later in the book.

Simmel noted that the traditional distinction between primary groups and secondary groups may need to be modified, to the extent that group membership can be voluntary or involuntary. For example, some types of primary groups such as families, are certainly characterized by involuntary membership (at least for children), while other types of primary groups, such as friendship groups, are for the most part voluntary. Although most secondary groups are characterized by voluntary membership, some are not. A good example is the young man or woman conscripted into military service. Keeping in mind this voluntary/involuntary distinction, Kurt Back has argued that

> There is a residual of other groups that have members and whose variety helps to integrate society and assure its continuation. We may call these "circles" or "sociability groups" because one of their main origins seems to be voluntary social interaction among the members.[26]

Back's position is consistent with Simmel's classic statement on the web of group affiliations and his attempt to deal more systematically with the nature of voluntary or informal memberships across a variety of group contexts.[27] Using a geometric analogy consistent with his formal sociology, Simmel referred to these various kinds of informal or voluntary groups as "social circles." As Simmel explains,

> there exists an immeasurable number of less conspicuous forms of relationship and kinds of interaction. Taken singly, they may appear negligible. But since in actuality they are inserted into the comprehensive and, as it were, official social formations, they alone produce society as we know it. To confine ourselves to the large social formations resembles the older science of anatomy with its limitation to the major, definitely circumscribed organs such as heart, liver, lungs, and stomach, and with its neglect of the innumerable, popularly unnamed or unknown tissues. Yet without these, the more obvious organs could never constitute a living organism.[28]

Simmel's organic analogy is offered as a warning to those researchers who would choose to concentrate on the largely formal and more visible contexts of group life, including the work group and the community. Attention to such "official" groups may diminish our understanding of the perhaps more basic, underlying structures of social life which are constituted in the everyday, mundane acts of sociation by which human beings make and remake their world.

Following from what has been said so far, there are five basic ways that small groups (or simply *groups*) enable or constrain individuals in everyday life.[29] *First*, groups provide the important basis of primary socialization, first within the context of the family, then within schools, neighborhoods, and among same-age peers. Through socialization, individuals learn the standards of the community. *Second*, groups can be the impetus for social change to the extent that some groups may challenge the prevailing cultural standards and ways of living in a given society. In these instances, social control may be contested. The activities of small groups can even snowball into full-blown social movements, some of which may contribute to the social welfare, while others (such as Emperor's Dilemma-type phenomena) may be injurious to it. *Third*, small groups provide members with what network theorists term "strong" ties, that is, relationships that are deep and abiding, and which give members a sense of "we-feeling" or belonging.[30] For example, when people were asked in a survey what "community" meant to them, they mentioned family and friends most often, followed far behind by co-workers.[31] And, as we have seen, friends and family are the stuff of which primary groups are made. *Fourth*, groups provide for the development of a collective identity, which can be an important source of social solidarity. For example, collective identity can be forged around a family name or lineage, a broader ethnic identity, a friendship group connected with a neighborhood or school, a church or religious organization, or even a youth gang. *Fifth*, groups provide members with an individual identity to which status and other kinds of social markers attach. For example, families provide a range of ascribed statuses to individuals, including sex, race or ethnicity, and social class location.

As we see, then, small groups – especially of the primary kind – play a prominent role in socialization, in the conferring of personality and identity, in the development of collective identities, and in the development and maintenance of informal social control more generally. A theoretical perspective known as dramaturgical theory, developed by Erving Goffman beginning in the 1950s, is one of the best single perspectives for anchoring understandings of what goes on in face-to-face interaction, the realm within which much informal control is accomplished. We turn next to an analysis of the key concepts and ideas of Goffman.

Erving Goffman and dramaturgical theory

Erving Goffman received his PhD from the University of Chicago in 1953, an institution that already had a well-established tradition of personal ethnographies of the city (primarily of Chicago itself) conducted largely from a situational or interactionist perspective. Even so, the interpretive or symbolic interactionist strand of Goffman's thinking was counterbalanced by a strand of thought heavily influenced by functionalist anthropology (e.g., Durkheim, Malinowski, and Radcliffe-Brown) as taught by Chicago anthropologist W. Lloyd Warner. Indeed, it was Warner who sent Goffman to the Shetland Islands to collect data for his dissertation "Communication Conduct in an Island Community," one of the first glimpses into Goffman's developing dramaturgical perspective.

In his dissertation Goffman argued that face-to-face interaction represented a domain of activity that deserved to be studied in its own right. He called this domain the "interaction order." Some thirty years later, in his presidential address to the American Sociological Association, Goffman described the *interaction order* as the relatively stable sequence of events and activities that is generated whenever persons enter into each other's immediate presence.[32] When people are in each other's immediate presence, whatever joint activities are to be undertaken – whether talking with a friend, asking the time of day from a stranger, playing a game of baseball, working in an office, or sitting at the dinner table at home with the rest of the family – are understood on some level as always involving risks or at least uncertainties. These risks and uncertainties are of course always assumed to be minimized or held in abeyance when interacting with members of primary groups or in locations that are familiar and cozy – such as in one's home or, say, the front yard of a neighbor – but on some level occasions for face-to-face gatherings always expose our bodies and minds to vulnerabilities. As Goffman explains,

> So there are enablements and risks inherent in co-bodily presence.
> These contingencies being acute, they are likely everywhere to give
> rise to techniques of social management; and since the same basic

contingencies are being managed, one can expect that across quite
different societies the interaction order is likely to exhibit some
markedly similar features.[33]

These "techniques of social management" amount to all the ways in
which persons in their everyday lives present themselves before a
group of others. In other words, persons are always concerned about
the figure they are cutting before a group of co-present others, and they
comport their actions to fit with the expectations of this perceived
moral universe. The *presentation of self* – which was the title of
Goffman's first book[34] – is one of the overriding preoccupations of individuals (and of groups as well).

In some ways Goffman's dramaturgical theory is consistent with
Shakespeare's assertion that "all the world's a stage." As in the theater,
persons in everyday life perform on the *front stage,* and steal away
backstage to rehearse for their public performances or simply to kick
back and relax. For example, a professor who is delivering a lecture to
his or her class does so on the front stage, and his or her audience are
the students. And the professor prepares his or her lecture backstage,
either in his or her office or at home away from the spotlight of
the front stage. Because persons are concerned with self- and team-
presentations, they are always alive to the nature of the audience in
front of whom they are acting or performing, and seek to come across
as well-demeaned individuals or groups. A professor, for example,
seeks to fulfill the tacit expectations of a competent performance,
which involves having a command of the material, engaging in "free"
talk rather than scripted talk, being able to use jocularity in appropriate ways, speaking clearly and varying the tone and tempo of his or her
speech, and so forth.[35] (For a summary of how the theater compares
with real life, see table 3.2.)

An important and omnipresent strategy within self-presentation is
impression management, which is simply the effort by individuals in
interaction to put their best foot forward. This amounts to emphasizing
the positive aspects of self while downplaying or minimizing potentially discrepant information about oneself. For example, persons on
first dates usually invest a good deal of time preparing, which may
include buying a new set of clothes, getting their hair done, tidying up
their car or apartment, and rehearsing points of discussion – including

Table 3.2 *Goffman's dramaturgical theory*

The theater	Real life
Actors playing parts on a stage before an audience	People performing roles in a setting before a group of others

flattery – all of which are calculated to make the best first impression possible.

The important thing to keep in mind is that impression management is not reserved only for first dates, job interviews, or other key events in a person's life. It is a pervasive feature of everyday life. For example, even among our family and closest friends, impression management through self- or team-presentations occurs with regularity. Even that most intimate act that takes place between a man and a woman, sexual intercourse, is a staged performance. Note also that most persons most of the time act with civility and decorum even among perfect strangers whom they are likely never to see again. Those that do not – beggars, prostitutes, the homeless, criminals, the mentally ill, and other assorted street characters that are a fixture in most urban industrial societies – are cast into the realm of the deviant, the disreputable, the incompetent, or the criminal.

Human beings have a range of tools in their interactional repertoire by which they can convey to others that they are not a threat, are "normal" according to the expectations of the situation, and are competent role performers who can carry out their self- or team-presentations without a hitch. One such class of role resources for maintaining decorum and normal appearances are *interaction rituals*, which are sometimes fleeting or perfunctory acts by which persons convey to others in interaction that they are ratified participants in whatever activities are the focus of attention.[36] For example, when two people are conversing, the person who is in the role of listener will usually provide a steady stream of ritual support for the speaker in the form of nods of the head, a visible focus of attention such as maintaining eye contact, and verbal utterances such as "uh-huh," "yeah," "Oh really?," and "I hear you." Another kind of interaction ritual that is used in public places is the nod of the head or the perfunctory "Good day" whenever persons pass each other on the street or sidewalk. Notice also that most persons will greet even very casual acquaintances with a "Hello" and often a "How are you doing?," even though the person asking the question may not really care at all how the person is doing.

Why would most persons be prompted or feel compelled to display these interaction rituals almost always and without exception? The reason is that persons are desperate to convey to others that they are well-demeaned individuals who are deserving of the kind of ritual support and considerateness that they have offered up to others through their own displays of deferential and accommodating conduct. This aspect of propriety in interaction is especially noticeable in two other types of management devices, namely civil inattention and role distance.

First, *civil inattention* (or studied non-observance) is the practice of acting as if you didn't see something when you really did.[37] Like interaction rituals, civil inattention is pervasive in everyday life. Consider the following example. One of the tacit norms of party-going is that you shouldn't be the first to arrive. Being first on the scene may display an unhealthy eagerness to have a good time, implying that you are lacking in this department on some level in your own life. Being aware of this, as you set out for the party you look for signs that guests have already arrived, such as the number of cars parked in front of the host's house. When you arrive and do indeed notice few if any cars parked in front of the house, you are likely simply to drive past and occupy yourself with other things for the next twenty or thirty minutes.

When you arrive back at the house you are relieved to find that a number of additional cars are now parked in front, signaling that it is safe to make your appearance. You ring the doorbell, the host greets you and lets you in, and everything is wonderful. It looks like it's going to be a great party. But unbeknown to you, the host happened to be looking out a window and spotted you driving by the first time. The host does not tell you of course, because to do so would be a breach of the framing rules of civil inattention.

Civil attention is often invoked whenever territories of the self are brought into play, for example, when a person has a brief lapse in control of his or her own bodily functions. The classic example is the fart: the tacit norm for dealing with an audible fart on the part of the perpetrator is to admit to nothing, while those co-present others who heard the fart are expected to act as if they didn't hear or smell it either. Indeed, it would be a breach of civil attention to say "Excuse me" after farting, for even the mere acknowledgment of the fart would bring embarrassment to all those assembled there. (Notice, however, that when someone belches at the dinner table an "Excuse me" is often permitted and expected, which points to the fact that different aspects of the territories of self have different interactional norms corresponding with them.) Embarrassment is contagious and can spread like wildfire, thereby posing one of the greatest dangers to the viability of focused or unfocused face-to-face gatherings.

A second interactional resource, aligned somewhat closely with civil inattention, is role distance. *Role distance* is the tendency to place distance between one's authentic self and one's virtual self-in-role in particular situations.[38] An *authentic* self consists of all those attributes that a person can be shown to actually possess, while a *virtual* self consists of imputations made about a person, gleaned from the immediate situation, before verifications can be made as to the accuracy of those imputations.[39] For example, persons confined in *total institutions* such as asylums, prisons, monasteries, boot camps, and similar types of all-encompassing organizations are often stripped of personal identity and made to conform to various forms of stigmatization as mandated by the organization, stemming largely from custodial arrangements concerning dress, behavior, communication, the types of recognition afforded to inmates, and so forth. Although some patients or inmates certainly acquiesce to the identity being foisted upon them by the institution, many rebel against the stigmatizing label however they can. Granted, they may give lip service and "play the game" as they comport their behavior to the expectations of line staff – this being their virtual self – but deep down they retain some fundamental essence, some conception of who they "really" are, and bide their time until or when they can more fully utilize and present their authentic self.

Role distance is not confined, however, only to the situation of inmates or to custody arrangements more generally. It is also a technique for managing interactional difficulties in everyday life. One day in a hotel lobby I noticed a young boy – perhaps no more than five or six years of age – being led by the hand into the women's restroom by a woman I presumed to be his mother. The boy was whining and resisting slightly, but when he saw that I saw him, he became more agitated and tried to break free from his mother's grip. She eventually dragged him into the restroom literally kicking and screaming.

A few minutes later I saw the boy and his mother emerge from the restroom, and I glanced away quickly so as to afford the boy as much civil inattention as possible. Out of the corner of my eye, however, I saw the boy approaching, and when he reached me he said, "Uh, mister, my Mommy needed help with something and my Daddy wasn't around."[40] This was a remarkable display of role distance, insofar as the boy was attempting to distance himself from the "virtual" self he was identified with by way of the bathroom incident. The human condition, then, is rife with various types of repair work, invoked whenever selves are in jeopardy, to uphold the definition of the situation, or to preserve the sanctity of social gatherings.

Conclusion

Goffman's dramaturgical theory is the premier theory of informal social control. Through careful study of face-to-face interaction over a career spanning some thirty years, Goffman identified a wide range of folkways and mores by which persons attempt to maintain and preserve local social order. The lesson to be learned from Goffman's insights is that the social order of everyday life is fragile indeed, and this is why persons tend to go along with prevailing group sentiment. Absent good reasons to do otherwise, persons are inclined not to rock the boat, to work hard to maintain normal appearances, to send clear messages to others that they are sane and can be trusted, and to control information with the aim of presenting the most flattering self-image possible.

Notice, however, with all this attention to self-presentation, impression management, and information control, persons also possess the ability to present distorted and even inauthentic images of themselves and their plans of action.[41] In other words, persons who are competent in the knowledge of a culture's folkways and mores regarding proper conduct in interpersonal relations can use this knowledge to fabricate frames of deception, dissemblance, or outright fraud. In this sense, secrecy is as important as open and honest communication.[42] The folk-ways of everyday life both enable and constrain the realization of the good life or the just society. Rather than being gross perversions of everyday life, then, emperor's dilemmas coexist alongside and within it.

Suggestions for further reading

Centola, Damon, Robb Willer, and Michael Macy. 2005. "The Emperor's Dilemma: A Computational Model of Self-Enforcing Norms." *American Journal of Sociology* **110 (4): 1009–40.**
This paper introduces the concept of the Emperor's Dilemma, and provides an explanation for the development of self-enforcing norms that the majority of group members do not support and wish would go away.

Goffman, Erving. 1959. *The Presentation of Self in Everyday Life.* **New York: Anchor Doubleday.**
This book contains Goffman's earliest formulation of the dramaturgical theory of action, which is one of the most useful perspectives for under-standing the world of everyday life, and especially of informal social control.

Harrington, Brooke and Gary Alan Fine. 2000. "Opening the 'Black Box': Small Groups and Twenty-First-Century Sociology." *Social Psychology Quarterly* **63 (4): 312–23.**
An excellent summary and overview of prevailing sociological under-standings of small groups. The authors argue that the study of small groups will continue to be a thriving area of study in sociology for the foreseeable future.

Shibutani, Tamotsu. 1962. "Reference Groups and Social Control." pp. 128–47 in *Human Behavior and Social Processes: An Interactionist Approach,* **ed. A. M. Rose. Boston: Houghton Mifflin.**
A useful paper which links the reference group to broader issues of social control.

Simmel, Georg. 1950. *The Sociology of Georg Simmel,* **trans. and ed. K. H. Wolff. New York: Free Press.**
One of the best compilations of Simmel's thought. In developing a perspective on sociology that emphasized the forms of human associ-ation, Simmel was one of the pioneers of the study of groups and group relations.

4 Medical Control

Introduction

In 1851 Samuel A. Cartwright, a respected Louisiana physician, published a paper in the *New Orleans Medical and Surgical Journal* in which he claimed to have discovered a new disease which he called "drapetomania." At the time in southern states such as Louisiana it was legal to own slaves, and drapetomania was supposedly a condition which caused slaves to run away from their masters.[1]

Cartwright provides one of the earliest modern examples of *medicalization*, which is the process by which personal and social problems are redefined as psychiatric or medical problems. Medicalization is one aspect of *medical social control*, which may be defined as

> the ways in which medicine functions (wittingly or unwittingly) to secure adherence to social norms – specifically, by using medical means to minimize, eliminate, or normalize deviant behavior.[2]

Medical terminology, discourses, and ways of thinking are pervasive and omnipresent especially in Western society, due largely to the high status physicians enjoy relative to other occupations or professions. As Renée Fox has argued, doctors are imbued with a "cloak of competence" that sets them apart from most of the other learned professions, including law, education, and even the clergy.[3] Medicine acts powerfully as a normalizing discourse, and medical practitioners – as well as a growing legion of non-physicians who have adopted medical discourse and terminology as their own – speak authoritatively about such things as disease, illness, pathology, syndromes, health, wellness, and pathogens, to name a few.[4]

As discussed in previous chapters, the earliest human societies relied on informal methods of control. In the most primitive hunter-gatherer stage, humans relied largely on superstition and tribal customs to ensure conformity of their members. With the rise of the early Greco-Roman city-states (third century BC), the legal and ethical philosophies of thinkers such as Plato viewed most social ills – including crime and vice more generally – as arising from ignorance. As Williams and Arrigo explain, "More precisely, virtue is knowledge, while vice is ignorance."[5]

By the early Middle Ages, philosophical inquiry was replaced by theological speculation. The earlier "crime as vice" perspective, which was inferred from the determination of the virtuous life as formulated within the context of ethical and political theorizing, was replaced by a "crime as sin" perspective fueled by the growth of Christianity, and especially of Catholicism. Even as this transition from "crime as vice" to "crime as sin" occurred between the Greco-Roman era and the Middle Ages, both of these eras were similar in that small groups such as the family, clan, or tribe effectively held individuals in check. This system of collective responsibility for the control of deviance and the mainte-nance of social order has aptly been described by Michel Foucault as *the many watch the few.*[6] The "many" refers to society-at-large, while the "few" refers to those persons, infrequent in number, who dare violate the normative order. If only a few persons are deviating, this means that the system of informal, group-based control is effective. With crime rates low or non-existent in early societies, there was very little thought given to the need for experts or specialists who would carry out control duties for society.

[handwritten margin note: Informal Control]

In earlier societies characterized by mechanical solidarity, shared orientations toward the sacred provided the groundwork for truth, knowledge, and wisdom concerning all matters religious and secular. Indeed, religion was one of the first systematic forms of social control and, as Charles Ellwood argued,

[handwritten asterisk mark in margin]

> The religious sanction for conduct, being a supernatural sanction, all human experience shows, has been one of the most effective means of controlling the conduct of normal individuals. The desire to come into right relations with a deity, who represents in the earlier stages of [societal] development the ideal of personal character, has been an effective means of preventing too wide a variation in conduct in individuals.[7]

As Michel Foucault and others have argued, in the transition from the primitive to the modern era, societal perspectives on deviance have changed as well.[8] The earliest societies (from human antiquity through the 1600s) tended to view deviants as ignorant (lacking ethics or virtue) or *sinful*; the era of early modernity (from the 1600s through the mid-1800s) tended to view deviants as *bad*, either rooted in bad genes (the biological explanation) or because persons simply chose to act in non-conforming ways (the utilitarian explanation); and in later modernity and postmodernity (from the mid-1800s until today) deviants tend to be viewed as *sick* and in need of treatment or rehabilitation rather than punishment. (As we will see in chapter 8, however, since the 1970s reha-bilitation as a goal of the criminal justice system has declined in favor of harsher and more punitive sanctions such as incarceration. Nevertheless, the therapeutic ethos remains a prominent feature of Western societies outside of the context of formal corrections, as will be illustrated below.) It is this latter stage of development of modernity within which medical social control rises to prominence, concomitant to the growth of medicine and allied professional and occupational groups. Although medicine competes with law for dominance in the realm of formal control, as we shall see it is often complicitous with law as well.

This chapter is concerned with providing a comprehensive overview of the nature of medical control. We begin by explaining the nature and form of social control exerted by a variety of medical as well as non-medical actors across various institutional spheres (the family, schools, community, and so forth). Although the contemporary trend is toward a continuing growth of medicalization, the introduction of such concepts as demedicalization, remedicalization, and biomedicalization will illustrate that medicine acts in neither a unitary nor a unidirectional fashion with regard to its control function. Even so, one thing that continues to facilitate the growth of medicalization is the therapeutic ethos of modern Western societies, a cultural orientation which places great emphasis on the self and self-fulfillment, and especially on the emotional and physical well-being of its citizens. Further, we will examine to what extent medical control impacts men and women differently, if at all. Lastly, we will spend some time examining aspects of the "dark side" of medicalization and medical control.

Medicine and social control

In his article titled "Medicine as an Institution of Social Control," Irving Zola provides one of the earliest and clearest statements on the growth of medicine and its role as a social control agent in modern society. As Zola explains,

> medicine is becoming a major institution of social control, nudging aside, if not incorporating, the more traditional institutions of religion and law. It is becoming the new repository of truth, the place where absolute and often final judgments are made by supposedly morally neutral and objective experts. And these judgments are made, not in the name of virtue or legitimacy, but in the name of health. Moreover, this is not occurring through the political power physicians hold or can influence, but is largely an insidious and often undramatic phenomenon accomplished by "medicalizing" much of daily living, by making medicine and the labels "healthy" and "ill" *relevant* to an ever increasing part of human existence.[9]

Over the last thirty years social policy and law arenas have reflected the continuing concerns that nation-states have with regard to the health and well-being of their citizens. In concert with the insurance industry, unprecedented steps have been taken to minimize losses due to accidents, illness, and death. These health policies and initiatives, incorporated into civil, criminal, and administrative law at the federal, state, and municipal levels, operate at both the group and the individual level. The two branches of medicine that are particularly well suited to taking up and overseeing the health of the citizenry are psychiatry and public health.

[handwritten margin note: Medicine as an institution]

Psychiatry functions primarily at the individual level, insofar as the aim is to instill prosocial adjustment in persons who are suffering from any number of recognized mental illnesses as documented in the *Diagnostic and Statistical Manual of Mental Disorders* (or *DSM*), the "bible" for psychiatric and mental health practitioners. In this sense, psychiatrists have purview over the medical aspects of the mind, subjectivity, and social behavior, just as doctors for many years have held a monopoly over the medical aspects of the body. Both psychiatry and regular medicine employ a case-method approach, seeking to return to health individual minds or individual bodies.

At the group or societal level is the *public health* approach or model, which may be defined as the "art and the science of preventing disease, prolonging life, and promoting health."[10] Through routine surveillance of populations or segments of populations that are considered to be at risk, data are gathered for purposes of ascertaining which antecedent factors are associated with unwanted health or behavioral outcomes. Based upon such data, interventions are implemented which presumably reduce or eliminate the social harm connected with these unwanted activities or processes. Some of the better known public health programs that have been initiated over the years include the campaign to reduce smoking; battles against infectious or non-infectious diseases such as typhoid, heart disease, cancer, and arteriosclerosis; removal or reduction of environmental hazards such as asbestos or lead paint in homes, businesses, and schools; needle-exchange programs to combat the transmission of HIV; and condom distribution in schools to reduce both unwanted teenage pregnancies and the spread of venereal disease.

We will examine the public health model more closely in a later chapter, but here it is important to note that successful public health campaigns against infectious diseases and other medical conditions have emboldened proponents of public health to expand their mandate to include a variety of social problems. Instead of medicalization, in this context we may suggest that a sort of *hygienization* or even *public healthification* is occurring.[11] A recent example is the controversy surrounding country singer Gretchen Wilson's use of smokeless tobacco in the video for her song "Skoal Ring."[12] The title of the song refers to the "worn-out circle" that results from users keeping a can of tobacco in their pants pocket. After Wilson played a concert in Nashville, Tennessee, where jumbo screens showed scenes from the video, the state attorney general ordered the country singer to stop "glamorizing" the use of chewing tobacco at her concerts. The reason this became an issue is that public displays of the video may violate the 1998 settlement between states and tobacco companies which prohibits the targeting of tobacco ads to young persons. Tennessee Attorney General Paul Summers informed Wilson that because many young people attend her concerts she could unduly influence them to take up cigarettes or other tobacco products. US Smokeless Tobacco

Co., the maker of Skoal, and party to the 1998 settlement, had agreed not to sponsor concerts under this or other tobacco-related brand names. It is indeed bizarre, yet in keeping with the logic of public health, that a state attorney general's office would threaten to halt or sanction musical or artistic performances in this way. Anything that is seen as promoting injurious or unhealthy activities or lifestyles is subject to legal, quasi-legal, or administrative controls in the name of public health and safety.

It should be noted in addition that psychiatrists are also attempting to expand their mandate beyond the treatment of sick individuals. Instead of diagnosing only individuals as suffering from mental disorders, some prominent members of the American Psychiatric Association are urging the establishment of a new category of mental illness that pertains to groups such as families, peer groups, work groups, or even terrorist organizations. If accepted for inclusion in the next edition of the *DSM*, this new class of "relational disorders" would view otherwise healthy individuals as "unhealthy" within the context of certain relationships or group settings.[13]

Medicalization, demedicalization, and remedicalization

Although medicalization refers to the process by which a growing number of social and personal issues are converted into medical problems, by no means is the growth of medicalization unidirectional or unilinear. Medicalization is more aptly described as growing in fits and starts, with some areas of society falling under the auspices of medical control faster than others.[14] Occasionally areas that were previously the province of medical expertise and intervention are *demedicalized*, meaning that medical understandings and treatments of the condition no longer apply or take precedent. A prime example of both medicalization and demedicalization is homosexuality.[15] Since 1968, the year in which the second edition of the *Diagnostic and Statistical Manual* was published, homosexuality had been listed as a type of "sexual deviation" with identifiable etiology and symptomology. In other words, for many years the field of psychiatry understood and treated homosexuality as a mental illness, the behavioral and cognitive manifestation of which was sexual attraction between persons of the same sex.

All the great pioneers of psychiatry, including Sigmund Freud, Carl Jung, and Alfred Adler, viewed homosexuality as a mental disorder, but scientific consensus on the matter began eroding by the 1960s. Interestingly enough, this changing perception of the status of homosexuality as a mental illness was not the result of dramatic new breakthroughs in the scientific evidence concerning this "disease." Rather, external factors such as changing social mores concerning the acceptability of homosexuality (as a concomitant to the sort of political activism embodied in the gay rights movement of the 1960s) were much more decisive. Indeed, in 1974 the nomenclature committee of the American Psychiatric Association voted to remove homosexuality as a mental illness, but decided to retain a category known as "egodystonic homosexuality," or sexual orientation disturbance, which included male or female homosexuals who were uncomfortable with their sexual orientation. The committee even went so far as to make a number of policy recommendations, including:

> be it resolved that the American Psychiatric Association deplores all public and private discrimination against homosexuals in such areas as employment, housing, public accommodation, licensing and declares that no burden of proof of such judgment, capacity, or reliability shall be placed upon homosexuals greater than that imposed on any other persons. Further, the American Psychiatric Association supports and urges the enactment of civil rights legislation at the local, state, and federal level that would offer homosexual citizens the same protections now guaranteed to others on the basis of race, creed, color, etc. Further, the American Psychiatric Association supports and urges the repeal of all discriminatory legislation singling out homosexual acts by consenting adults in private.[16]

When the third edition of *DSM* was published in 1980, homosexuality was dropped for good as a category of mental illness. Just like drapetomania a century earlier, homosexuality disappeared from the official lexicon and imagination of medical practitioners. The immediate consequence of this demedicalization of homosexuality was that it was left as an issue for other realms of control, most notably those of everyday life and of law and politics, to grapple over, define, and respond to.

Since 1980 competing discourses in the arenas of politics, science, religion, the mass media, gay rights activism, and the lay public have produced an unsettled and still contested picture of the nature of homosexuality. The APA was an effective instigator in the thrust or direction of this discourse with its dropping of homosexuality from the *DSM* and its law and policy recommendations for acknowledgment of the civil rights of gays. To combat religious views of homosexuality as sin or lay public views of it as merely a lifestyle choice, gay rights activists in concert with sympathetic members of the scientific community pursued a biological explanation for homosexuality. The search for a "gay gene" continued through the 1980s and 1990s, and a "born gay" philosophy emerged as the best strategy for assuring fairness and equal protection for homosexuals under civil rights law.

This embrace of biology and genetics has acted as a two-edged sword, however, because it opens up the possibility of a *remedicalization* of homosexuality.[17] Besides interest in a possible genetic basis for sexual orientation, however, there is also the fact that, at least early on, AIDS was considered a "gay" disease, and this early "treatment and prevention of HIV/AIDS was engendering a remedicalization of homosexuality."[18] Although some further stigmatization of homosexual lifestyles occurred as a result of this – including heightened medical surveillance of gay men especially – a complete remedicalization of homosexuality has yet to occur.

In addition, with increasing attention to the biological and genetic underpinnings of human phenomena, including of course human social behavior, some authors argue that a second great transformation of medicine has occurred. The first social transformation of medicine, running from approximately 1890 to 1945, saw the emergence of medicine as a leading profession comprised not only of physicians, who were at the top of the status hierarchy within the profession, but also nursing and an array of allied health services. During this time there also emerged technological and pharmaceutical innovations that helped to further professionalize medicine, as well as specialized structures such as hospitals, clinics, and private medical practices which provided the worksites for doctors to perform their craft.[19] Again, it was during this period that medicalization began, owing to the growing status of physicians and allied health practitioners who, as a group, felt emboldened to expand their areas of expertise to include not only the body but also the mind, social behavior, and society more generally.[20]

Biomedicalization and "selling sickness"

The second great transformation, mentioned above, began after 1945, as continuing advances in science, technology (especially computer technology), and pharmaceuticals gave rise to innovations such as molecular biology, biotechnologies, genomization, transplant medicine, cloning, and the extension of not only life expectancy but also the quality of life to levels never before imagined.[21] The term for this transformation is *biomedicalization*, which inexorably renders less relevant the human element in medical care and treatment while elevating to prominence the use of technological and pharmaceutical interventions. For example, more than thirty years ago Henry Gadsen, the head of Merck, one of the world's biggest drug companies, told *Forbes* magazine that he would like to expand his clientele beyond just sick people to include virtually everybody. Indeed, his dream was to market and sell drugs to everyone.[22] With the continuing rise in prominence of the medical and allied professions, the acceptance and use of the disease metaphor in everyday life, the near obsession with reducing risk and harm by governments and everyday citizens, and the emphasis placed on "quality of life" in public health, medicine, and even community policing, that dream of Gadsen's has come true. Human beings are turning with increasing regularity to the use of drugs for even the most minor aches and pains associated with modern living. This is at the heart of biomedicalization, an increasingly prominent form of medical control.

Tying in with the issue of biomedicalization, it should be noted that medicalization is spurred on not so much by the purposive efforts of self-interested doctors and allied health professionals. As Frank Furedi argues, medicalization is no longer a top-down phenomenon (if it ever truly was), but instead a grassroots phenomenon being prodded along by growing legions of "patients" who insist on medical interventions for a variety of everyday difficulties.[23] And given the presence of this growing number of discerning and informed individuals clamoring for medical and drug treatments, drug companies have been more than willing to oblige them in their quest to become – and remain – patients. Hence, "selling sickness" has become big business, and a sort of *disease mongering* has arisen, a situation whereby individuals are informed about and seek drug treatments for such things as male pattern baldness, erectile dysfunction, social anxiety disorder, and emotional trauma, as well as a growing list of addictions and phobias.[24]

Public health and public safety

With the rise of the nation-state and the concept of citizenship, human beings began being assessed and understood more and more in economic terms, that is, in terms of their being "resources" that the state may use to pursue collective political and social goals. It begins with such things as taxation (forced payments to the state to offset operating expenses) and conscription (forced military service), but then expands into more areas of social life, including the idea that persons ought not to do things that jeopardize their own or others' safety. Since medicine had already been on the scene to provide authoritative pronouncements about the nature of human health and illness, it was only natural that the professional complex of medicine would be placed in the service of the state, largely through the granting of licensing for the provision of medical services, but also for informing legislative bodies about the health risks citizens faced.

In the United States the history of public health initiatives was at best haphazard and sporadic at least through the early twentieth century. In the southern United States especially, public health initiatives were not embarked upon in any systematic fashion until full-blown health crises emerged. For example, it was not until the 1870s that full legislative efforts to implement public health measures were enacted, this in response to a deadly plague of yellow fever which had been introduced through the port of New Orleans and which had spread as far north as Ohio.[25] By an act of Congress the port was eventually quarantined, in stiff opposition to local politicians and citizens who saw it as an unwarranted intrusion of federal authority and control.

Nevertheless, precedents established in law tend to take on a life of their own, and over time more and more federally mandated medical interventions emerged, based on the success of many such programs implemented in the southern United States and elsewhere. Unlike the uneven and erratic impetus toward public health law that emerged in the United States, however, England's public health initiatives happened earlier and on the whole were better planned and managed. The Public Health Act, passed in England in 1848, was in response to

the gross damage to human life engendered by the industrial revolution. To seek work and financial security, there was mass emigration
from rural into urban life. The towns were not prepared for this and the
consequent overcrowding, squalor and poverty created serious misery
and disease affecting a large proportion of the working population.
Over time, this threatened to engulf English society as a whole as
disease spread across the poverty line into "polite" society.[26]

Some of the earliest mapping of cities occurred in Britain, as citizens
and especially city administrators increasingly became concerned with
the public health of industrial conurbations. In 1842 Edwin Chadwick,
secretary of the Poor Commission, published a detailed map of such
cities as Leeds and also Bethnal Green in London, indicating by color
"less clean houses" (in brown) but also outbreaks of diseases such as
cholera (in blue). Authorities could, in effect, exert social control
through political surveillance of cities, not only keeping tabs on
publicly avowed health issues, but also enabling "cartographic surveillance of centres of social radicalism."[27]

Largely because of public health – including such health innovations
as sanitation, waste disposal, clean water technologies, and milk
pasteurization – mortality in the United States declined by 40 percent
from 1900 to 1940, while during the same period life expectancy at birth
rose from forty-seven to sixty-three years.[28] These quite substantial
advances in the health of human populations led inexorably to the
increased application of medical and public health techniques and
operating assumptions to many more areas of life not tied directly to
the physiological aspects of health and wellness. This is why today, in
modern or postmodern society, there are increasing numbers of legal,
administrative, or quasi-legal regulations pertaining to the reduction of
accident, injury, and death, but also an ever-expanding array of "risky"
behaviors, including gambling, aggression and violence, drug use,
sexual promiscuity, stalking, using the Internet, watching television,
and so forth. With regard to medicalization, the discourse of "addiction" has attached itself to these and many other social activities.

As mentioned earlier, medicalization moves forward and advances
not necessarily because doctors are pushing an agenda for medical
expansionism or imperialism.[29] Indeed, medicalization is often pushed
forward by other personnel, agencies, and institutions. Within the vast
healthcare system of the United States, for example, only about 8
percent of personnel are medical doctors; the vast majority are support
staff (such as in clerical or administrative work and nursing), pharma-
cists, medical social workers, medical sociologists, and a wide assortment of counselors and therapists, most of whom are not psychiatrists.[30] Social institutions such as education and business have
personnel that mimic the role and functions of physicians. For example, although schools have school physicians and nurses on staff, they
also typically have school social workers and non-medical counselors.
Many business organizations, especially those that practice human

resource (or HR) management, have employees that act like doctors or psychiatrists even though they are more likely to have management rather than medical degrees. Paradigmatic of this are so-called employee assistance programs (EAPs), the aims of which are to provide counseling and other services to employees who are struggling with such issues as drug or alcohol use, stress, nervousness or anxiety, difficulty in getting along with co-workers or supervisors, tardiness or absences, reduced productivity, malingering, and so forth.[31]

Whereas at the level of individual case management the preeminent values are those of harm and risk reduction, at the collective level the overriding medical value is that of *public safety*. At both the individual and collective levels, medical values are utilitarian in that the goal of medical intervention and oversight is to maximize the good (health) and minimize the bad (illness and pathology) for the greatest number of people. The medical goal of *utility*, and its instantiation in the policy value of public safety, should be compared with the primary value of the criminal justice system, which is *justice*. Historically the criminal justice system has been a reactive system of control, in that police response to crimes occurs for the most part only in those instances where citizens feel sufficiently compelled to file a complaint or make a report. Conversely, the medical model of individual case management as well as the collective model of public health act (ideally) in a proactive fashion, attempting to head off adverse health consequences before they have a chance to become severe through routine surveillance of individuals and populations. This is the ideal of preventive maintenance, which the criminal justice system has only recently attempted to implement by way of community-oriented and problem-oriented policing (these will be covered in more detail in later chapters).

The interesting thing about the medical or public health value of public safety and the criminal justice system value of justice is that the two values – public safety and justice – are not necessarily compatible, and often come into conflict with one another. In the criminal justice system, defendants who are being charged with a crime have available to them a range of due process procedural safeguards to ensure their fair and equitable treatment as a check against the arbitrary and potentially illegitimate use of state power against them. This means that the value of justice demands a sometimes lengthy series of appeals and other legal maneuvers before the state can impose a sanction against the defendant.

On the other hand, the value of public safety demands quick and swift actions on the part of agencies and oversight personnel in order to ameliorate whatever situation is at hand. From the public safety perspective, for example, it makes more sense to fast-track a criminal defendant charged with drug possession into treatment for his or her "own good," rather than have them go through the usual range of pre-sentence hearings and other technical aspects of court procedure. In other words, from the public safety perspective, due process procedural safeguards act as impediments standing in the way of the defendant getting "help" for his or her "condition" or "sickness."[32]

This conflict between the values of utility and justice is especially acute regarding a whole range of social behaviors or activities that are illegal, specifically so-called victimless crimes. *Victimless crimes* – for example drug use, gambling, various forms of sexual activity, seatbelt laws, bans against assisted suicide, and so forth – are criminalized by way of *mala prohibita* laws, which are laws that make things illegal by decree, that is, by passage of an ordinance specifying which acts are considered to fall under the jurisdiction of legal control. *Mala prohibita* laws are contrasted against *mala in se* laws, the latter of which are laws which make illegal a range of acts which presumably most reasonable persons can agree are bad in and of themselves, including things such as murder, rape, assault, robbery, and theft. The point is that there is not a high level of citizen consensus regarding the extent to which *mala prohibita* or victimless crimes are truly criminal in nature.

Crimes that can be characterized as *mala prohibita*, such as drug use and sexual behavior, are more likely than other crimes to be caught in a tug-of-war between proponents of medicalization on the one hand, and proponents of criminalization on the other. For example, is drug use a crime, a sickness, or perhaps both? Is the best response to drug use the public safety response which seeks to treat offenders rather than punish them? This might mean a complete circumvention of their due process rights in favor of fast-tracking them into drug treatment "for their own good." Or is the best response the standard law and order and crime control responses of the criminal justice system, where drug defendants are tried as criminals for their drug-related behaviors, but also are afforded the full gamut of legal protections by the state which must bear the highest level burden of proof, namely "beyond a reasonable doubt"? Which forms if any of "deviant" sexuality are we willing to criminalize or medicalize, and how far should it go? For example, should prostitution best be viewed as a crime, an illness, or neither (such as the case of decriminalization of prostitution in certain counties in Nevada)?

The debate over medicalization versus criminalization could become entirely moot if societal attitudes toward *mala prohibita* crimes continue tipping toward the position that many acts currently classified as criminal should be redefined as illnesses. For example, the "psychopathology of crime" perspective argues that all forms of crime and deviant behavior fall under the category of psychopathology insofar as crime or deviance is not "normal," whether in a statistical, a moral or a legal sense. In this most radical version of the argument, treatment tribunals would replace judges and criminal courts, culminating in what many refer to as the therapeutic state.[33] In the next few sections we will examine the idea of the therapeutic state – and the ethos or culture lying behind it – in somewhat more detail.

The therapeutic ethos

It was mentioned earlier that medicalization proceeds and is prodded along largely at the behest of persons who do not themselves hold medical degrees. However, it is not only in the areas of service provision in business and other major institutional settings that we see a proliferation of quasi-medical personnel in support of legitimate medical personnel. The cultures of modern Western society – especially those of the United States and Great Britain – are also thoroughly suffused with the language, terminology, and epistemological assumptions of sickness, disease, wellness, rehabilitation, and recovery. James Nolan has referred to this as the *therapeutic ethos*, a cultural orientation in which, in their interpersonal dealings with others, persons are apt to interpret and act upon situations in terms of the assumptions of mental health, emotivism, developmentalism, and a "confessional" mode of problem-solving which emphasizes the talking out of "feelings" or other presumably private, internal matters.[34]

In earlier times, when the church was the leading source of morality, wisdom, and truth, priests tended to the spiritual needs of true believers through the private confessional. This normalizing discourse has of course over time been transformed into the normalizing discourses of medicine and psychiatry, where persons put themselves on public display through the sharing of feelings and emotions, especially when untoward activities are associated with an individual. Back in 1997 sportscaster Marv Albert was accused of throwing his former girlfriend, Vanessa Perhach, on a bed in a Virginia hotel room and biting her on the back more than a dozen times.[35] Albert, who resigned as television announcer for the New York Knicks and New York Rangers and was fired from NBC sports, pled guilty to a misdemeanor assault charge, and the judge ordered him to continue the mental health treatments – primarily anger-management therapy – which he had voluntarily begun when the charges first surfaced. Whether or not these sessions really did anything to cure or ameliorate his "sickness" will never be known. However, Albert made a public appearance in which he stated, "Through these regular sessions I feel I've learned more about myself than at any point in my life." Making a clean break of things in the therapeutic culture means being willing to tell others how new insights about one's self gained as a result of mental health interventions have transformed the individual presumably for the better.

The operation of the therapeutic ethos is evident in other cases beyond those which involve a person's attempt to repair a criminal or deviant identity through public confessionals and self-presentations. In a women's college basketball game played on Tuesday, February 24, 1998, between the University of Connecticut and Villanova University, Connecticut player Nykesha Sales was allowed to score a basket unchallenged by the other team.[36] A few nights earlier Sales, who was only one point away from become the leading scorer in the history of

Connecticut's women's basketball program, ruptured her Achilles tendon in a game against Notre Dame. The injury ended her season and her career, and presumably any hopes of her attaining the scoring record.

But in a deal pre-arranged by the coaches of both teams, and with the blessings of Big East commissioner Mike Tranghese, at the opening tip Villanova lined all of its players on its end of the floor while Sales, wearing a large knee brace and positioned under the basket, was passed the ball from one of her teammates and scored easily. On the next possession Villanova was allowed to go back down the court uncontested to score their two points.

The two points allowed Sales to pass Kerry Bascom as the all-time scoring leader in Connecticut women's basketball. Connecticut coach Geno Auriemma said, "She never asked to score a lot of points, and she never asked to break the record. It was the right thing to do for all she has done for UConn the last four years." If this is indeed the "right thing to do," it makes sense only if the assumption is made that it is more important to attend to feelings, emotions, and the shoring up of fragile self-esteem than it is to maintain the integrity of competition in sporting events. Indeed, one of the interesting things about the self-esteem training that routinely occurs in a number of schools (typically in grades K through 8) is that keeping score of sporting events is viewed as potentially damaging to self-esteem because of the way it lumps individuals into the categories of "winners" and "losers." As a consequence, some schools have moved toward a policy of not keeping score of games, at least not among the younger age groups.[37]

In the case of Sales and the arrangement to allow her to score the basket which made her Connecticut's all-time leading scorer, the game was of course being scored, and points were important – indeed, the whole purpose of the special arrangement was about points – but they were important for the wrong reason. The points were important primarily to make persons feel good about themselves – Sales, the coaches, the league commissioner, and everyone in the stands who gave Sales a standing ovation after she was allowed to score the two points. The whole event was something akin to a group hug. Paying homage to feelings in this way is the hallmark of the therapeutic culture.

The therapeutic state

Closely allied to the concept of therapeutic culture or ethos is the therapeutic state. The term *therapeutic state* refers to the ascendancy of the medical model of disease as the prevailing ideology of the modern welfare state. Within the therapeutic state medical terms such as "syndrome," "pathology," sickness," "illness," "disease," "addiction," and "therapy" tend to dominate social, legal, political, policy, and even informal (that is, everyday life) arenas of discourse.[38] The structure of therapeutic states is tied to the development and establishment of psychology (from the non-medical side) and psychiatry (from the medical side) as legitimating or normalizing discourses in those societies.[39] For example, within law and legal studies there recently has emerged a movement known as therapeutic jurisprudence (TJ). *Therapeutic jurisprudence* is a perspective that is concerned with using social and behavioral science research to study the extent to which a legal rule or practice promotes the psychological well-being of participants in the criminal justice system.[40] The aim is to maximize therapeutic and minimize anti-therapeutic outcomes of law and legal rulings.[41] For example, a judge who is sympathetic to TJ principles may, during jury instructions, inform the jury members that, because deliberations are often stressful and contentious, they can reduce such pressures and difficulties by acting more collaboratively and with more compassion, patience, and tolerance toward one another, and turning to each other for emotional support during this "trying" time.[42] An instruction of this sort effectively aims to turn jury deliberations into a group therapy session.

Indeed, over time law and court proceedings have become more emotional. In the original blueprint for the modern criminal court, cases would be decided by the sober collection of evidence in an adversarial system where the state on the one side would seek a conviction against the defendant, supported by his or her legal defense team, on the other. Any evidence or testimony deemed to be too emotionally charged would be excluded from the court proceedings, in that anything that inflamed the passions of the jury could get in the way of the sober, rational quest for the "facts" as based on the evidence at hand. This meant that for the most part victims were left on the sidelines while legal representatives of the state argued for a conviction. This move was made for purposes of eradicating, as much as possible, emotionalism and subjectivity from courtroom proceedings.

Today, however, as reflected in the victims' rights movement, the criminal court is attempting to incorporate victims into the legal process in more meaningful ways. One way this occurs is through the allowing of victim impact statements during the sentencing phase of the criminal trial. Other innovations such as the recent creation of a category of criminal offense known as "hate crimes" has further granted legitimacy to emotions within the modern courtroom.[43]

In a modern, enlightened and technologically advanced society, there is a strong belief that many of the bad things that happen in life – accidents, disease and sickness, death, broken hearts, unsatisfying marriages, uncertainty, being bullied, feeling sad, anxious, nervous, jittery, stressed out, or traumatized – can be reduced or even eliminated with the proper application of cutting-edge scientific, medical, social scientific, and behavioral science knowledge. Modern nation-states have a vested interest in the maximization of the life chances, productivity, and happiness of their citizens, primarily through the private business sector's ability to create such life-enhancing products and services for those among the middle class who can afford them. Those that cannot attain the ideal of a middle-class lifestyle are serviced by the welfare apparatus of government, and although for many years welfare programs have been run by the rather sober logic of economics and policy analysis, even welfare of late has become medicalized.

For example, under President Clinton's welfare-to-work initiatives – especially as instantiated in the Personal Responsibility and Work Opportunity Reconciliation Act of 1996 – those on welfare are now expected to get off benefits within a specified period of time. In order to do this, welfare recipients need to be made "job-ready" so that "rapid attachment" to the workforce may occur. But instead of nuts-and-bolts educational and job-training programs – the so-called hard skills of training and job competencies – under the increasingly medicalized welfare-to-work programs welfare recipients are more likely to be given "soft skills" training, namely, behavioral "tips" or guidelines for fitting into the social relations of the workplace.[44] Whereas previously welfare caseworkers acted more like employment counselors or "job coaches," now they act more like therapists involved in intensive case management of "patients," assessing and monitoring their progress toward integration into the workplace.

Another area of growth in the therapeutic state revolves around the issues of trauma and stress. Specifically, post-traumatic stress disorder has become the highest profile form of stress in media, policy, and legislative circles. It originated from the ongoing effort to comprehend the Vietnam War experience by many of the veterans of that war.[45] Many Vietnam veterans were having trouble adjusting to normal routines and social activities upon returning from the war, and as they were appearing in greater numbers at veterans' hospitals and mental health clinics complaining of a range of symptoms – restlessness and sleeplessness, aggressiveness and proneness towards violence, inability to sustain close relationships, suicidal thoughts, drug and alcohol use, isolationism, panic attacks, and mistrust toward others – psychiatrists and psychologists began taking notice. A set of diagnostic criteria for a new mental illness, post-traumatic stress disorder (PTSD), was soon developed and first appeared in *DSM-III* in 1980. Since that time, however, application of PTSD to a widening array of complaints and conditions – not just to war-related trauma – has grown exponentially.

One area in which the discourse of PTSD has been most noticeable is natural or human-made disasters. Although today it is commonplace to assume that persons who have experienced such disasters – such as hurricane Katrina in 2005 which devastated portions of Louisiana, Mississippi, and Alabama – often show classic symptoms of PTSD, this has not always been the case. As Frank Furedi has argued, until the 1980s the British people faced disasters with stoicism, rugged determinism, fortitude, and a "stiff upper lip." After the Aberfan disaster of 1966, an industrial tragedy that took the lives of 116 children and twenty-eight adults, there was no talk of psychological distress among the survivors. Indeed, within several weeks the surviving children of the town resumed their education, and first responders and others at the scene noted that the children seemed normal and well adjusted. The villagers had in effect managed the situation well with little help, and without much hand-wringing over the grief and trauma that may have lingered afterwards. As Furedi cogently observes,

> Today, such a response to a major disaster would be unthinkable. There would be an automatic assumption that every survivor in the area was deeply traumatized and inevitably scarred for life. Sending young pupils back to school so soon after a tragedy would be scorned as bad practice. The very attempt by the community to cope through self-help would be denounced as misguided since such victims could not be expected to deal with such problems on their own.[46]

Interestingly enough, in today's world, where disorders such as PTSD are the analytical frames for understanding or making sense of the aftermath of disasters, reactions to disasters like the one that occurred at Aberfan simply cannot be accepted. Organizations such as the National Center for PTSD have a "psychological first aid" manual ready to be distributed to survivors alongside life essentials such as food, clothing, temporary living quarters, clean water, getting electricity and sewage systems back on line, and preparing for physical reconstruction of the area.[47] Indeed, there is quite a bit of revisionist history going on with regard to Aberfan, as researchers are "helping survivors to reinterpret their experiences through the language of trauma."[48]

Gender and medicalization

If indeed, as the medicalization thesis suggests, medicine has grown more powerful as a narrative or discourse for defining and regulating social behavior, does medicalization impact men and women differently? We would expect that in patriarchal societies, where males tend to garner the lion's share of valued social resources at the expense of relatively deprived and oppressed females, medical control would be directed more at women, and have a more profound impact in terms of regulating and circumscribing women's lives. Although this thesis has a certain intuitive appeal, it is not quite this simple or straightforward. For a more nuanced account of the impact of medicalization on women, let us look at the work of Elianne Riska.[49]

Riska argues that, beginning in the 1970s, the impact of medicalization on women has passed through three phases or stages. The first phase was *gender neutrality*, meaning that in its earliest stages medicalization proceeded in a general fashion without necessarily acting in a way that discriminated against women. For example, the precursor to the modern medicalization thesis was the anti-psychiatry movement of the 1950s and the 1960s, which was a broad-based critique of the practice of warehousing social misfits – males and females alike – in total institutions such as the insane asylum. In the asylum, psychiatrists were criticized for being able to pass judgments – often uncontested – on the alleged problematic behavior of persons being confined there. In addition, advances in medical technology had produced a range of drugs that acted to facilitate behavior management and modification, and since psychiatrists and physicians were the only ones who could legitimately prescribe such drugs, their power increased accordingly with only minimal checks in place. In addition, patients in these asylums were exposed to degrading and dehumanizing conditions, including the stripping of personal identity, isolation from the outside world, being confined in close living quarters with other patients who were sometimes violent, and exposure to drug regimens and surgical procedures (such as lobotomies or electro-shock) the aims of which were to pacify and stultify patients even at the expense of their health.

The growth in the number of mental illnesses appearing with each new edition of the *DSM* was another point of criticism among proponents of the medicalization thesis, yet again early on these criticisms rarely focused on gender issues per se. For example, in the therapeutic state behavior modification and control through drug treatment continues to be emphasized, and, as more and more drugs are linked up with the treatment of specific unwanted behaviors, there is a concomitant growth of *DSM* categories of mental illness. Among school children, fidgeting, inattention, hyperactivity, and not paying attention may lead to a diagnosis of attention deficit hyperactivity disorder (ADHD), and the drug of choice for treatment of this "disease" is Ritalin. There is also explosive growth in the diagnosis of depression, which is treated by a number of anti-depressants including Zoloft, Prozac, Paxil, and Wellbutrin.

It was not until the second phase, which Riska refers to as *women as victims*, that explicit attention to gender issues began appearing in the medicalization literature. Much of this was tied to the second wave of feminism which began in the 1960s and which made inroads into academic writing and by the 1970s had spawned a vast feminist literature. Examples of topics appearing during this phase include:

- the medicalization of childbirth, whereby the largely male-dominated medical specialty of obstetrics displaced the traditional methods of prenatal care and birth delivery, such as midwifery, which were female-dominated;
- the explosive growth in plastic surgery, performed by male surgical specialists on a predominately female patient population;
- maladies such as pre-menstrual syndrome and surgical procedures such as hysterectomies, which pathologized the normal bodily processes of females.

Here, feminist critique merged with the critique of medical control embodied in the medicalization thesis, making problematic in more specific and focused terms the control of women's bodies and lives by a male-dominated medical profession.

Riska refers to the third phase as the *revival of reductionism.* In the early stages of the growth of medicine as a profession, the great majority of research studies on a variety of medical conditions used male subjects as the test population. This meant that medicine developed presumably general and universal understandings about illness and disease which were based on an invisible male standard. In some sense, then, the first phase of gender neutrality was reductionist in that it reduced all categories of persons to the invisible male standard, even as medicine was claiming the generalizability of its findings to all members of the human population. With the second phase of medicalization, the phase that raised the "women's issue" and tended to view women as "victims" of male-dominated medicine, the invisible male standard was shattered, whether explicitly or implicitly.

But since this second phase, where so much attention had been devoted to women's health issues as well as critiques of the male-dominated medical establishment, there is more explicit attention being devoted to men's health. For example, public health advocates have raised something that might be called the "men as endangered species" hypothesis.[50] This is generated from the reality or the perception that certain diseases or conditions are unique to, or disproportionately affect, males. In most human populations, for example, males have lower life expectancy than females. Coronary heart disease is much more prevalent in males as well, and at least initially this was traced to stress and the fact that, as breadwinners in a patriarchal society, males are forced to compete with other males for the economic security of their families. This gave rise to the theory of the Type A personality – the hard-working male breadwinner – which effectively medicalized the moral aspects of heterosexual masculinity.[51] Also, with so much new focus on men's sexuality, especially with regard to sexual functioning (e.g., heightened awareness of male impotence, made famous by Bob Dole's "erectile dysfunction" commercials, as well as media sensationalism over the drug Viagra), men's health issues tend to be viewed not as social or psychological issues, but as biological issues. This marks a reintroduction of reductionistic biological thinking, but instead of operating with an invisible male standard, it has now been made explicitly biological.

Conclusion: the dark side of medicalization

Many humanitarians (most often falling on the left or liberal side of the ideological or political divide) support some aspects of medicalization to the extent that what is judged to be deviant behavior may not actually be the fault of the deviant. Instead, it may be the result of a medical condition. If so, the deviant cannot properly be held accountable for his or her actions. From the humanitarian vantage point, for these reasons it is preferable to conceptualize deviance as sickness as opposed to badness.[52]

If something like a "medicalization of life" has happened, as suggested by Ivan Illich,[53] it has happened at least in part because persons in their everyday lives find it expedient or advantageous on some level. As Lawrence Schneiderman explains,

> People who are preoccupied with the ordinary fatigues and aches and pains of living, [Illich] charged, rarely want to acknowledge that they are unhappy with their jobs or their relationships, or despondent because they are trapped in stressful, unfulfilling life pursuits, or experiencing existential despair. They want to hear that they are physically ill. They want to hear that their sadness and fatigue, their aches and their pains are ailments for which medicine must assume responsibility.[54]

This quote sums up nicely the first negative aspect of medicalization, namely the *dislocation of responsibility*.[55] By defining behavior as a medical problem, individuals are absolved (at least partially) of responsibility. However, they also get labeled as having a sickness, which of course can have its own consequences above and beyond the issue of responsibility.

A closely related problem is that medicalization tends to turn more and more persons into victims, thus contributing to a growing *culture of victimization*. As more and more bad acts are understood as not being under the conscious control of individuals, persons are apt to claim, whenever they are caught in deviant or criminal acts, that they are a victim of their socialization, or genes, or hormones, or addictions.[56] A famous example of this sort of "abuse excuse" was the trial of the Melendez brothers, Erik and Lyle, in Los Angeles.[57] The brothers murdered their parents using a shotgun to end what they claimed were years of physical, sexual, and emotional abuse. Although the first trial ended in a hung jury, they were convicted of murder in the second trial.

Connected with the promotion of a culture of victimization is the fact that the growth of mental illnesses is bound to continue because of the internal logic of medical thinking. There are two basic types of error that can occur in medical diagnosis (as well as in hypothesis testing more generally). A doctor who judges a sick person to be well has committed a Type I error, while a doctor who judges a well person to be sick has committed a Type II error. When a doctor is examining a patient and attempting, based upon the range of symptoms presented, to determine whether the patient is ill, on close calls the doctor is more likely to view the patient as ill rather than as healthy. This is because, all things being equal, there are many more negative consequences associated with not doing something for a patient who is really ill, versus doing something for a patient who is not really ill. We may understand this tendency for medical practitioners to assume illness where perhaps none exists as the *Type II error problem*.[58] Because they are more ephemeral and hence resistant to empirical verification,[59] mental illnesses will produce more such "close calls" than physical illnesses, hence doctors (or non-physician practitioners offering mental health services) will give patients the benefit of the doubt and diagnose illness in greater numbers of cases, even where no such illness actually exists.

In sum, in the area of mental health diagnosis especially, mental health providers are likely to commit the Type II error (diagnosing illness where none exists), and as growing legions of persons are assumed to suffer from some form of mental illness this contributes to both a culture of victimization and the dislocation of responsibility. This medicalization of mental life has the ultimate effect of imperiling the ethics of personal responsibility.

Another problem with medicalization is the assumption of the *moral neutrality of medicine*. Professionals such as doctors ideally act in an affectively neutral way, putting the interests of their patients (or "clients," according to the service delivery model of managed health care) ahead of their own personal interests. Also, diagnoses and other technical aspects of patient care are presumably universalistic in nature, meaning that the particular characteristics of patients play no part in determining how doctors handle each case.[60] This view of how doctors go about their work is highly idealized and excessively optimistic. When medicine was limited to making authoritative statements about the human body and its physiology and functioning, it was at least plausible that moral and normative considerations played a minimal role in medical knowledge. But as the mandate of medicine expanded to include determinations of normal and deviant social behavior, so too did the role of values and morals. As Conrad and Schneider state, "Defining deviance as a medical phenomenon involves moral enterprise."[61]

Another problem with regard to medicalization is the *domination of expert control*. To the extent that more and more social behaviors fall under the mandate of medical control, persons in their everyday lives are disempowered since they lose the ability to negotiate the conditions of their existence collectively. In other words, they lose the ability to apply lay or local knowledge and understandings to their own lives. This contributes to the general impoverishment of communication, but also to heightened cynicism toward and distrust of major social institutions.[62]

Yet another manifestation of medicalization is *the individualization of social problems*. With the ongoing rationalization of society and the continuing move away from an emphasis on the group to an emphasis on the individual, there is a tendency to define and respond to social problems from the perspective of the individual. In other words, when a problem is medicalized the tendency is to isolate and respond to sick individuals rather than to acknowledge that most problems are complex and systemic. Personal behavior that does not meet with the approval of society may indicate a problem in the social structure of society rather than merely a case of individual pathology or deviance that is amenable to medical diagnosis and treatment.

From the previous point follows the problem of the *depoliticization of deviant behavior*. One of the best ways to reduce or eliminate ideas or actions that are deemed to be threatening or dangerous to the status quo is to label as medically ill those who hold such ideas or engage in such actions. As Conrad and Schneider explain, "Medicalizing deviant behavior precludes us from recognizing it as a possible intentional repudiation of existing political [or social] arrangements."[63] For example, a student fidgeting and not paying attention in class may not have the disease of ADHD, but instead may simply be the product of a visual culture characterized by the rapid movement and transient images of video games and the Internet.[64] This may indicate that children need to spend more quality time with real flesh-and-blood human beings, a potentially problematic suggestion given the modern realities of the two-parent working family and continuingly high divorce rates.

A final problem for which medicalization is at least partially culpable is the *exclusion of evil*. In earlier times, when religion was the leading source of truth, wisdom, and goodness, deviant acts were understood as sinful or evil. The religious worldview provides an unshakeable moral template grounded in the word of God or the gods, and as a consequence the world is seen in black and white, as a struggle between good and evil. There are no shades of gray. But with the rise of Enlightenment thought and the deterministic explanatory systems of science, secular explanations were sought for all sorts of phenomena, including social behavior. If people's actions are not caused by God or by evil forces, they must originate in the person, or chemicals, or the environment, or society more generally, or some complex combination of worldly elements. If crime and deviance are illnesses, it makes no sense to say that such behavior is evil or that the person willingly engaged in it. Excluding evil in this way is a logical extension of the scientific worldview which suggests that all phenomena have worldly causes, thereby denying the metaphysical speculation that the human species may still harbor deep and dark – indeed evil – aspects even in an age of enlightened reason.[65]

This sentiment appears whenever human beings perpetrate horrendous and gruesome acts against one another. A lay sentiment toward serial killers, for example, is that no "sane" person would do something like that. We may attribute the acts themselves as evil, but still maintain that the person perpetrating the acts is "sick." The recent case of Dennis Rader, the so-called BTK killer (for "bind, torture, and kill") in Wichita, Kansas, is a case in point. By the time he was finally arrested in 2005, Rader had killed ten people over a thirty-year period, during which time he would occasionally send letters to the local newspaper taunting them over the killings and providing cryptic clues of who he was and his motivations for the acts.

At his sentencing, which occurred on August 18, 2005, Rader was informed that he would receive concurrent life sentences for each of the ten murders. (Although Kansas reinstated the death penalty in

1994, Rader was not eligible for capital punishment since the murders occurred before then.) When he was given the floor to speak, Rader spoke "matter-of-factly" about his victims and the techniques he used to subdue and eventually kill them. He referred to his victims as "projects," and explained how he selected them, beginning with a "trolling" phase and then moving into an active "stalking" phase if the "project" looked promising. He acquainted himself with the neighborhood within which his victims lived, observing their daily routines and social relationships. Rader preferred to break into a victim's home and wait for the person to return, at which time he would bind and gag the victim, then before murdering him or her (usually her) sometimes engaging in various forms of torture. He would occasionally take pictures with his Polaroid camera of the body in various poses of his choosing. He sometimes also masturbated on his victims.

During all this time Rader maintained the outward appearances of a normal life. He was married to the same woman for thirty years, he attended school and worked in the community, and he even became president of Christ Lutheran Church in Park City (a suburb of Wichita). He is now serving time in the El Dorado Correctional Facility in Kansas, where he is allowed three showers a week. He does not have access to television or radio and his reading materials are limited to legal documents related to his case. He is being held in an 80-square-foot cell with a concrete slab bunk, metal shelving and a chair, sink and plastic trash can. He will wear a brown jumpsuit and blue slip-on shoes, and his meals will be delivered through an opening in his cell door.[66] He believes he will eventually be redeemed when he faces God on his judgment day.

His current isolation in the facility is presumably for his own good. If he were to be integrated into the general prison population, he would likely meet the same fate as another notorious serial killer, Jeffrey Dahmer, who was murdered by a fellow inmate while assigned to latrine duty. Serial killers are near the bottom of the inmate status hierarchy.

Although Rader frequently referred to himself as a sexual predator and suggested that he was driven to these acts for reasons unknown to him (he sometimes invoked "Factor X"), his defense team chose not to use the insanity defense. Rader also waived his right to a jury trial, because, as he stated at the sentencing hearing, the evidence was overwhelming and "there was no way that I was going to get out of this." Although many people believe Rader is sick, especially with regard to the sexual fetish aspect of the killings, it is probably more accurate to say that he is simply evil, and leave it at that. But, as a therapeutic society, we cannot stop there. We want to dig deeply into the "tormented" minds of this and other serial killers so that we may discover the "true" reasons impelling such bizarre behavior, with an eye toward eventually "curing" this "sickness" of serial killing once and for all. Resigning ourselves to the fact that evil still exists in the world is simply not an option.

Suggestions for further reading

Conrad, Peter and Joseph W. Schneider. 1980. *Deviance and Medicalization: From Badness to Sickness.* St Louis: C. V. Mosby.

A book that thoroughly examines the variety of ways that everyday life, including those acts that could be considered deviant, has become medicalized.

Nolan, James L., Jr. 1998. *The Therapeutic State: Justifying Government at Century's End.* New York: New York University Press.

A thorough examination of the rise of therapeutic sensibilities in many areas of life, including government, schooling, the family, the church, the courts, and everyday life.

Riska, Elianne. 2003. "Gendering the Medicalization Thesis." *Gender Perspectives on Health and Medicine: Key Issues. Advances in Gender Research* 7: 59–97.

In this paper Riska offers a three-stage model of the impact and nature of medicalization applied specifically to the case of women.

Starr, Paul. 1982. *The Social Transformation of American Medicine.* New York: Basic Books.

Starr's analysis of the social transformation of medicine from the 1800s to the present remains an essential and authoritative resource on the subject.

Zola, Irving K. 1972. "Medicine as an Institution of Social Control." *Sociological Review* 20 (4): 487–504.

One of the earliest articles that made the explicit argument that medicine acts as an important form of social control in modern society.

5 Legal Control

Introduction: the criminal justice system

Among the three major forms of control – informal, medical, and legal – it is the last which captures more of the public imagination, which is depicted most prominently in popular culture, and which people share stories about with each other in their everyday lives. The lynchpin of legal control is the *criminal justice system*, comprised of three major subsystems, namely, police, law and the courts, and corrections. The criminal justice system of the United States is huge and costly. For example, in the fiscal year 2003, federal, state, and local governments spent over $185 billion for police protection, corrections, and judicial and legal activities, which represented a 10 percent increase over 2001.[1]

In this chapter we will examine the operation of the criminal justice system as it relates specifically to the issue of social control. The police, the courts, and corrections each has its own unique issues of control that are connected with how these subsystems operate within the broader system, and what major functions each serves. To simplify a very complex and expansive process, the *police* detain suspects and make arrests, the *courts* pass judgment on whether or not a person actually committed the crime or crimes with which he or she is being charged, and the *corrections* system punishes those convicted of crimes in criminal court.

The history of criminal justice: from informal to legal control

As discussed in the last chapter, in England up to AD 900 the mainte-nance of the social order was the responsibility of persons in their local communities.[2] By the time of the Norman Conquest in 1066, however, a sort of community policing known as the *frankpledge* system emerged. This was a system in which citizens formed volunteer teams with nine other neighbors, and this ten-member team would watch over each other to ensure everyone stayed out of trouble. This surveillance-based form of discipline worked because of the incipient forms of solidarity already found in the village or folk society as a result of the likeness and familiarity between its members.

If a member of a frankpledge group observed a law being broken he or she would engage in *hue and cry*, namely, yelling out to other members of the community that a violation had occurred.[3] All able-bodied persons would then be expected to respond to the hue and cry.

However, because frankpledge was more often than not based on neighborhood ties rather than on kinship ties per se, it was not a purely informal system of control. A level of formality was introduced especially with the requirement that members of frankpledge teams provide a *tithing* or a payment, which created a pool of funds that could be drawn on to pay to the court or, more frequently, the constable or sheriff of the district to help offset whatever damages were caused by wayward members of the team. This form of collective responsibility represents a transition point between the pure forms of informal control, based in kinship and primary groups, and the later formal systems of control represented by criminal justice.[4]

This system of control, marked by group surveillance based on neighborhood solidarity and tithings paid to sheriffs for infractions committed, remained in place in medieval England with only slight variations for the next five centuries. (At the time the position of sheriff was unpaid, hence tithings helped remunerate them for their services.) Members of local communities acted as their own police forces, and sheriffs acted more or less merely as figureheads for the king, who wielded almost unbridled power over the various shires of his kingdom. For the most part misbehavior in the community was handled informally, led by male heads of well-established families of yeomen or resident gentry. By the 1300s, however, the frankpledge system was augmented by *leet courts*, lesser public courts which rested upon presentment juries comprised of twelve or more men – generally no women were allowed to serve – who were sworn to present a collective report regarding problems of interest to the community.[5] Complaints making their way to these early leet courts included such things as scolding (a broad category of offenses, often charged against women, which included malicious gossiping, backbiting, and spreading rumors), eavesdropping, nightwalking, sexual misconduct, disorderly alehouses, "evil reputation," poverty, and illegal gaming.[6]

This system of control began breaking down with calls for law reform in England beginning in 1620. The main focus of the law reforms, in England as well as in New England in colonial America, was bringing to an end the Tudor ideology of the divine right of kings.[7] One of the most radical manifestations of this attempt to end the English monarchy was the execution of King Charles I in 1649. The execution of King Charles is notable to the extent that it serves to illustrate the way persons routinely tolerated what would today be considered gross violations and incivilities in the areas of aesthetics, human relations, and the value placed on human life.

Up to this time and at least into the late 1700s, at which point various writers began criticizing the practices of capital punishment and making a public spectacle of punishment in general, how a person died was important. As Donald Siebert explains, "It was expected that good people would die well, and that the good *and* great would die greatly."[8] The day of his execution the king dressed warmly to guard against shaking from the cold, which could give the impression that he was afraid. When he faced the executioner the first thing he asked him was "Is my hair well?" The king looked at the chopping block and reprimanded the executioner that "you must set it fast" and that "it might have been a little higher." He also showed the executioner the hand signal he would give to deliver the fatal blow, to which the executioner replied, "Yes I will and it please your Majesty." When the signal was given, with one blow the king's head was severed from his body, the head was held up and shown to the crowd, then placed in a casket with the body and put into a coffin covered with black velvet.[9]

The execution of King Charles I was a symbolic and dramaturgical event, one that displayed the triumph of popular justice over royal majesty.[10] Although still under British rule, the colonial Americans attempted also to implement aspects of popular justice even while necessarily borrowing a number of features of British law. For the Puritans of the Massachusetts Bay Colony, the law was designed to ensure public and private morality.[11] Consistent with Durkheim's conception of mechanical solidarity, offenses against God such as blasphemy could bring the death penalty, both for the Puritans as well as the Quakers of Pennsylvania. Punishments were overwhelmingly punitive and repressive, because deviance and crime were seen as abominations in the eyes of the Lord. As a result brandings, mutilations, and public whippings were common forms of punishment. Public humiliation was also important. We have already seen that executions were highly public performances, and pillories and the stocks were used for this purpose as well. The collective, open, and public nature of punishment in colonial times served to identify offenders to the entire community. Unlike the modern impulse toward rehabilitation as a goal of punishment, there was no pretense of changing offenders in colonial America.[12]

The American colonies declared themselves independent from England in 1776, and from that time until 1781 the Americans engaged in a desperate war against the British crown for their own liberty and freedom. British criminal justice was monarchical and authoritarian, and the king was considered the "fountain of justice." But for Puritan leaders and others in the American colonies, this was a flawed idea. Rather than the king, it was God who was the ultimate source of justice. As vigorously as America repudiated England's royal theory of justice, it nevertheless maintained a major feature of English law, and this was the common law.[13]

There are several characteristics of *common law* worth noting. First, under the doctrine of the supremacy of law no one is above the law, not even the king. Second, common law is law based on precedent, that is, on past court decisions. This is the doctrine of *stare decisis*, meaning "stand by the decided matter." Third, in keeping with the spirit of popular justice embedded in common law, criminal cases may be and often are decided by a jury of one's peers. Fourth, unlike other legal systems, common law places great emphasis on the spoken word.[14] As discussed previously, the criminal trial is an adversarial system in which two sides – the state as plaintiff and the criminal defendant and his or her team of defense lawyers – argue their case before a presiding judge (bench trial) or a jury. In order to win a conviction, the state must prove its case beyond reasonable doubt, the highest burden of proof among all forms of legal trial. Hence, much emphasis is placed on the oratory skills and knowledge of the law of lawyers, while the judge acts as a "referee," making sure that procedural rules are followed throughout the trial. Judges do not like having the decisions of their court overturned on appeal.

The Enlightenment, and changing ideas about justice and punishment

The *Enlightenment* was an eighteenth-century philosophical movement that emphasized the application of reason, experience, and the scientific method rather than dogma (religious or otherwise), superstition, and other such speculative and untestable ideas in the explanation of the physical and social world. The Enlightenment's triumph of science and rationalism pushed the search for universal laws of natural and social phenomena, including, within the social realm, procedural and substantive law founded on precedents established in judicial decisions. The notion of the "universality of law" meant that treatment of persons under the auspices of the criminal justice system was supposed to be equal, fair, and transparent. Instead of the rather arbitrary and oftentimes harsh and brutal treatment of criminal defendants characteristic of earlier times, the Enlightenment ushered in new ways of thinking concerning the punishment of prisoners.[15]

By the middle of the eighteenth century in Europe a *Classical School* of criminology found its beginning in the writings of such thinkers as Cesare Beccaria, Jeremy Bentham, and John Howard. Firmly located within the Enlightenment movement of thought, these and other thinkers emphasized the importance of reason and experience while denigrating theological forms of reasoning.[16] Let us first turn to a brief summary of Beccaria's thought.

Cesare Beccaria

This new impulse toward penal reform was initiated by Italian lawyer Cesare Beccaria, who published *On Crimes and Punishment* in 1764. Beccaria was appalled at the harsh and brutal punishments characteristic of European and American penal systems, including capital punishment, torture, banishment, transportation, and exorbitant fines out of proportion to the seriousness of the offense. As it was being practiced up through the middle of the eighteenth century, punishment was irrational in that it was arbitrary, often left to the whim of the sitting judge or to more informal systems of control, such as vigilantism, mob rule, blood feuds, lynchings, and even remnants of oaths and ordeals. Punishment was also irrational because it was excessively cruel and inhumane. This led Beccaria to suggest that capital punishment ought to be abolished, and that incarceration or imprisonment should replace many of the "irrational" punishments mentioned above. He further argued that, rather than the severity of punishment, what should be emphasized is the certainty of punishment. If certainty of punishment is to be achieved, this would require systemization, upgrading, and expansion of resources in all areas of the criminal justice system, not just corrections.[17]

Jeremy Bentham

A contemporary of Beccaria was British philosopher, economist, and jurist Jeremy Bentham. Unlike most of the thinkers of his time, Bentham believed that the common law was deficient because of its conservatism. Since common law relies overwhelmingly on the past decisions of judges, the doctrine of precedence is stultifying in that law changes only incrementally, if at all. The traditionalism of common law stands in the way of developing a truly scientific theory of law and legal process. For Bentham, a truly scientific approach to law would be grounded in the basic forces impelling human beings to act, namely pleasure and pain. According to Bentham's notion of the *hedonic calculus*, persons will act to maximize their pleasure and minimize their pain. The scientific approach to law, then, would incorporate this basic insight into human behavior, and hence the best laws would be those that ensured the greatest good for the greatest number of people. We see, then, that Bentham made explicit the utilitarianism already contained in Beccaria's thoughts on penal reform.

For Bentham, the quality of law is to be judged on its *utility*, that is, its ability to secure the greatest good for the greatest number of persons. This emphasis on utility, rather than on justice per se, led to the later medicalization of law, especially with regard to the value of public health or safety as discussed in the previous chapter. During Bentham's time, however, the penal goal of rehabilitation had not yet been formulated or made explicit, yet we can see its beginnings here.

By 1791, Bentham had conceptualized a new prison design which he called the Panopticon. The *Panopticon* was a prison envisioned as a circular structure with jail cells running around the circumference, while the jailers would be positioned in an elevated spire or steeple in the middle of the structure. From this middle, elevated position the jailers could easily monitor the activities of all the inmates. Further, the jailers' quarters would be constructed in such a way that the inmates could not tell if the observation tower was occupied. Because they had to assume they were being watched, inmates would in effect engage in self-control, which contributed to the prison's goal of assuring social control through the willing compliance and docility of the inmates.

Bentham hoped that the Panopticon design would catch on in all future prison construction, but it really never did. In 1794 a bill passed the British parliament to build such a prison at Battersea. Insufficient funds and the landowner's resistance to selling the land upon which the prison was to be built effectively scuttled the project.[18]

John Howard

Movements of thought such as the Enlightenment ideal that social progress was attainable through the application of the scientific method, as well as humanitarian and religious impulses toward the amelioration of human misery, had by the last quarter of the eighteenth century led to some laws being passed in the area of prison reform represented in the efforts of Beccaria, Bentham, Elizabeth Fry, William Blackstone, and others. For example, in 1773 parliament authorized magistrates to appoint chaplains in their jails.[19] There were also arguments made in favor of the abolition of solitary confinement, the education of prisoners, and other general improvements in the incarceration conditions of inmates, some of which were implemented into law as well, but on a limited and sporadic basis.

John Howard, an English philanthropist who was a contemporary of both Beccaria and Bentham, attempted to move the agenda of penal reform even further. When he was appointed high sheriff of Bedfordshire in 1773 he began the routine practice of visiting gaols (jails), prisons, and other correctional institutions with an eye toward ascertaining prevailing conditions in these facilities. In 1777 he published *State Prisons in England,* a report on these visitations. Howard was shocked by the conditions he saw in prisons, especially in the jails, which were rife with corruption (especially in the fee system by which jailers got paid), and general levels of filth, squalor, and unhealthiness. The momentum from this book, as well as Howard's earlier testimony before the House of Commons on the conditions of jails and prisons, led him to draft a "penitentiary act" which he hoped would be seriously considered by members of the British parliament.

The draft included several principles which Howard felt needed to be implemented for any meaningful prison reform to occur. The first things he proposed were improved sanitary conditions in living quarters, as well as improvements in the quality of prison food. He believed that the current fee system, where prisoners were responsible for paying for their own incarceration with fees going to their jailers, should be abolished. Additionally, Howard believed that prisons could be used to reform, and since many prisoners were being held because of drunkenness, he argued that no liquor should be allowed in jails and prisons. He also recommended the classification and segregation of prisoners by sex, age, and the types and severity of crimes committed.

Further, Howard argued that idleness was a cause of criminality, and urged that prisoners be taught "industriousness," although he did not advocate compulsory prison employment. Finally, on account of his deeply religious convictions (he was a Baptist), Howard believed that religious instruction was crucial for the reform of inmates.[20]

Howard's draft document, along with the efforts of other prison reformers such as William Eden and Sir William Blackstone, led to the British parliament passing the Penitentiary Act of 1779. This represented the most extensive and far-reaching change in law regarding the practice of state-sanctioned punishment in the Western world up to that time. For example, shortly after passage of the Act, use of capital punishment declined, the transportation of prisoners to the American colonies diminished considerably, and the use of imprisonment as a primary sanction increased significantly.[21]

Consolidation of state power and the emergence of policing

In America by the early nineteenth century similar changes in law, policing, and corrections were underway. After gaining its independence from Great Britain, the United States experienced substantial population growth. For example, in 1790 no American city had more than 50,000 inhabitants, but by 1830 almost half a million people lived in urban centers of that size or greater.[22] After 1830 industrial development and manufacturing grew as well, and continued to expand after the Civil War, marking a so-called Gilded Age of economic affluence for owners of industries in steel, transportation, rubber, and oil.

During this time immigration increased as well, initially primarily from Anglo-Saxon countries such as Ireland, Germany, and Great Britain, and many were arriving to seek employment opportunities in the newly industrializing areas of the American northeast. However, there was also the beginnings of a westward expansion, as Americans and others arriving in the country were attempting to settle the western frontier in search of gold, land, and whatever other opportunities awaited them there. Obviously, there was much lawlessness on the Overland Trail, and the California gold rush of 1848 produced some extreme forms of violence, malfeasance, and organized criminality.[23]

Even so, forms of self-help such as collective violence, rioting, and vigilantism were not confined to the western frontier. Beginning in the 1830s, riots became commonplace in America, especially in the east, growing out of class antagonisms fueled by a growing disparity between the haves and the have-nots in early industrial America, but also because of the political instability produced as a result of newly gained independence. During the Jacksonian era, the balance seemed to swing away from the sovereignty of the individual (embodied in the idea of rugged individualism and the Protestant work ethic) and toward the growth, centralization, and consolidation of state power. Even though

America was a society of laws, there was nevertheless a strong current of public scorn toward the law and toward lawyers specifically. In his *Vice Unmasked*, a book written in 1830, P. W. Grayson wrote about the uneasiness with law that ran throughout life in Jacksonian America. According to Grayson, although the United States had brought an end to tyrannical rule, the legal system that survived nevertheless still harbored elements that impeded human freedom. Grayson's main indictment was the way the rule of law had injured humanity's moral essence, that is,

> the way it debased man's sense of self and social responsibility by turning him from his high moral potential to a tricksy tailoring of conduct to avoid legal prosecution. In short, law was generally a tool of the cleverly vicious, a snare for the simply virtuous, and a burden on everyone, crippling human decency and progress.[24]

It was within this play of factors – increasing centralization of state authority, the real or perceived rise in unlawful and criminal activities (predominantly public order offenses), and growing class antagonisms in an era of industrial expansion – that impetus grew for the establishment of a paid, professional police force. As was the case for both corrections and the law, the American municipal police would be based on a British model as well, that of the "new police" of Sir Robert Peel.

Peel's "new police"

Robert Peel, a Tory politician, was appointed Chief Secretary for Ireland in 1812. The Irish government was especially concerned about a group of agrarian terrorists called the "banditti," who through collective violence sought to lower rents and tithes. Rural law enforcement in Ireland was magistrate-based, but when uprisings of the sort the banditti were fomenting occurred there was little officially that could be done. Indeed, by the time of Peel's arrival many of the local magistrates had abandoned their posts. Peel believed that, rather than suppressing violence and crime, more emphasis needed to be placed on prevention.

In order to solve the problem of agrarian violence, Peel established the Peace Preservation Force, a more coercive response to the problem than previously attempted.[25] Through the employment of the coercive powers of the members of the Preservation Force as well as the implementation of a fining system which placed hardships on those communities within which the disturbances were occurring, Peel was successful in quelling banditti violence, although by 1817 he had abandoned the fining system in favor of a shared responsibility arrangement where England would bear two-thirds of the cost of Preservation Force operations while local communities would pay the other third.

Successful in this venture, Peel returned to England in 1818 and began thinking about implementing such a system of policing in his home country. What Peel had accomplished in Ireland was taking law enforcement out of the hands of amateurs and placing it in those of the professionals.[26] Peel worked for the next decade on putting his vision into practice, and in 1829 parliament passed the Metropolitan Police Act. The Police Act placed 3,000 police officers under the control of the Home Secretary. This was the first full-time, paid police force, modeled largely after features of military bureaucratic organization, including a rank system for purposes of hiring and promotions, as well as a chain of command. Officers would wear uniforms, and each was readily identifiable by a copper badge worn over the left breast. The "new police," sometimes referred to as "peelers" or "bobbies," were expected to walk a beat to ensure close familiarity between patrol officers and members of the local community. Further, officers were not equipped with handguns, although they did carry truncheons or "billy clubs." Finally, police officers had broad powers of investigation and arrest, and were entrusted with high levels of discretion, ostensibly because of their status as full-time government employees and upstanding members of the community.

Policing in America: three eras

The United States soon followed the lead of the British, with Boston being the first city to establish a professional police force, in 1838, but it was not until 1854 that the department took on many of the characteristics of Peel's "new police." The New York City police force was established in 1844, followed later by Philadelphia in 1856, Chicago in 1861, Detroit in 1863, and Cleveland in 1866. By 1880 most of the larger American cities had done likewise.

From the beginning of the establishment of municipal policing in America to the early 1900s the police were as or more likely to respond to citizen demands for public order and urban social services than to actual criminal offenses. In other words, police were likely to respond in many areas beyond crime control per se, including order maintenance and many other situations engendered by the less formal relations that existed between citizens and police in the early stages of the establishment of modern policing. For example, beginning in the Jacksonian era (which ran from 1830 through about 1850), Americans began losing faith in punishment (specifically those of the harsh and brutal colonial forms) as a way of dealing with crime and deviance, and started looking to other solutions for reassuring or reestablishing the social order.[27] This is why in Jacksonian America almost simultaneous to the rise of the penitentiary there was also the rise of insane asylums, almshouses for the poor, orphanages and houses of refuge for wayward or abandoned youth (the forerunner of the juvenile justice system), safehouses and shelters for women in distress, and workhouses for men who were deemed either unemployable or simply lazy, "shiftless," or irresponsible (but not necessarily criminal).[28] The emergence of these various total institutions set up ostensibly for dealing with a range of perceived social ills – but most importantly those of public order disturbances – was also reflective of the continuing centralization and consolidation of state power, including the establishment of municipal police forces.

In the earlier years of operation, then, American police in particular and the criminal justice system in general had a diffuse focus on all kinds of people, not just criminals. As historian Eric Monkonnen explains, during the nineteenth century,

> Police dispensed welfare; jails and prisons housed the insane; jails sometimes held more witnesses than offenders awaiting trial. During the first two decades of the twentieth century, the focus of the system began to sharpen. As a result, demands for organization responses to crime became more closely tied to the actual rates of crime because the system no longer attended to problems that were not related to crimes.[29]

With regard to the municipal police, then, the general trend from 1830 to the present has been the increasing formalization, bureaucratization, specialization, and (later) professionalization of its operations. Focusing specifically on developments in police operations since the 1840s, three eras or phases have been identified.[30]

The first phase of modern policing, running from the 1840s until the 1920s, is referred to as the *political spoils* era. Police departments that were emerging in nineteenth-century America were controlled largely by the political administration of the city or municipality that happened to be in office at the time. For example, in most larger cities the chief of police was a political appointee of the mayor, and since there were no official standards for recruitment of police candidates the mayor basically handpicked whomever he wanted. Oftentimes these choices were made on the basis of political loyalties, informal ties and familiarity with either the recruit himself or his family, and ethnicity and other ascribed characteristics. As a result, patronage abuses and corruption ran rampant largely because the ties between municipal governance and the police were simply too close and "chummy."

The second policing era, running from the 1930s into the 1970s, is termed professionalization. Because of the many problems associated with the previous era of political spoils, during the second era of *reform and early professionalization* there were attempts to place more distance between city government and the operation of the police force. In most major American cities the informal system of police recruitment was being replaced by a more formal system, including written guidelines for the recruitment, retention, and promotion of police officers, but also the creation of tight organizational structures where bureaucratic control over police activities was emphasized. This involved the promulgation of many more operational rules and regulations, affecting not only the bottom-rung line staff (patrol officers and administrative staff) but also mid- and upper-level management, including the chief of police himself.

The ideology of professionalization also meant greater specialization, the implication of which was that police departments began defining their mandate more narrowly to include only law enforcement, while other activities that police had traditionally performed (such as order maintenance, peacekeeping, and social services) were not officially recognized. Following Foucault, the gradual transition from informal control to the establishment of police vested with the coercive powers of the state meant that the conditions of control shifted from "the many watch the few" to *the few watch the many*. Here, the "many" are the growing throngs of persons labeled as deviant or criminal (represented, for example, in rising crime rates beginning in the 1960s), while the "few" are those professionals who specialize in legal control, namely the police but also key players within the court system (e.g., district attorneys) and corrections.

Another aspect of professionalization was taking police officers off traditional foot patrols and placing them in squad cars. This created greater distance between police and citizens, a situation that was perceived to be warranted given the corruption of the previous era. This second era is described as "early" professionalization because during this time there was still little thought given over to increasing educational requirements of cadets or providing extensive training for them. The consensus even into the 1940s and 1950s was that, rather than being a full-blown profession, policing was overwhelmingly a blue-collar occupation that did not require formal education or the mastery of a body of esoteric knowledge. This aspect of professionalization would not be fully realized until the third era.

This third era of policing, running from the 1970s to the present, is known as community-oriented or problem-oriented policing. *Community-oriented policing* (COP) and problem-oriented policing (POP) emerged out of the turbulent 1960s, which was an era notable for openly hostile relations between police and citizens, especially for those citizens involved in such social movements as anti-war protest, civil rights, gay rights, and the women's movement, as well as youth and campus protests. Much of this open conflict took place in urban metropolitan areas characterized by growing cultural heterogeneity as well as ethnic and racial diversity, and the old bureaucratic form of "professional" policing was badly out of step in its inability to understand the needs of diverse populations. Out of this came the call to increase the education and training of police candidates, but also to recruit more women and persons of color into policing so that police forces would match more closely the sociodemographic characteristics of the populations they served.

Another important element in what was to become known as community- or problem-oriented policing was the effort to repair strained relations between citizens and police, hence police departments started putting more effort into getting their officers more noticeably involved in their communities, and not just as crime fighters or law enforcers. Because a better class of person was being brought into policing – presumably better educated, more literate, more culturally aware, and better able to handle a wide range of interpersonal situations – police in this third era were expected to be multitaskers who could fulfill multiple roles in the communities that they served. In both community- and problem-oriented policing, the police are acting like psychologists, counselors, social workers, and teachers as much as they are crime fighters. Examples of community policing activities include:

- Drug Abuse Resistance Education or DARE, a seventeen-week program taught by uniformed police officers in elementary schools (typically fifth graders);
- Gang Resistance Education and Training or GREAT, a ten-week program to teach middle-school seventh graders skills of conflict resolution and how to resist peer pressure;
- Eddie Eagle Gun Safety Program, gun safety education for elementary-school children emphasizing the motto "Stop, Don't Touch, Leave the Area, Tell an Adult"; and
- Police Athletic League or PAL, dedicated to positive development of youth to prevent juvenile delinquency through supervision of organized activities.[31]

Although these and other programs give the impression that community-oriented policing is a marked improvement over earlier forms of policing, problems nevertheless remain. These problems will be picked up in the next section where, in addition to the specific topic of community-oriented policing, we will examine other aspects of the "dark side" of legal control, including net-widening; class, race, and gender bias in the criminal justice system; and conflict over the death penalty.

The dark side of legal control

Community-oriented policing and fear of crime

Since its inception in the mid-1980s, community-oriented policing has experienced steady growth, and today a majority of municipal police departments characterize themselves as COP or POP departments. A typical statement on the characteristics and goals of community policing is provided by the police department of Akron, Ohio:

> In the 21st century, the law enforcement mission continues to expand from simply making arrests to taking a much broader community-based problem solving approach for dealing with crime and disorder issues. More than ever, community stakeholders want and expect the police to form partnerships with them in order to address issues of mutual concern that cause them fear, anxiety and affect their quality of life. This change in strategy is referred to as (COPPS) Community Oriented Policing and Problem Solving. COPPS is a philosophy that promotes proactive problem solving and police–community

partnerships that address the causes of crime and fear of crime as well as other community issues.[32]

The above statement is typical of how cities portray the great advantages of adopting community policing strategies. But many of the above assertions appear more self-serving than factual. For example, is it really the case that a growing number of citizens "want and expect" police to form partnerships with them, or might it actually be the other way around? That is, perhaps it is the police who feel that greater citizen input into daily police operations is needed in order to help legitimate police services in an era of declining crime rates and general public funding for the police. Also, is "fear of crime" really as big an issue for citizens as community policing advocates suggest it is? It might actually be the case that governments, by enumerating and making public the nature of crimes and the crime rate through "official" measures such as the Uniform Crime Reports, serve to instill greater fear of crime in citizens, even if the crime rate is actually in decline. Then, as disciplines such as criminology and sociology assume that fear of crime is a stable "social object" to be analyzed and studied in its own right, a looping or feedback effect is produced which helps perpetuate a fear of crime industry, encouraged immensely of course by continuous coverage of sensational crime stories by the mass media. Finally, police departments, and especially those employing community policing strategies, may be complicit in fomenting fear of crime by making police officers a continuing and visible presence in the community (such as the presence of police mini-stations in neighborhoods, the creation of neighborhood watch groups, or even the encouragement of citizen patrols), in effect warning citizens about all the dangers that lurk just around each corner.[33]

Net-widening

Even with the emphasis on professionalization and upgrading of policing and police services that began in the third era of policing, there is also the assumption that informal control systems continue to weaken, thereby necessitating the continuing growth and expansion of legal control. For example, since 1973 "the number of police in America has grown by nearly 50%, the number of prisoners by 500%, and the number of probationers by 400%."[34] Much of this has to do with the continuing growth of community-based corrections, which arose in response to rising incarceration rates and prison overcrowding problems since the early 1980s. A range of alternative or *intermediate sanctions* – such as home confinement, residential treatment, boot camps, halfway houses, shock or intensive supervision probation, and community service – are available to judges for those defendants whose offenses do not merit incarceration.

Although this appears to be a more compassionate and reasonable form of sanctioning which also would appear to ease the problem of prison overcrowding, it has not worked out that way. This is because judges now have at their disposal a range of alternative sanctions which, because they are not as onerous in terms of their severity, are likely to be meted out simply because they are available. As the bar is lowered regarding what counts as an actionable offense, more persons are pulled into the criminal justice system, thereby contributing to the problem of *net-widening*.[35] Although net-widening by way of the use of intermediate sanctions has certainly increased the probation population – as noted above – it has the potential to increase the incarceration rate as well. This is because many alternative sanctions have conditions attached to them – similar to traditional probation – whereby violation of the conditions of the sanction, or so-called *technical violations*, may lead to more formal and serious punishments, thus expanding legal control.

The poor get prison

This example of net-widening points out how legal control, as embodied in the organization, roles, and activities of the criminal justice system, operates in ways that are injurious to citizens, thereby exposing the injustices of legal control. Many of these injustices reflect the racism, sexism, and classism of the criminal justice system. Jeffrey Reiman, for example, has argued that, because racial minorities and the poor are overrepresented in the criminal justice system in terms of arrests and convictions, the force used by representative of the system to apprehend, prosecute, and punish minority defendants is no more justified than the force used by common criminals against their victims. As Reiman explains,

> A criminal justice system is a system of justice to the extent that it protects equally the interests and rights of all and to the extent that it punishes equally all those who endanger these interests or violate these rights. To the extent that it veers from these goals, the criminal justice system is guilty of the same sacrificing of the interests of some for the benefit of others that it exists to combat. It is, therefore, morally speaking, guilty of crime.[36]

Contrary to the notion that persons are equal under the law, the sad fact is that those with more money can buy a more favorable brand of justice than those who have less or no money. For example, poor defendants who are assigned public defenders are more likely to be given the advice to plead guilty (often to a lesser charge through plea bargaining) than are those defendants who can afford to hire their own private attorneys. This means that the poor are more likely to be convicted of crimes than the wealthy, who have the resources to fight criminal charges. And because the poor are more likely to be convicted, they are also more likely to have a prior arrest record if stopped by the police. And prior arrest record is one of the important elements that influences a police officer's decision to arrest a suspect. In other words, given the same crime and same set of circumstances at the scene, police officers will more likely arrest a suspect with prior involvement with the criminal justice system than one with no such record of prior arrests.

The death penalty and racism

Explicit racial bias also shows up in the statistics on capital punishment. African-Americans comprise 12 percent of the US population, yet commit (or rather, are convicted of) more than 50 percent of the country's murders. Even so, African-Americans account for only 40 percent of the total death-row inmate population. This 10 percent gap might lead one to believe that the criminal justice system is acting in a race-neutral fashion, since the percentage of African-Americans on death row is smaller than the percentage of African-Americans who have been convicted of murder. In actuality, though, the data reflect the existence of a racial hierarchy operating within the criminal justice system. Specifically, a death penalty is about *three times* more likely to be imposed on defendants accused of murdering a white person than those accused of murdering a black person. In other words, within the criminal justice system the murder of a white person is treated more seriously than the murder of a black person. Considering all executions performed in America between 1930 and 1995, blacks who murdered whites comprised 35 percent of the total, whites who murdered whites comprised 22 percent of the total, whites who murdered blacks comprised 14 percent of the total, and blacks who murdered blacks comprised only 6 percent of the total.[37] The high percentage of executions of black offenders who murder whites (35 percent) in combination with the small percentage of executions of black offenders who murder blacks (6 percent) is reflective of an obvious racial bias in sentencing. This racial hierarchy

> stems in part from prosecutors' reluctance to seek death in cases involving black victims, and eagerness to seek death in cases involving black defendants and white victims. Because black offenders nearly always murder black victims, reluctance to seek death in black victim cases reduces black death row populations and more than offsets the propensity to seek death sentences for blacks who murder whites.[38]

Paternalism and status offenses

Sex bias also exists within the criminal justice system. In most patriarchal societies for many years – especially as evolving out of the nineteenth-century Victorian era of sexual prudishness – a "cult of domesticity" or a "cult of true womanhood" developed whereby women were relegated to the domestic sphere of home and neighborhood and family ties, while men reigned over the public sphere of work and business ties. In effect, the patriarchal arrangement of males as breadwinners and women as homemakers and child-rearers meant that separate and unequal social spheres developed. In short, in everyday life women were much more heavily supervised and their range of activities much more restricted in comparison to men. Because women were assumed to be the "weaker sex," social control of women tended also to be paternalistic, in that the natural "purity" and "virtuousness" of women needed to be protected against the vulgarities and profanations of males and male-related activities.

The greater supervision and restriction of movement of women in everyday life meant that women's opportunities for both legitimate and illegitimate activities were diminished. As a consequence historically women have engaged in (or at least been caught in) less crime and deviance relative to men. Although the gap in rates of offending between males and females has been narrowing somewhat recently, for the most part men continue to dominate most of the crime statistics, especially those crimes which require physical strength and/or endurance, such as robbery, assault, and burglary. But when women engage in serious crimes such as murder, this tends to be viewed as a gross perversion of women's natural tendencies toward nurturing, empathy, and caregiving. As a consequence, the criminal justice system tends to punish women less severely than men for the same or a similar offense. In essence, women's criminality is viewed through the eyes of a paternalistic and patriarchal society as a "sickness," or certainly as an "aberration."[39] On the other hand, because of this same paternalistic supervision and oversight of females, girls tend to be punished more harshly than boys for status offenses. For example, 57 percent of those arrested in 1994 for running away were girls, and between 1985 and 1994 arrests of girls for curfew violations increased by 83.1 percent, while arrests for boys increased by only 44.7 percent. Girls are more likely than boys to be arrested for status offenses, because activities such as curfew violations and running away from home are assumed to be more of a threat in that they might promote girls' sexual promiscuity.[40] For adolescent boys, of course, sexual interest and aggressiveness is assumed to be normal or at least tolerated, reflected in notions such as "he's just sowing his wild oats."

Foucault, the Panopticon, and governmentality

Calls for prison reform in the eighteenth century and the rise of the penitentiary in the nineteenth century, by which time incarceration replaced other punishments that were considered barbaric or inhumane, reflected the progressive spirit of Enlightenment rationalism as well as secular humanism. For the most part, then, the changes occurring during this time were interpreted as positive steps toward the expansion of fairness and human decency in dealings with criminal defendants and convicted prisoners. But Michel Foucault takes issue with the assertion that, with the rise of the prison, punishment shifted from harsh, cruel, and barbaric to measured, proportionate, and reasonable. Foucault turns much of his critical attention to Jeremy Bentham's idea of the Panopticon.

Foucault argues that the transition from harsh, retributive punishments that focused on the body to more "humane" punishments that emphasized the incapacitation of deviants in penitentiaries, asylums, and similar custodial institutions was not as humanitarian and progressive as many observers have made it out to be. Rather, the penitentiary as a holding institution was punishing better or more effectively, using techniques of science, including measurement, calculation, observation, segregation, classification, and surveillance, to produce docile and more controllable inmate populations. What was introduced with the idea of the Panopticon was a field of power at the disposal of custodians of these total institutions, generated by their ability to watch and monitor the activities of many persons simultaneously. Previously power was not so widely dispersed but localized. For example, although the power of the king or sovereign was put on public display whenever condemned persons were hanged or beheaded or dismembered before a gathered crowd, the actual effect of the power was directed at the body of the condemned. Although there were hopes that such public displays of power would act as a general deterrent whereby citizens would refrain from unlawful behaviors, the only certainty was that particular condemned persons' bodies were being brutalized, ravaged, or ultimately destroyed. The public spectacle – the many watch the few – was being converted to the more private enclosures of custodial institutions, generating a new and improved control effect, namely, the few watch the many. This also meant that little or no direct contact with bodies was needed. Instead, power worked its effects from afar, through the constant gaze of the prison keepers. As Foucault explains,

> The Panopticon functions as a kind of laboratory of power. Thanks to its mechanisms of observation, it gains in efficiency and in the ability to penetrate into men's behavior; knowledge follows the advances of power, discovering new objects of knowledge over all the surfaces on which power is exercised.[41]

Another aspect of the Panopticon is that it is polyvalent, meaning that it can be applied to a wide assortment of groups of persons for whatever reasons custodial functionaries deem appropriate. In effect, the Panopticon can now be used not only to reform prisoners, but also to treat patients, instruct schoolchildren, confine the insane, and put beggars and idlers to work.[42] This means that the ethos of the Panopticon becomes a generalizing effect in society at large; the principles of identification, investigation, isolation, and surveillance are not limited to confines of a physical structure. For Foucault, then, the prison constituted merely one aspect of the *carceral society*, a society concerned with formulating and applying a wide range of disciplinary mechanisms to rapidly expanding categories of persons. According to Foucault, "The prison transformed the punitive procedure into a penitentiary technique; the carceral archipelago transported this technique from the penal institution to the entire social body."[43]

This returns us to the issue of society's greatest challenge, namely, the production of self-controlled individuals. Religion was the single most powerful and effective guarantor of the social production of self-controlled individuals. Through the positing of an omniscient being who is all-knowing and who watches all persons all the time, even in their most intimate moments, persons were apt to refrain from illicit conduct whenever tempted simply by reminding themselves that "God is watching." With the secularization of society and the waning of religious affect, the assurance of self-control was diminished as well. Because of the perception or the reality of rising rates of crime and deviance, people began losing faith in the informal system of socialization and primary group control, and a search was launched for a secular alternative to an all-seeing, all-knowing God. Group- and even neighborhood-surveillance systems – such as the frankpledge – were limited because of the physical limitations of human vision. But Bentham's idea of the Panopticon promised a return of sorts to the "eye in sky" surveillance that was so effective under the sway of religious and theological solidarity.

But because of the polyvalent nature of the Panopticon, because it can be applied to a wide range of groups and settings, even extending beyond the confines of physical structures to society itself, the power of the custodians can potentially become too great. With more and more disciplinary mechanisms fanning out across society in general – Foucault referred to this as the "swarming" of disciplinary mechanisms – persons are apt to internalize norms of control through surveillance as part and parcel of the good life, as part and parcel of what it means to be a unified self. According to Foucault's notion of *governmentality*, more and more persons are running around acting like government functionaries, whether the police, auditors, accountants, lawyers, doctors, therapists, managers, teachers, scientists and professors, or what have you.[44] The logic of community policing ties in nicely with the idea of governmentality, as the police hope that everyday citizens take on more and more of the features, orientations, and attitudes of sworn law-enforcement personnel.

When Panopticon principles escape the confines of custodial institutions and spill over into a society's culture, thereby producing the conditions for governmentality, another transition in the nature of social control is generated: rather than "the few watch the many" we now have *the many watch the many*. The first "many" refers not only to the police, but to virtually all citizens who are now acting like the police. The second "many" refers to the fact that crime rates and deviance remain as high as (or higher than) in the second control phase, namely the few watch the many. Indeed, now that surveillance has become widespread, general, and constant, more people are caught in deviance simply because they are being watched more carefully and continuously. Modern camera surveillance is one of the most effective tools in this new condition of governmentality and the carceral society. The internalization of the norms of governmentality, and hence the production of a governable self, are made explicit in such sayings or attitudes as "I'm not opposed to surveillance because I've got nothing to hide."

Conclusion

This very big and important topic of modern surveillance will be returned to in later chapters. For right now, it is worth pointing out that none of the goals of punishment which have been experimented with or pursued over the centuries – whether deterrence, incapacitation, rehabilitation, shaming, or even retribution – have done much to reduce crime rates or reform deviants.[45] As David Garland has argued, it is "only the mainstream processes of socialization that are able to promote proper conduct on a consistent and regular basis."[46] Formal punishment is at best a backup, a stopgap measure to be applied wherever and whenever the informal system fails to produce desired levels of control.

But what happens when a society has given up all hope that the informal mechanisms of control can do their job? For example, what happens when a critical mass of people believe that the modern family system has fallen into disrepair and likely cannot be fixed? The rhetoric of "families in crisis" and "children at risk" creates an opening for the encroachment of "experts" into more and more areas of life, to speak definitively about the ramifications of the loss of this most important and primary institution of informal social control.[47] But if indeed "nothing works" at the formal level of punishment and control, and if indeed the family is irreparably damaged as a mechanism for assuring the production of self-controlled individuals, what then?

About all that is left is either (1) a full-blown commitment to governmentality and the carceral society, where the assumption is made that everyone is "bad" and thereby deserving of constant surveillance for purposes of catching and isolating those who will eventually deviate; or (2) a more vigorous commitment to medicalization, and especially to public healthification, whereby surveillance of the population is undertaken to determine the characteristics of those "at risk" and to fashion interventions to reduce public harm accruing from their actions. Notice that these two options – governmentality and public health – converge on the technique of mass surveillance of the population.

In the next three chapters, critical case studies will be presented with regard to each of the three categories of control. The next chapter will kick things off with case studies of informal social control.

Suggestions for further reading

Foucault, Michel. 1977. *Discipline and Punish: The Birth of the Prison,* trans. A. Sheridan. New York: Vintage Books.

An examination of the rise of the prison, tracing the changing nature of punishment from the 1600s to the present. This and other works of Foucault introduced a number of terms still in currency in criminology and penology, including governmentality, docility, Panopticism, swarming of disciplinary mechanisms, and the carceral society.

Manning, Peter K. 1997. *Police Work: The Social Organization of Policing,* 2nd edn. Prospect Heights, IL: Waveland Press.

This book offers a dramaturgical analysis of modern policing and police organizations, emphasizing the ritual, dramatic, and rhetorical features of police work.

McIntosh, Marjorie Keniston. 1998. *Controlling Misbehavior in England, 1370–1600.* Cambridge: Cambridge University Press.

A careful and thoroughgoing historical analysis of the changing nature of social control in England from medieval times to the early modern period.

Reiman, Jeffrey H. 2004. *The Rich Get Richer and the Poor Get Prison: Ideology, Class, and Criminal Justice,* 7th edn. Boston: Allyn & Bacon.

Now in its seventh edition, this book is one of the best-known indictments of the American criminal justice system's racism and classism. Although strident at times, on balance it contains more truths than errors.

Rothman, David J. 2002. *The Discovery of the Asylum,* rev. edn. Hawthorne, NY: Aldine de Gruyter.

Rothman's book, originally published in 1970, provides a thorough conceptualization of the rise of total institutions (such as prisons, mental asylums, and almshouses) in America from the colonial period to the late 1800s. His follow-up book, *Conscience and Convenience,* picks up the story from the Progressive Era (beginning in the 1890s).

PART II

CASE STUDIES IN SOCIAL CONTROL

6 Informal Control: The Urban Underclass, Housing Segregation, and the Code of the Street

Introduction

In this chapter we will explore a range of issues in the theory and conceptualization of informal control. Specifically, a select group of sociological and criminological theories are discussed to illustrate how informal systems of control – those associated with the socialization process and with group pressures to conform in everyday life – are often imbedded and play an important role in theories of legal control. By examining such theories, we are in a better position to understand the linkages between informal and legal control.

A basic insight to keep in mind is that, as persons age over the life course, the nature of informal control – but also legal and medical control – changes as well.[1] As discussed in chapter 3, from early childhood into the teenage years the primary agents of informal control are parents, schools, and peer groups, while the dominant institution of legal control is the juvenile justice system. For example, even controlling for such factors as the quality of the school and students' age, race, gender, and socioeconomic status, delinquent students are much more likely than non-delinquent students to be held back a grade, have poorer attendance records, make lower grades, and receive more disciplinary actions.[2] Children experiencing such educational deficiencies typically also experience difficulties in other areas of life (in their families and neighborhoods, with same-age peers, and so forth), indicating poor social bonding to conventional institutions and individuals and, hence, the weakening of informal controls.

In young adulthood, the primary institutions of informal control shift to higher education and vocational training, work, and marriage, with the criminal justice system replacing the juvenile justice system in the legal control realm. Finally, from middle adulthood and beyond the salient forms of informal control are work, marriage, parenthood, and investments in the community.

The main point to take away from this discussion of the shifting bases of informal control over the life course is the importance of persons' ties to others, or so-called *social bonds*, first within the context of primary groups and then expanding outward as persons age, become more autonomous, and begin contacting a greater diversity of individuals through schooling, work, and other activities. First, then, it is important to review perhaps the major theory of social bonding developed, namely Travis Hirschi's control theory. After this, we will examine how the social bond has been conceptualized, beginning in the early 1980s in the guise of social capital. After having established the social bond as the fundamental element in informal control, we will then be in a position to examine critical case studies of informal control in three areas: the urban underclass, housing segregation, and the code of the street.

The importance of social bonds

As we saw in chapter 1, Emile Durkheim argued that social order is assured to the extent that persons are tied or attached to others in meaningful ways. In earlier times, social solidarity – so-called mechanical solidarity – was assured through cultural homogeneity and the subordination of individuals to the will of the group. But with the growth of population, industrialization, urbanization, mobility, and increasing migration from a variety of countries, all of which served to further diversify the United States and European nations, attachments between individuals were jeopardized as greater anonymity made informal group-based control less effective. As Durkheim stated, "as society spreads out and becomes denser, it envelops the individual less tightly, and in consequence can restrain less efficiently the diverging tendencies that appear."[3] Even so, informal control does not simply disappear; rather, group control is augmented by other forms of control, including medical and legal.

Durkheim's emphasis on the importance of attachments in assuring social order is located within a tradition of thought known as *mass society theory*. As Irene Thomson explains,

> Mass society theory saw industrialization, urbanization, bureaucratization, and the sheer scale of modern society as destroying the strong group ties – of church, clan, guild, and local neighborhood – that had previously brought order to society and meaningful participation for individuals. The absence of such ties was viewed as leaving individuals alienated and vulnerable to manipulation by elites, demagogues, or extremist social movements.[4]

Intimate and intermediate groups such as families, friendship groups, neighborhoods, and community organizations provide the basis for persons to be connected with others in shared activities, and the cross-cutting loyalties and obligations that persons feel as members of these collectivities effectively hold them in check, thereby reducing deviance among group members.[5] The rise of the modern urban metropolis introduced various forms of social disorganization, as new social conditions effectively cut some of the crucial linkages between persons and their supportive groups. Within sociology, a theoretical perspective known as *social disorganization* developed at the University of Chicago and flourished between 1920 and 1935.[6] Chicago had experienced rapid population growth beginning in the 1850s, and this previously rural community was transformed in only a few decades into a thriving urban metropolis.

From social disorganization to social control

Through their empirical research taking place in Chicago and surrounding communities beginning in the 1920s, the social disorganization theorists documented that socially disorganized communities – those characterized by economic deprivation, high population turnover, low rates of home ownership, family disruption, and the like – tend also to be plagued by high rates of crime and delinquency. Albert J. Reiss, a University of Chicago sociologist who published and researched in several areas including community analysis, family studies, and delinquency, was the first person to articulate the criminological theory that came to be known as control theory. In essence, control theory emerges out of the broader social disorganization orientation, in combination with the continuing professionalization and scientization of family studies.

Reiss set out to isolate a set of personal and social controls that, when absent or weak, are associated with higher levels of delinquent recidivism.[7] Of special interest here is the problem of control in primary groups, most importantly, factors associated with the ability of families to control or provide for the needs of their children. As Reiss stated, "Primary groups are the basic institutions for the development of personal controls and the exercise of social control over the child."[8] An important part of "family control," according to Reiss, is the ability of the family to meet the needs of its members. The types of informal or primary group controls that Reiss found most significantly correlated with juvenile recidivism (operationalized as probation failures) were these:

- family economic status (as status decreases recidivism increases)
- marital relationships of natural parents (the weaker the affective ties between parents, the higher the recidivism of children)
- moral ideas and techniques of control (parents who provide their children with non-deviant role models, and parenting styles that are neither too lax nor too authoritarian or punitive, are associated with lower recidivism)
- institutional or foster home experience (children who have been institutionalized are much more likely to recidivate than children with no previous experiences in foster or institutional homes).[9]

Reiss and later control theorists (such as Travis Hirschi) assume that persons are "bad" and will deviate unless significant obstacles are put in their way that, in essence, keep them from doing so. This is a change from ecological and social disorganization orientations, which tended to assume that persons are "good" but can be "made bad" as a result of family or marital disorganization, bad schools, disorganized communities, difficult economic times, and so forth. In assuming people are bad, control theorists must bank heavily on those social, personal, and institutional controls in place in any society which, it is claimed, steer people toward conformity and away from deviance.

Utilitarianism, natural right, and natural law

Most control theories are also at heart utilitarian, as the assumption is made that human beings are by their nature solitary and brutish, and will seek to maximize their own interests and gratifications (often at the expense of others) if left unconstrained.[10] The Hobbesian solution to avoiding this inevitable war of all against all is the evolution of the rational faculty by which human beings overcome their basic selfish and hedonistic urges. In other words, in the evolution of society, human beings reach a point at which they realize it is in their own best interests to forego the unbridled pursuit of gratifications in exchange for the state's guarantee to step in and regulate everyone else's pursuit of self-gratification. This constraining force is the state, which Hobbes referred to as the Leviathan.

Hobbes argues that, in the original state of nature, human beings pursued their own individual gratifications as they saw fit. This is the notion of *natural right,* namely, the liberty of every person to do whatever seemed most expedient for self-preservation. In the condition of natural right, there are no conceptions of right and wrong or just and unjust. It is simply life ruled by the passions. Later, with the rise of the rational faculty, natural right is replaced by natural law. *Natural law* is discovered through the power of reason, that is, the power to understand that maximization of self-preservation can occur only if social conditions are created in which all others realize that the unbridled pursuit of self-interest will ultimately destroy everyone. Natural law imposes three fundamental precepts:

- Human beings must escape from the state of actual or potential war, seeking peace and observing it.
- Human beings must abandon their natural right to whatever it is they wish to possess or acquire.
- All promises must be kept, otherwise the state of nature will return.[11]

Since individual persons would have trouble consistently abiding by these ideals, they enter into a social contract whereby the state and its agents of formal control are acknowledged as legitimate enforcers of these precepts, as embodied in legal statutes.

Hirschi's control theory and elements of the social bond

Indeed, consensus theorists, utilitarians, functionalist theorists, and control theorists all posit the importance of informal ties to groups and commitment to shared norms and values as the best guarantor of social order and stability. Travis Hirschi's social control theory is in essence an extension and refinement of Durkheim's notion that persons are more likely to deviate when they are poorly integrated into ongoing group relations.[12] Indeed, Hirschi cites approvingly the following passage from Durkheim:

> The more weakened the groups to which [the individual] belongs, the less he depends on them, the more he consequently depends only on himself and recognizes no other rules of conduct than what are founded on his private interests.[13]

Hirschi further suggests that the social bond consists of four crucial elements or dimensions. These elements are attachment, belief, commitment, and involvement. *Attachment* is the emotional, affective, or expressive aspect of the social bond. It is synonymous with concepts such as the internalization of norms (Durkheim), the superego (Freud), or moral conscience. Proper internalization of the norms of conventional society orients individuals toward a feeling of respect and admiration for, or devotion toward, parents, school, and peers. Hirschi argues that one must first have such an emotional attachment – a cathexis, in Freudian and Parsonian terms[14] – toward social objects before one can accept (or believe in) the rules they promulgate or represent.[15]

This brings us to a second crucial element of the social bond, namely *belief*. Belief is the evaluative, cultural dimension of the social bond. Hirschi explains that control theory assumes the existence of a common value system within society whose norms are sometimes violated.[16] He assumes there is variation in the extent to which people believe they should obey the rules of society. Although most persons most of the time believe they should follow the rules of their society, which in itself points to a value consensus among the citizenry over right and wrong, moral and immoral, and good and bad, some do not. The less a person believes he or she should obey the rules, the more likely it is that he or she will violate them.[17]

Another element of the social bond is *commitment*. Commitment represents the cognitive dimension of the social bond. It is the rational calculation a person engages in concerning how much time and energy to invest in certain lines of activity. For example, presumably someone who has spent many years studying to be a doctor would be less inclined to risk it all by engaging in some form of deviance, whereas another person with lower or no "stakes in conformity," such as the unemployed, the uneducated, or the petty street criminal, has very little to lose if caught in a deviant or criminal act. Hirschi invokes Freud again here, stating, "If attachment to others is the sociological counterpart of the superego or conscience, commitment is the counterpart of the ego or common sense."[18]

A final element of the social bond is *involvement*. Involvement is the behavioral dimension of the social bond. The idea is that the more time

Table 6.1 *Elements of the social bond*

Level	Element	Description
BEHAVIORAL	INVOLVEMENT	Time spent in conventional activities
COGNITIVE	COMMITMENT	Rational calculation of the costs of lawbreaking for future goals
AFFECTIVE	ATTACHMENT	Emotional closeness to family, peers, and schools
EVALUATIVE	BELIEF	Ideas that support a conventional orientation

Source: Adapted from Hirschi (1969) and Livingston (1996).

people spend in conventional activities, the less time they will have to engage in delinquent or deviant activities. Hirschi's control theory is summarized in table 6.1.

In summary, then, Hirschi suggests that the more *attached* persons are to other members of society, the more they *believe* in the values of conventional society, and the more they *invest in* and are *involved in* conventional lines of activity, the less likely they are to deviate.

Hirschi devotes an entire chapter to youths' attachment to parents, and a brief summary of these findings are in order.[19] As Hirschi states, "Control theory assumes that the bond of affection for conventional persons is a major deterrent to crime."[20] Children's attachment to their parents is, according to Hirschi, one of the single best predictors of delinquency: as attachment to parents weakens, delinquency increases. Granted, being attached or bonded to a parent means that the child is likely to be more heavily supervised and more often in the presence of parents than children with weaker bonds. But delinquent acts do not take much time to commit, so this sort of "direct control" explanation is only partial at best.

At least as important, if not more so, is the *moral* element in the attachment, the idea that, even though a parent may be physically distant from a child who is considering committing a deviant act, the parent nevertheless could be psychologically present when such temptations arise. A child who, at the moment of temptation, asks him- or herself, "What will my parents think?" tends to exhibit more strongly the moral component of attachment than a child whose conscience does not prompt him or her in the same way. This sort of "indirect control" is more important with regard to the attachment element of the social bond than the direct, supervisory activities of parents seeking to restrict the activities of their children.

Another element in attachment that is important in reducing delinquency is the quality of the communication between parents and their children. The level of so-called intimate communication, where children freely and routinely share their thoughts and feelings with their parents or talk to them about their future plans, or even where parents explain their actions or feelings to their children, is strongly related to the commission of delinquent acts. In sum, parent–child relationships that lack intimate communication are associated with higher levels of juvenile delinquency.

Yet another important element of attachment is a child's affectual identification with a parent or parents. One question in Hirschi's self-report study of youths that was especially strongly related to delinquency was "Would you like to be the kind of person your mother (father) is?"[21] As Hirschi summarizes: "the present data indicate that the closer the child's relations with his parents, the more he is attached to and identifies with them, the lower his chances of delinquency."[22] Children who affectually identify with their parents also tend to view them as role models, which thereby reduces their involvement in anti-social behavior. Beyond the level of any single concrete family, one may also observe that across a community, as more and more families are characterized by parents acting as positive role models for their children, a sort of *collective socialization* occurs at the network level whereby communities are better able to reduce or hold in check child anti-social behavior.[23] Social (or community) disorganization occurs, then, where such community networks are weak or non-existent.

The move to self-control

In their *A General Theory of Crime*, published in 1990, Michael R. Gottfredson and Travis Hirschi abandoned explicit reference to social bonds in favor of self-control as the primary factor in the explanation of crime and delinquency.[24] By admission of Hirschi and Gottfredson as well as outside commentators, it appeared that the move from social control (by way of the social bond) to self-control was radical, something akin to an epistemological or analytical rupture.[25] Why was this change made? Hirschi explains that,

> After examining age distributions of crimes and analogous acts, Gottfredson and I reversed my original position, concluding that these acts are, after all, manifestations of low self-control on the part of the offender.[26]

According to the original social bonding theory of Hirschi, delinquency and crime were more a manifestation of the strength or weakness of the social bonds between the offender and others than of the particular characteristics of the offender. For Gottfredson and Hirschi, the stable differences in crime rates across group and individual levels that they discovered seemed to suggest that the explanation of crime, rather than being to do with social bonds, the strength of which can fluctuate over time, and with changes in the social and economic situations of individuals, would more likely be found in one's level of self-control.[27]

But where does self-control come from? Gottfredson and Hirschi admit that it begins early in life and is relatively impervious to change later in life. Indeed, the authors adopted a "child-rearing model" to account for the origins of (or conversely, the failure to learn) self-control.[28] This move places great emphasis on the importance of primary groups and especially the socialization function of the family. However, Gottfredson and Hirschi never traced out the implications of the continuing importance of the family not only for the formation and stability of social bonds, but also for the establishment of self-control.

It is clear that, in the earlier control theory of Hirschi, the concept of attachments, or being embedded in a network of relationships, is the major element protecting persons from engaging in criminal or deviant behavior. Here control is a relational concept, insofar as those who have the right relationships – secure attachments to conventional others and beliefs in the propriety of conventional institutions and activities – are less likely to deviate. The theory states in no uncertain terms that, when working properly, the socialization process and the system of informal controls guarantee social order and stability. To the extent that these systems work effectively, there is less need to call forth formal control mechanisms such as police, courts, and corrections.

In their later version of control theory, Gottfredson and Hirschi argue that attachments are less important in explaining levels of crime and deviance, because self-control is relatively invariant and, on its own, accounts for rates of offending, not just with regard to criminality but to other forms of offending or deviance as well.[29] Persons who smoke or drink to excess, who are rude, loud, and boisterous, who are physically aggressive, who get into trouble with gambling and other vices, and who commit crimes of any sort (ranging from assault or theft all the way up to murder) are theorized as having lower levels of self-control than those who do not engage in such behaviors.

According to Gottfredson and Hirschi the following are major characteristics of people with low self-control.

- They are impulsive and seek *immediate gratification*, and criminal acts often fulfill this need.
- They prefer acts that provide *easy and simple* gratification of desires, for example, sex without courtship, money without work, and so forth.
- They prefer acts that are *exciting, risky, or thrilling*, and many types of criminal and deviant acts are of this type.
- Since they seek immediate gratification, they often engage in criminal activities that provide *few or meager long-term benefits*.
- Since crimes often cause victims loss, pain, or discomfort, persons who perpetrate these acts tend to be *self-centered, indifferent, or insensitive* to the suffering of others.[30]

Recent research suggests that "bad" parenting is indeed criminogenic, to the extent that inadequate monitoring and supervision of children, as well as a lack of positive role modeling, may produce children possessing an especially destructive combination of aggressiveness and low self-control.[31] However, contrary to Gottfredson and Hirschi's argument, low self-control is not the single factor leading to delinquency and other forms of deviance. Rather, self-control is one among a number of factors that can vary with variations in parenting skills.

The concept of social capital

One of the problems with the various utilitarian theories discussed above is they tend to take the atomistic social actor for granted. This is especially the case for Hirschi's self-control theory, in which it is argued that a particular psychological endowment – low self-control – explains much about deviance and criminality.

Since the 1980s or so a new way of talking about the relationship between the individual and society has emerged in the social sciences, one which attempts to overcome the individualistic bias of much of these earlier theories. This concept is known as *social capital*, which stands for "the ability of actors to secure benefits by virtue of membership in social networks or other social structures."[32] Social capital has to do with the nature of relationships or social ties between individuals. For example, person A may be able to accomplish things person B cannot, simply by virtue of the social contacts enjoyed by person A. As Robert Putnam has put it, "Just as a screwdriver (physical capital) or a college education (human capital) can increase productivity (both individual and collective), so too social contacts affect the productivity of individuals and groups."[33]

Whereas attachments are important as a protection against deviance at the individual level, social capital theorists shift from the individual to the collective level of analysis by arguing that certain features of neighborhoods or societies – those that have high levels of social capital – are better able to secure the collective goals of the citizenry. Especially important is the idea that citizens ought to be involved in civic participation, whether joining voluntary organizations, being actively involved in their communities, and/or being involved in group activities beyond the level of the primary group (for example, political organizations, hobby groups, sports activities, and so forth). The condition of maximal social capital characterizes citizens as having high levels of trust with regard to their dealings with other citizens, and these mutual sets of obligations create a tapestry of informal control which thereby also facilitates the pursuit of collective goals.

Putnam's decline of social capital thesis

From the field of political science, Robert Putnam has developed the thesis that American civil society has declined significantly over the last two decades. When Alexis de Tocqueville visited the United States in the

1830s, he was impressed with Americans' propensity toward civic participation. Regardless of their social class, ethnic or racial background, religious beliefs, or political outlooks, Tocqueville saw evidence that Americans were willing to work together to build and sustain democracy. Much of this work appeared in the form of the endless associations Americans were forming. Since that time, research has shown that, indeed, sustained civic engagement of the citizenry in such areas as "voter participation, newspaper readership, membership in choral societies and football clubs" indicates a vibrant and healthy region.[34]

However, a countervailing tendency has been developing in Western societies, one which emphasizes individualism at the expense of community-building. Putnam sees evidence of the increase of unhealthy individualism and a concomitant detachment from civic participation in a number of areas. From the high-water mark of the 1960s, voter turnout through the 1990s declined by a quarter. The percentage of Americans who reported that they had attended a public meeting on town or school affairs fell from 22 percent in 1973 to 13 percent in 1993. Americans also disengaged psychologically from politics and government over the same time period. The proportion of Americans who said they trusted the government only "some of the time" or "almost never" rose from 30 percent in 1966 to 75 percent in 1992, and this trend has continued to the present day. In a poll conducted by the Pew Research Center for the People and the Press, the public's rating of the federal government had fallen from 59 percent favorable in 2004 to only 45 percent favorable in 2005. And the Department of Defense, which had a favorable rating of 76 percent in 1997, fell to a 56 percent favorable rating in 2005 (although it is certainly the case that the unpopular war in Iraq had much to do with this decline).[35]

There has also been a decline in regular churchgoing; in union membership; in the number of parents involved in and regularly attending school PTA meetings; in the joining of volunteer organizations such as the Boy Scouts or the Red Cross; and in the number of Americans joining fraternal organizations such as the Elks or the Jaycees. Putnam notes that, although the number of bowlers in America increased by 10 percent between 1980 and 1993, during the same period the number of Americans participating in bowling leagues *declined* by 40 percent. For Putnam, bowling alone is symptomatic of a more general decline in American social capital. People simply aren't doing as many things together as they once were.

With this decline of commitments and attachments to intermediate groups there has been a concomitant increase in membership in mass organizations such as the American Association of Retired Persons (AARP), environmental groups such as the Sierra Club, and various lobbying groups based in Washington, DC. But these groups hold few local meetings, and hence there is little face-to-face interaction among members. Indeed, for many of these mass organizations the only membership activities involve paying dues or reading a newsletter.[36]

For Putnam, mass membership organizations do little to stem the tide of social capital decline.

Finally, Putnam notes that self-help and support organizations have proliferated during the period of the alleged social capital decline. But because organizations such as Alcoholics Anonymous, Because I Love You parent support groups, Overeaters Anonymous, and Smart Recovery focus overwhelmingly on the self-betterment of individuals, there is little if any social capital generated. And communitarian fads such as "paying it forward" – acting proactively to do something nice for someone who may never be in a position to return the favor – are just that: fads. Phenomena such as paying it forward are consistent with the individualistic, therapeutic ethos which is geared more toward making people feel good about themselves than contributing to the broader public good.

Postindustrialism and the rise of the urban underclass

The problem of the decline of social capital, and hence of informal control in communities, can be tied directly to major structural changes occurring in the United States and elsewhere. Since the 1960s especially, the economies of the United States and Western Europe have experienced a profound transition. The backbone of the industrial economy was manufacturing, with coal, steel, textiles, oil, plastics, and rubber industries leading the way. Many of America's urban metropolises, especially those located in the northeast, were built on the physical labor of blue-collar industrial workers which, in combination with machine automation, gave rise to factory mass production servicing the needs of a growing middle class. But even with the introduction of automation in plants and factories, industrialization was always labor intensive, and one way owners of industry began cutting costs was exporting their manufacturing operations overseas to take advantage of cheap labor in other (often third world) countries.

This is one among a number of factors that has contributed to the transformation of industrial economies into so-called *postindustrial* economies, characterized by a move away from manufacturing as the primary mode of production to a bifurcated system in which service and hi-tech jobs prevailed. Under industrialism and manufacturing, a person who was willing to work hard could secure a middle-class wage and lifestyle without a formal education. But with the disappearance of manufacturing jobs and the transition to a postindustrial economy, a formal education became necessary in order to acquire an income that could support a middle-class lifestyle. Since manufacturing jobs were concentrated in the urban metropolis, and since a large percentage of the African-American population lived in these urban centers, largely as a result of the great black urban migration that began after World War II, the problematic aspects of the transition to the postindustrial economy disproportionately affected blacks.

Poverty became an urban phenomenon after the 1960s, and the racial aspect mentioned above became visible with the emergence of the black urban ghetto. In 1969, the proportion of those living in poverty in America's central cities stood at 12.7 percent, but by 1982 it had risen to 19.9 percent, a 57 percent increase over that time period.[37] As William Julius Wilson and Robert Aponte explain,

> in urban areas "postindustrial society" occupational positions that usually require levels of education and training beyond the reach of poor inner-city residents have significantly increased. Shifts in the urban job structure have accompanied changes in the demographic composition of large central cities from predominantly European white to predominantly black and Hispanic, resulting in a decrease both in the total population of central cities and in aggregate personal income levels.[38]

As Philip Cohen has argued, in metropolitan areas where the black population is larger proportionate to the white population, increased minority size provokes a more hostile collective reaction from whites (the visibility-discrimination hypothesis). Also, larger minority work-forces under conditions of occupational segregation lead to lower wages for minority workers (the crowding hypothesis).[39] Structural changes in the economies of advanced nations indicated by a number of phenomena – the concentration of the poorest of the poor in urban ghettos; educational failure; underemployment and job insecurity; social and spatial isolation; welfare dependency; teenage pregnancy and motherhood; the absence of the father from the home and dwindling numbers of positive male role models for young boys in these neighborhoods; racial discrimination; and a propensity to engage in criminal and disorderly behavior – have given rise to a so-called urban *underclass*.[40] Members of this underclass – to whom William Julius Wilson refers collectively as the "truly disadvantaged" – are characterized as living in chronic poverty, with little hope of escaping from it, because of a lack of income-producing employment.[41]

Besides economic disadvantages wrought by the transition to a postindustrial economy and continuing racism, both overt and institutional, the underclass is disproportionately black, ironically enough, because of the end of de jure housing segregation based on race. Although de facto housing segregation certainly still exists – a point we will return to shortly – it was not until recently that middle- and working-class blacks have had the opportunity to find housing beyond the confines of the ghetto, and those economically able to move have indeed done so.[42] As William Julius Wilson explains,

> Especially since 1970, inner-city neighborhoods have experienced an outmigration of working- and middle-class families previously confined to them by restrictive covenants of higher-status city neighborhoods and suburbs. Combined with the increase in the number of poor caused by rising joblessness, the outmigration has sharply

concentrated the poverty in inner-city neighborhoods. The number with poverty rates that exceed 40 percent – a threshold definition of "extreme poverty" neighborhoods – has risen precipitously.[43]

As a result, rather than being spread out across urban areas as in the past, the poor are now spatially concentrated in a subset of neighborhood locations, thereby being isolated from the social and economic mainstream. This concentration and *social isolation* of blacks in particular are the distinguishing features of the urban underclass.[44]

Use of linguistic cues in perpetrating de facto housing segregation

As was mentioned above, legal statutes such as the Fair Housing Act of 1968 have attempted to end *de facto* (or informal) housing discrimination. Although these laws have gone a long way toward minimizing such practices, there are still resources available in everyday life whereby renters, landlords, real-estate businesses, or mortgage companies can discriminate, on the basis of either race, sex, or class, or some combination of these. This means that, although much overt discrimination has been reduced, more subtle practices of racial exclusion have persisted.

A study by Doug Massey and Garvey Lundy analyzes these forms of informal control ostensibly aimed at excluding blacks from certain housing markets.[45] They begin with the observation that most Americans are capable of making fairly accurate racial attributions on the basis of linguistic cues alone. For example, most Americans can identify the race of someone speaking *Black English Vernacular* (or BEV), and also the race of code-switching blacks, those speaking standard English but with a "black" pronunciation of certain words (so-called *Black Accented English*). The authors hypothesize that much discrimination occurs over the phone, on initial calls to landlords, owner-sellers, and real-estate agents requesting information.[46]

Massey and Lundy recruited students in an undergraduate research methods course to pose as prospective buyers or renters, and were instructed to place calls for information to landlords in the Philadelphia area. Students selected for participation in the study were natural speakers of BEV, Black Accented English (BAE), or White Middle-Class English (WME). A phone script was prepared for all students to follow to control for interactional effects, and common sets of profiles were assigned to each caller. In 46 percent of the cases initial calls resulted in contact with some form of voice mail. Here, callers were instructed to leave a short request for a return call.

The results showed strong evidence for the existence of phone-based discrimination in the Philadelphia rental housing market.

- Blacks experience less access than whites do for units of rental housing.
- Females experience less access than males.

- Lower-class blacks (those speaking BEV) have less access than middle-class blacks (those speaking BAE).
- Race, sex, and class interact to influence rental outcomes.

This is further illustrated when looking at the likelihood of callers reaching a rental agent. The percentages of those who got through were as follows:

- 87 percent of white males
- 80 percent of BAE males
- 75 percent of white middle-class females
- 72 percent of BEV males
- 71 percent of BAE females
- at the low end, only 63 percent of BEV females.

Speaking to an agent is only half the battle, however. There is also the need to look at what prospective renters were told regarding whether or not a rental unit was available. The results for those being told a unit was available were as follows:

- 86 percent of white middle-class males
- 80 percent of white middle-class females
- 79 percent of BAE males
- 61 percent of BEV males
- and just 60 percent of BEV females.

The product of these two proportions – the share reaching a rental agent and the share being told a unit was available – indicates overall access to rental units in the Philadelphia housing market. The overall results were as follows:

- 76 percent of WME males
- 63 percent of BAE males
- 60 percent of WME females
- 57 percent of BAE females
- 44 percent of BEV males
- and just 38 percent of BEV females.

These same patterns held with regard to agents raising concerns of creditworthiness, and whether an application fee was charged (and, if so, how much). Just being considered as a potential renter cost on average $11 for WME males; $25 for BAE males and females; $32 for BEV males; and $43 for BEV females. It is clear from these figures that lower-class black females are especially disadvantaged, carrying the triple burden of race, sex, and class.

Informal justice: the code of the street

This summary of the economic transition which has given rise to the urban underclass, as well as the various forms of informal or "off the books" discrimination that can be perpetrated against members of this class, serves as the backdrop for examining the work of Elijah Anderson.[47] Anderson, like other researchers concerned with urban poverty and the crime and social disorganization that attends it, is particularly interested in the problem of inner-city youth violence. Anderson argues that youth violence springs from circumstances of life among the ghetto poor, including:

- lack of living wages
- limited public services (police, utilities, trash)
- stigma of race
- drug use and sales
- fatalism, or alienation and absence of hope for the future
- low or no stakes in conformity.

The combination of these circumstances creates a pervasive sense of despair which in turn spawns an oppositional culture among the ghetto poor. One key manifestation of this oppositional culture is the *code of the street*, a set of informal rules governing interpersonal public behavior, particularly those relating to violence.[48] Areas covered by the code include:

- proper comportment
- the proper way to respond if challenged
- regulating the use of violence
- that if the tacit rules of the code are violated, there will be consequences
- that ignorance of the code is not a defense.

At the heart of the code is the issue of respect. Being granted deference, being treated "right," and being accommodated are near the top of the value hierarchy of the code. Respect is hard-won but easily lost, hence the status system generated by the code is highly precarious. A person's status, respect, and sense of self must constantly be guarded. Gaining and keeping respect is important because those who are judged to be worthy of respect within the street environment are apt not to be bothered or "dissed."

This brings us to an interesting point. Within the street environment where the code is in effect and enforced, forms of "dissing" – such as maintaining eye contact too long, not wearing the right type of clothing, passing by too closely, or engaging in verbal insults – may seem trivial from the perspective of middle-class values. But on the streets of the inner city, "dissing" can become a matter of life and death. The idea is that in mainstream society there are plenty of places to go to get your ego stroked if someone treats you badly or calls you a bad name or whatever. But in the inner city, since respect and status are so precarious and since there is so little of it to go around, any challenges to it, even in the seemingly trivial cases of non-verbal behavior or talk which may be interpreted as offensive, are serious and deserving of vigorous defense.

Notice also that Anderson is working with the notion of status as a zero-sum phenomenon. Conceptualizing something as *zero-sum* implies that some valued thing – power, status, or prestige for example – is a finite resource, meaning that those who have a lot of it effectively keep others from acquiring their fair share. And among those who have very little of the valued resource to begin with – such as the inner-city poor in relation to power or respect – whatever little is available will be fought over tenaciously, with sometimes deadly consequences. The zero-sum perspective on power or status is contrasted with an alternative perspective which views these phenomena as resources that go through cycles of inflation and deflation. Following Talcott Parsons, let us call this the symbolic or *generalized medium* perspective.[49] Parsons viewed power not as a fixed or finite resource in society, but as a generalized medium seated in the polity which circulates throughout the social system. Power is in effect the instrument through which collective goals are pursued. As Parsons explains,

> Power, as a symbolic medium, is like money in that it is itself "worthless," but is accepted in the expectation that it can later be "cashed in," this time in the activation of binding obligations. If, however, "power-credit" has been extended too far, without the necessary organizational basis for fulfillment of expectations having been laid, then attempting to invoke the obligations will result in less than a full level of performance, inhibited by various sorts of resistance.[50]

The thing to be pointed out here is that those who hold to a zero-sum view of valued resources tend toward the liberal side of the ideological or political spectrum, while those who hold the generalized medium view tend toward the conservative side. In the case of respect or status, Anderson's zero-sum perspective decries the fact that persons in the inner city, often through no fault of their own, are not given the opportunity to acquire levels of status, respect, or living wages because the means for their acquisition are blocked or absent. Caught up as they are in the structural constraints and degradations of the inner city, some will turn to aggression and other forms of deviant behavior in reaction to their dilemma. Indeed, metropolitan areas with few quality jobs for less-skilled and less-educated workers are characterized by significantly higher rates of violent and property crime.[51] Although such individuals cannot be totally absolved of their behavior, there is the recognition that structural forces beyond the control of individuals – such as the change from an industrial to a postindustrial economy – are the root cause of such unwanted behaviors.

We see, then, that with regard to the code of the street, respect is a valuable form of social capital.[52] Within the inner city, there is a pervasive sense that the police cannot be relied upon to maintain order and respond to citizens' calls in a timely manner. Under these conditions, where formal controls are viewed as ineffective, self-help will come to predominate. The code of the street is the embodiment of this informal system of self-help. An especially important part of the code are those tacit norms dealing with the presentation of self. With regard to presence on the streets, young males especially must display a certain predisposition to violence. This may involve certain facial expressions, gait, talk, clothing (for gangs and street-oriented persons expensive athletic attire is preferred), jewelry, and grooming. To be respected, it is vital to have the right look. Those who have the "right" appearance according to the tacit norms of the code deserve a measure of respect, while those that do not uphold these appearance conventions are likely to be deemed socially deficient and thereby subject to challenge or attack.

As Anderson argues, this becomes a vicious cycle, trapping many poor ghetto youths. Ghetto youth must constantly "campaign for respect," and this means presenting a "tough" self. They learn at an early age to socialize competitively with peers, and they learn the social meaning of fighting. Physical and verbal aggression is taught at home, at school, and in the streets. In essence, might makes right; toughness is a virtue while humility is not.

Objects also play a crucial role in the social system of the street. Expensive jackets, sneakers, jewelry, and even firearms are objects persons must be willing to possess. Like respect, these objects are precious and in short supply, and thus require defending. For example, a youth who wears "unhip" attire runs the risk of being assaulted for being an "unworthy" person. This means that, in the inner city, a kid might not risk wearing a pair of generic or no-name sneakers from Wal-Mart for fear of being "dissed" or even worse. (Indeed, for inner-city youths being called "poor" is perhaps the most cutting insult of all.) As a measure of self-protection, inner-city youth would more likely choose Timberland, Tommy Hilfiger, or other accepted name brands.

On first blush this appears to be a classist or even racist position. After all, norms of fashion dictate to most everyone in the middle and upper classes that certain name-brand clothing or other items ought to be worn or purchased. It is not just the urban poor who are caught up in this one-upmanship regarding styles and fashion: virtually everyone plays the game on some level. The difference, though, is that those in the middle classes or higher typically do not risk physical assault for wearing unhip fashions.

Individuals shore up their precarious identities, then, by acquiring valued things. One may campaign for status by taking the possessions of others. The ability to violate somebody – to "diss" or "get in their face" – is valued. Within this violent system of give and take, raising oneself up depends on putting someone else down. This craving for respect, always in short supply, gives people thin skins and short fuses. It also serves to illustrate once again the zero-sum nature of respect within the social system of the urban ghetto.

It should also be noted that the code of the street is not limited to the physical confines of the streets of the inner city. It is also present in aspects of popular culture, particularly in rap music. Rap music lyrics consistently emphasize the theme of respect, asserting that violence is an appropriate and expected response and that disrespect cannot be tolerated. In this case, violence is a form of informal social control in the form of self-help.[53]

Linkages between informal and formal controls

Anderson makes the point that the code of the street exists not because all or even most of the inhabitants of urban poverty areas are invested in or approve of it. Indeed, the code proliferates even when the majority of families within the inner city could be characterized as possessing a *decent* orientation, namely, families that display and believe in traditional middle-class values of respect for others, optimism about the future, appropriate child-rearing practices, and the belief in the validity of major social institutions such as church and school. The code emerges and is sustained largely as a result of a minority of so-called *street* families, namely, persons who lack consideration for others, who hold only a superficial sense of family and community, who have difficulty coping with the demands of parenthood, who have a limited understanding of priorities and consequences of action, and who are invested in some degree in the drug trade.[54]

Because young males from street families tend to dominate the streets and other public places of the ghetto, their presence creates a tipping point whereby even youngsters from decent families must learn to handle themselves within the street environment. This means that a critical mass of persons on the streets display the outward appearance of investment in the code – especially through their clothing but also through styles of communication and aggressive presentations of self – even if most are not fully invested in it. In other words, the outward appearance of abiding by the code is for many a form of self-defense. (In some respects also this is akin to the Emperor's Dilemma, discussed in chapter 4.)

The point is that, even with the acknowledgment of the emergence and sustenance of a deviant system of self-help within urban ghettos, there are also more traditional systems of informal control in operation. Informal controls at the level of the neighborhood or community may include "neighbors taking note and questioning strangers, watching over each other's property, assuming responsibility for the supervision of youth and intervening in local disturbances."[55] As was noted, from the perspective of Hirschi's control theory a crucial element of informal control is children's identification with their parents. Children who have positive adult role models in the community, including parents as well as other conventional figures such as priests, teachers, same-age peers, and neighbors, are less likely to engage in anti-social behavior. Ideally, adequate levels of informal control can be maintained in a community to the extent that collective and legal socialization occurs across dense networks of families and other neighborhood associations.[56]

An important link between informal and formal control, mentioned above, is *legal socialization*, which refers to the process by which a person's moral values and orientations toward the legal system are formed. Although legal socialization starts in childhood, there are countless factors affecting a person's later attitudes toward the legal system. The extent to which one views the legal system as legitimate and is motivated to comply with law and legal authorities is of course moderated by the social contexts within which one's life develops. The kinds of persons one meets, one's family background, and one's neighborhood are a few of these social contexts.[57] Although for most persons developmental pathways over the life course are complex, one thing that appears certain is that young persons' experiences with the legal system – whether as a direct participant or as a result of knowing someone involved with the system – form a crucial factor in the development of negative or positive attitudes toward the police, the courts, and the correctional system. In other words, issues of *procedural justice*, namely, the perception of the fairness of the treatment of persons at the hands of the police or who come before the court, is perhaps the single most important factor in the formation of such attitudes.[58]

As we have seen in the case of the code of the street that emerges within the urban ghetto, those who live in such areas of concentrated disadvantage tend to have a more negative view of the police, and are also more tolerant of deviance, than persons living in middle-class neighborhoods.[59] Police response to socially disorganized and impoverished neighborhoods exacerbates the problems of high crime already in place, to the extent that, as a result of arrest and incarceration, young males are removed from these areas, which in turn reduces informal control because there are fewer males around to act as role models for neighborhood youth.[60] This means that residents of ghetto areas, who may already hold negative or cynical views of the legal system, as described above, may also hold negative views of the informal system of control.

To test this hypothesis, Dina Rose and Todd Clear examined how experiences with the criminal justice system affect attitudes toward both legal and informal control.[61] Rose and Clear surveyed residents of Leon County, Florida, and asked them whether or not they knew someone who had been incarcerated. They also asked these persons about their perception of the effectiveness of informal controls in their neighborhoods. There were two groups of questions pertaining to informal control. One group asked respondents how effectively members of the neighborhood made sure their children went to school, disciplined their children, and controlled their children in general. The other group of questions asked respondents to assess their neighbors' willingness to break up a fight, to intervene if someone were breaking into respondents' houses, and to intervene if someone were selling drugs to respondents' children.[62]

Results indicated that persons who report knowing someone in jail or prison are more likely to have low opinions of both formal and informal controls. With regard to race, blacks are more likely than whites to hold negative opinions about informal control in their neighborhood only if they have been exposed to incarceration (that is, knowing someone who is incarcerated). However, blacks who have *not* been exposed to incarceration hold no lower opinion of the effectiveness of informal controls than whites. The only difference, of course, is that, as a group, blacks were more likely than whites to have been exposed to incarceration, that is, were more likely to know someone who has been imprisoned (for reasons covered in chapter 5). As Rose and Clear explain, these results are significant because negative views of the police and the courts translate into a lesser willingness to comply with legal controls.[63] But such prison experiences may also cause people to have low opinions of informal controls, which in turn negatively impacts their ability to function within the community.[64] Indeed, newer initiatives such as community-oriented and problem-oriented policing have arisen largely from citizen dissatisfaction with the police and the perception that disorder and disorganization have increased, especially in impoverished communities because of the divestment in family and community services.

Conclusion

A number of criminologists and sociologists view the idea of social capital as an important corrective to earlier individualistic theories about crime, disorder, and deviance. The resources that accumulate as a result of family relations and within community social organization, and which also contribute to the positive cognitive and social development of children, are considered to be vital to the well-being of communities.[65] Although Anderson's theory concerning the code of the street, which explains why youth violence is likely to emerge within impoverished communities, has been shown to be correct for the most part, there are still some issues to be resolved.[66] For example, although it is suggested that frequent interaction between neighbors is an important form of social capital which ensures the continuing viability of informal controls, this may be somewhat overstated. Dense networks of neighbors interacting with and watching over each other may indeed be important for reducing certain types of crimes (most significantly burglary, motor vehicle theft, and robbery).[67] But communities characterized as dense networks may be somewhat cut off from resources available from more distant parts of the network, and this may work against the health of the community. For poor blacks especially, this is the problem of social isolation discussed above.

Even with the acknowledgment that many poor blacks within the ghetto are denied access to mainstream ties and institutions, thereby explaining persistent joblessness among the urban poor, this is not yet the whole story. One aspect of social capital is the ability of persons seeking jobs to request a reference from somebody who is in a position to vouch for their fitness for the position. Yet, under conditions of social isolation, persons are less likely to have access to other persons who could step in and provide references to assist in their job-seeking. This would then at least partially explain higher levels of joblessness among the ghetto poor.

But, as Sandra Smith has argued, persistent joblessness among the urban poor may be less an issue of social isolation and reduced access, and more an issue of functional deficiencies within their friendship networks. By *functional deficiencies*, Smith means "the disinclination of potential job contacts to assist when given the opportunity to do so, not because they lack information or the ability to influence hirers, but because they perceive untrustworthiness among their job-seeking ties and choose not to assist."[68]

Smith is arguing that the social capital deficiencies of the black urban poor with regard to job-seeking are caused not by access issues – most have plenty of contacts with persons who could potentially step in to provide references – but by motivation and mobilization issues. Her research indicates that job contacts expressed great reluctance to assist job-seekers. For example, persons were less likely to help out a job-seeker who was perceived as having an unstable employment history, or who was habitually tardy while employed. They were also concerned that job-seekers would "bring the street to the job,"

> which included, among other things, showing the effects of alcohol and drug abuse, acting raucously and boisterously, stealing, and intimidating authority figures and co-workers.[69]

This is synonymous with the street orientation described by Anderson, and it is with these issues of reputation and general behavioral orientations of job-seekers that job contacts are most concerned.

Suggestions for further reading

Anderson, Elijah. 1999. *Code of the Street: Decency, Violence, and the Moral Life of the Inner City*. New York: Norton.
Anderson's study of the code of the street, an informal system of control that arises out of the peculiar circumstances of life in the urban inner city, is located squarely within the tradition of Chicago School of sociology ethnographies stretching back to the 1910s and 1920s.

Hirschi, Travis. 1969. *Causes of Delinquency*. Berkeley: University of California Press.
Although widely known as a criminological theory, Hirschi's control or social bonding theory also provides a glimpse into the workings of everyday or informal social control.

Massey, Douglas S. and Garvey Lundy. 2001. "Use of Black English and Racial Discrimination in Urban Housing Markets: New Methods and Findings." *Urban Affairs Review* 36 (4): 452–69.

This article represents one of the single best studies illustrating the phenomenon of linguistic profiling. Although laws have been passed to stop overt forms of housing segregation, informal strategies, such as ascertaining the race of a person from the sound of his or her voice, are still widely employed.

Putnam, Robert D. 2000. *Bowling Alone: The Collapse and Revival of American Community.* **New York: Simon & Schuster.**

Although surely not the first treatment of its kind, Putnam's book nevertheless put the concept of social capital into wider circulation in scholarly, policy, and governance arenas.

Wilson, William Julius. 1987. *The Truly Disadvantaged: The Inner City, the Underclass, and Public Policy.* **Chicago: University of Chicago Press.**

Wilson's study, an analysis of the complex set of factors that has given rise to black inner-city poverty, was selected by the editors of the *New York Times Book Review* as one of the sixteen best books of 1987.

7 Medical Control: ADHD, Selective Mutism, and Violence as a Disease

Introduction

The critical case studies discussed in this chapter all relate to the medical control of youth. Two of them are taken from the wide range of mental disorders of childhood identified in the *Diagnostic and Statistical Manual of Mental Disorders* (*DSM*), namely, attention deficit hyperactivity disorder (ADHD) and selective mutism. A third case study examines the public health approach to the problem of youth and school violence, specifically focusing on how public health proponents are apt to conceptualize violence as a "disease."

These particular case studies of the medical control of youth were chosen for the following reasons. First, ADHD is perhaps the single best-known *DSM* category of "mental illness" afflicting young persons, and hence it was included because of the wide coverage it has received in both the mass media and the medical and social scientific literature. Second, in order to provide a contrast to this high-profile childhood affliction, I have chosen to cover selective mutism, a mental illness that, although virtually unknown to the general public, nevertheless vividly illustrates the continuing expansion of categories of mental illness of young persons. Third, the public health approach to school shootings provides a ready-made case analysis of the continuing tendency to invoke the language of disease and pathology when dealing with social problems.

In order to set the stage for this discussion, it is worthwhile noting that a number of prominent critics of psychiatry, such as Thomas Scheff, Thomas Szasz, and Erving Goffman (all of whom were pioneers in the "anti-psychiatry movement" of the 1950s and 1960s), argued that mental illnesses were merely labels applied to social deviance.[1] As summarized by Allyson Skene,

> Psychiatry, they agree, is the only branch of medicine which will treat a "disease" in the absence of biological abnormality and without a patient's consent. This, combined with the fact that the primary target of psychiatric interventions is behavior and psychological states, leads to the conclusion that psychiatry is a form of social control which represses socially undesirable behaviors.[2]

Skene is correct about the general animus directed toward the field of psychiatry by these authors and others within the anti-psychiatry movement. However, one need not take an overtly critical or even hostile stance toward psychiatry and its system of classifying mental disorders when pointing out its unmistakable social control function. The overriding concern of the discussions of selective mutism and ADHD in the next several sections will be to explore how and why these particular disorders became medicalized or, similarly, why informal control of and responses to these behaviors came to be deemed somehow inadequate.

Selective mutism

According to the *DSM-IV-TR* (published in 2000), selective mutism (313.23, formerly "elective mutism" in earlier versions of the *DSM*) is listed as an Axis I mental disorder "usually first diagnosed in infancy, childhood, or adolescence." The essential characteristic of *selective mutism* is the failure of a child to speak in situations where there is a social expectation that the child should speak (such as, for example, in the classroom). Additionally, the child's silence in these social settings cannot be attributed to any speech impediments (whether physiological or neurological). In other words, when a child who is able to speak refuses to do so in certain situations or social settings, the child could be diagnosed with selective mutism.

Research on the "disorder" finds that it typically begins during the pre-school ages, is more common among girls than boys, and although rare (affecting between 1 percent and 3 percent of the childhood population, and only 0.01 percent of the general population) is found at all levels of society.[3] Before the release of the fourth edition of the *DSM* in 1994 and later *DSM-TR* (or "text revision") version released in 2000, clinicians consistently found that one of the early developmental "risk factors" for selective mutism was "a history of immigration."[4] This is clearly absurd insofar as an immigrant child newly arrived to the United States (or any other host country) would likely not yet have full proficiency in spoken English (or other host tongues) and hence might very well not speak much, if at all, in a classroom or other formal setting. Here, given the social circumstances of newly arrived immigrants, the mutism or silence would be normal, not pathological. The acknowledgment of this oversight is included in the latest version of the diagnostic criteria for selective mutism:

- consistent failure to speak in specific social situations (in which there is an expectation for speaking, e.g., at school) despite speaking in other situations;
- the disturbance interferes with educational or occupational achievement or with social communication;
- the duration of the disturbance is at least 1 month (not limited to the first month of school);
- the failure to speak is not due to a lack of knowledge of, or comfort with, the spoken language required in the social situation; and

- the disturbance is not better accounted for by a communication disorder (e.g., stuttering) and does not occur exclusively during the course of a pervasive development disorder, schizophrenia, or other psychotic disorder.[5]

Selective mutism is presently classified as an Axis I "other" disorder of infancy, childhood, and adolescence because the etiology of the disorder is thought to be complex. Earlier researchers suggested that selective mutism was a motivational disorder, insofar as children were using silence as a way of manipulating persons and the immediate environment. This is, in effect, a variation of the "silent treatment," a strategy used in informal relationships, often most effectively employed by females against male friends or partners for their perceived wrongdoings. Extending this idea from the realm of informal control to that of medical control, children who choose to be silent may be understood as motivated out of the anxiety of having to face situations where speech is expected.[6] Other studies suggest family dysfunction may play a role, such as enmeshment between mother and mute child, a distant or detached father, strained marital relations, or a history of shyness in the family.

All things considered, the current consensus among psychologists, psychiatrists, school personnel, and other clinicians who deal with selective mutism on some level is that it is an anxiety disorder, and should probably be classified as such. The shyness mentioned above is considered to be the major contributor to anxiety disorders that may in turn become manifest as selective mutism. In essence, we have in selective mutism the pathologization of shyness, and this has occurred overwhelmingly within the context of school assessment and evaluation.[7] Just as the use of drugs such as Ritalin to treat ADD or ADHD has experienced explosive growth within the past fifteen years (to be discussed more fully below), so too have drugs (primarily antidepressants such as Prozac) been recommended for the treatment of selective mutism. As far as children are concerned, and especially insofar as social control within the schools is considered tenuous and in desperate need of shoring up (because of, among others things, the alleged decline of the family; the proliferation of violent television, film, and video games; the changing sociodemographics of public schooling; the diminution of teachers' authority within the classroom; and the tragic phenomenon of school shootings), the biomedicalization of youth continues unabated.[8]

Proponents of a biomedicalized view of childhood ills tend to agree on the biological, hormonal, or neurological underpinnings of various disorders, including selective mutism. The extent to which they favor drug treatments, however, depends on the ability of particular clinicians or therapists to provide drug treatments to patients or clients. Since doctors and psychiatrists own a monopoly on drug treatments, other non-medical personnel are limited to providing various types of "talking cures" such as behavioral or cognitive-behavioral therapy, social learning or self-modeling approaches, play therapy, family systems approaches, social skills training, or psychoanalysis more broadly defined.[9]

A few researchers have offered warnings about how far this pathologization and biomedicalization of youthful conduct could go if left unchecked. For example, as Neil Gordon argues,

> Although elective mutism may be one end of a spectrum from shy children to those in whom there is a presumptive cause, such as immigration, unhappiness at school, or anxiety over some social disaster, it will be important to reserve management and treatment to those in whom the problem is significantly affecting the child, and or, the parents. Otherwise, as stressed by Kolvin and Fundudis, a lot of children will be labeled unnecessarily who are reacting not unreasonably to a strange situation, such as a reception class in school, and who will soon be talking normally.[10]

One of the reasons that a seemingly innocent behavior such as shyness could be interpreted as pathological and brought under the orbit of selective mutism is that a critical mass of mental health and school professionals assume that shyness itself is biologically based. This means that, when shyness becomes excessive and is deemed to "interfere" with the activities of children within (primarily) school settings, it is subject to drug treatment or other types of clinical interventions. Indeed, children who possess a "shy biological temperament" and who exhibit the various diagnostic criteria of selective mutism are apt to be viewed by clinicians and health providers as suffering from a childhood anxiety order that is biologically based.[11]

For the most part school personnel appear to be thoroughly committed to the notion that selective mutism is a "real" mental disorder and that it has a biological basis. Consider the case of a thirteen-year-old student who since the age of five and a half had remained virtually speechless within classroom settings.[12] Early on elementary-school teachers and school psychologists had attempted to get him to speak, but to no avail. He was placed in a learning disability classroom, but this did not help. He maintained his muteness. By the time he was thirteen teachers had become so frustrated by this student's lack of progress that school administrators threatened legal action against his parents because they would neither seek nor consent to psychological services for their son. Under the threat of legal action, the parents relented and the student was put into a multi-modal treatment plan involving therapists, school personnel, family members, and peers. After one and a half years of treatment the student began speaking and made a successful transition from junior high school to high school. The treatments were deemed a resounding success, targeted as they were to the reduction of his social anxiety which was believed to be fueling his mutism.

However, claims of the efficacy of these and other interventions aimed at "curing" the "disorder" of selective mutism need to be critically examined. First, the fact that the student graduated to high school is not necessarily an indication of the effectiveness of the treatment. Notice for example that throughout his school career, during which time the student was presumably afflicted with selective mutism, he still managed to graduate on time at each grade level. Second, in order to assess the efficacy of the treatments a standard A-B design was employed, but these are notoriously problematic with regard to questions of external validity. Since no controls were utilized in the research design, there is no scientific basis upon which to assert that the intervention itself was actually what caused the student to start talking again in school settings. In other words, with no adequate controls in place there is no way to rule out a host of other factors that could have actually brought about the desired outcome, including the very real possibility that the student was likely to start talking on his own regardless of the treatments.

Disvalued versus disordered conditions of childhood and adolescence

Perhaps the most enlightening discussion concerning the problematic aspects of childhood disorders such as selective mutism – and to be discussed shortly, ADHD – has been provided by Jerome Wakefield.[13] According to Wakefield, the concept of mental disorder must satisfy at least two conditions: (1) the disorder is due to some internal dysfunction within the individual, and (2) a value judgment is made that the behaviors associated with the disorder are harmful to the individual or to society. Value judgments per se regarding the nature or level of harm associated with some unwanted behaviors are not problematic, insofar as the realms of law and everyday life (legal and informal control respectively) make the same sort of value judgments about social harm as well. Where the concept of mental disorder runs into trouble is in the tendency, while lacking an independent means of verification, to view unwanted or disvalued behaviors as indicative, *ipso facto*, of some underlying or internal dysfunction within the individual. To restate, oftentimes disvalued conduct is taken as evidence that an internal dysfunction within the individual is driving the conduct, when in fact no such internal dysfunction is present or reasonably can be shown to exist using the methods of the empirical sciences. Even further, even if an internal dysfunction can be shown to exist in some instances, the diagnostic criteria are overly inclusive, meaning that many false positives (the Type II error discussed in chapter 4) are produced, leading to an overestimation of the extent and severity of the disorder in the population.

As Wakefield argues, especially in the case of the myriad mental disorders that apply particularly to children and adolescents – who are relatively powerless and cannot speak for themselves regarding their being labeled mentally disordered – it is simply too easy to mistake disvalued conditions for disordered conditions.[14] Getting back to the case of selective mutism, the diagnostic criteria for determining whether an internal dysfunction actually exists within the child or adolescent make it too easy to conflate disvalue with disorder. Wakefield provides a useful example:

> a girl who refuses to talk because a bully has accused her of being teacher's pet and has threatened to beat her up if she opens her mouth in class can still be diagnosed as disordered under these [diagnostic] criteria.[15]

The production of these and other types of false positives leads reasonable persons to suspect that, rather than its being a mental disorder, selective mutism serves more a social control function, especially within school settings.

Attention deficit hyperactivity disorder

According to the *DSM-IV*, attention deficit hyperactivity disorder (ADHD) is a neurological condition marked by a person's inability to regulate attention, or impulses, or both. According to the most recent diagnostic criteria for ADHD, some of the symptoms of inattention include:

• difficulty in sustaining attention in play or task activities;
• not listening when spoken to directly;
• difficulty organizing tasks and activities; and
• being easily distracted.

Some of the symptoms of hyperactivity include:

• fidgeting with hands or feet or squirming in seat;
• often leaving seat when remaining seated is expected;
• often being "on the go" as if "driven by a motor"; and
• often talking excessively.

And some of the symptoms of impulsivity include:

• often blurting out answers before a question has been completed;
• often having difficulty waiting one's turn; and
• often interrupting or intruding on others.

It is further stated that some minimal constellation of symptoms must be present for at least six months, and that the symptoms constitute "clinically significant impairment" in the social, academic, or occupational functioning of the afflicted person.[16] An important class of indicators of such "impairment" is of course negative evaluations on the part of teachers who are dealing with the sometimes unruly and disruptive behavior of young boys in their classrooms. But why are fidgeting in one's seat, looking out the window, blurting out answers, or not paying attention considered symptoms of a mental disorder? How in the world has this happened?

Insofar as the history of the concept of attention deficits has developed in the United States, it is safe to say that "the cure preceded the ailment."[17] That is to say, before the disorder was even named, drug treatments had been developed to subdue children's unruly behavior. For example, in 1937 physician Charles Bradley discovered that amphetamine drugs had a paradoxical effect on school children: instead of stimulating them, as is the case in adults, these drugs actually subdued their behavior.

Over the next two decades the medical literature was rife with studies which lauded the clinical utility of stimulant medications for so-called childhood behavior disorders.[18] In 1957 the disorder was first named by Maurice Laufer and associates as "hyperkinetic impulse disorder." Around this same time a new drug called Ritalin was synthesized, and it became the drug of choice in the treatment of childhood behavior disorders because it had many of the qualities of amphetamines without the undesirable side effects. Later, hyperkinetic disorder began being referred to simply as hyperkinesis, and by the 1970s it had become the most common child psychiatric problem.[19]

Hyperkinesis is now referred to as attention deficit disorder (ADD) or, when hyperactivity is part of the syndrome, attention deficit hyperactivity disorder (ADHD). As mentioned previously, Ritalin is the drug of choice for the treatment of ADHD, and in the United States its use has grown astonishingly over the last twenty years. For example, between 1989 and 1994 the US consumption of Ritalin and associated stimulants showed a fourfold increase. Depending on estimates, boys are four to ten times more likely than girls to be diagnosed with ADHD, and currently about 12 percent of all male school children in the United States take the drug. The United States leads other countries by a wide margin in consumption of these stimulant drugs, as its citizens now consume over 90 percent of production worldwide.[20]

The medical discourse on ADHD, and hence biomedicalization of the disorder, continues to strengthen as the schools use their administrative clout, in concert with health professionals employed either within the school system (such as school social workers or psychologists) or from without, to exercise pressure against parents or other family members who may be reluctant, at least initially, to accept the diagnosis of attention deficits. Just as in the case of selective mutism mentioned above, schools may often use the threat of legal action as a wedge to gain compliance from parents who resist submitting their children for evaluation who are believed to be afflicted with ADHD. A number of studies have examined the initial uneasy alliance between parents of an ADHD child, the school system, health professionals, and the legal system.[21] The important thing to note is that the power of the disease discourse tends to win out over the initial objections of the family. Parents in fact often acquiesce to the discourse of disease assembled within the shared framework of the schools, medicine, and the law. Indeed, in many cases parents become some of the strongest proponents of the disease view of hyperactivity, networking with other parents of ADD or ADHD children to form support groups and working to reduce the stigma associated with this particular "mental illness."

Considering all that has been said, it may not be farfetched to suggest that ADHD has been invented rather than discovered. The fact that some children are fidgety, inattentive, or easily excitable may simply be due to normal fluctuations about the statistical mean of human behavior. Indeed, the tradition of early childhood schooling in Western countries may actually represent a massive constriction of normal childhood activity, so behaviors that meet the diagnostic criteria of ADHD may actually be a normal response to these constraints.[22] Related to this, our societal values – in particular the Protestant work ethic – may simply demand that a disorder like ADHD exists. In a society that favors the delay of gratification and the efficient use of time and energy to attain positions of wealth and power, labeling children with a disease who are distractible, seemingly lack motivation, or are impulsive may simply be a way of protecting and reinforcing cherished social values.[23]

Both selective mutism and ADHD are psychiatric disorders which are defined and responded to within the framework of the medical case model of individual pathology or disease. In the third critical case study to be discussed beginning in the next section, we illustrate how medicine may respond to pathology at the collective or group level. The public health model and its propensity for turning social problems into medical problems has a parallel at the individual level, namely the medical case method, which has a similar propensity for labeling various forms of deviant or disvalued behaviors as mental disorders. We will illustrate the operation of the public health model in its approach to the issue of violence. Specifically, the public health model attempts to make the case that violence is a "disease."

The problem of school and youth violence

Much recent scholarly attention devoted to the problem of school violence emphasizes a so-called proactive approach. Indeed, proactivity is one of the newest and hottest buzzwords in school research and social policy more generally. Proponents of proactivity in school policy assume that this is a new and better approach that improves upon earlier, merely "reactive" approaches to any number of pressing school issues.[24]

In this section I examine the rhetoric of proactivity in recent scholarly writings in one particular area of school operation and policy, namely school violence. It is especially important to examine the claims being made by proponents of proactive school policy in this area in light of the string of highly publicized and tragic school shootings that began in earnest in 1999. As a result of these events, there appears to be a broad consensus among scholars, policy analysts, teachers and administrators, and the lay public that a "crisis" or "epidemic" of violence has descended upon our schools, and that something needs to be done quickly. It is no longer sufficient, argue proponents of proactivity, merely to react to incidents of school violence after they have already occurred. With our "scientific" (read: medical, psychoanalytical, or psychological) knowledge about human behavior firmly in hand, we should be able to construct "proactive" approaches to school violence that in effect get at its root cause (or "etiology"). In other words, by knowing the environmental conditions of schools and local communities as well as the individual traits or characteristics of perpetrators of school violence, we should be able to predict and thus reduce or eliminate its occurrence.

The invocation of proactivity assumes that there has been a startling leap forward in new techniques or knowledge that effectively renders current, merely "reactive" approaches obsolete. However, the evidence to support such assertions is lacking. Indeed, we will see that, more often than not, proactivity is ritually invoked to provide comforting reassurance that some area of the social world that is under siege or problematic – as is certainly perceived to be the case with school violence – is being tended to and ameliorated thanks to the latest cutting-edge advances in the field. In this sense, proactivity in social policy provides a rhetorical flourish but in reality is little more than wishful thinking.

The public health model revisited

I shall now turn to several discussions of proactivity within the school violence literature. One of the clearest and most forceful articulations of proactive policy is embodied in the broad public health model of social problems, which was introduced in chapter 4. To reiterate, the public health approach includes "both the art and the science of preventing disease, prolonging life, and promoting health."[25] Since violence and aggression cause or lead to injuries and death, proponents of the public health model are apt to treat violence as if it were a "disease" with identifiable stages: etiology or onset; developmental pathways of the "disease" after onset; characteristics of the population "at risk" of "contracting" the disease; and interventions at the individual or group level that purport to reduce or eliminate the disease of youth/school violence.

From the public health perspective, both the earlier models of punishment and rehabilitation (or treatment) were reactive in that they dealt with criminals or clients only after their offending or problematic behavior came to light or was "diagnosed." Although public health proponents acknowledge that interventions aimed at rehabilitating defendants/clients who have already offended is an improvement over the criminal justice emphasis on punishment for the sake of deterrence, retribution, or justice, the treatment model does not go far enough. Rather than intervention, the public health model's primary objective is *prevention*, that is, ensuring that the disease never arises in the first place.[26]

The idea that violence – school, youth, or otherwise – is a "disease" that can and should be conceptualized as a public health issue is widespread. A sampling from a large literature includes the following pronouncements:

- "Youth violence is an important national and public health problem."[27]
- "Violence is a public health problem that can be understood and changed."[28]
- "Though crime rates have been decreasing in recent years, violence continues to be a public health problem in the United States."[29]
- "Violence is one of America's most challenging and concerning public health problems."[30]
- "Violence is a major public health problem in the United States and elsewhere."[31]

All of these quotations appear as first lines or within the first few pages of a journal article or book. The style and placing of the statements function rhetorically to make the sober, authoritative point that youth violence is perhaps the single most serious and significant public health problem we face today. It is not simply a social problem; it is a *public health* problem. It is important to make whatever persuasive appeals are necessary to sell the notion that something is a public health problem, and this is because of the higher levels of invasiveness and surveillance of the population that is implied in the public health model as compared to other models of justice or treatment. Indeed, Deborah Prothrow-Stith suggests that the first stage of the public health mission involves the setting up of surveillance systems which, in the case of interpersonal violence, means collecting data on "who is being hurt and under what circumstances."[32] The public health model, then, is utilitarian at heart, because even though stepping up surveillance of the population for purposes of monitoring and (hopefully) eradicating yet another "disease" is potentially harmful or debilitating to some groups – especially children, I would contend – in the end what counts is "the greatest good for the greatest number of people." That is, proponents of the public health model argue that whatever costs are incurred in the process of defining and treating violence as a disease are outweighed by the expected future benefits, namely, reducing or eliminating violence.

Three stages of prevention

The public health model conceptualizes a tripartite classification of prevention into primary, secondary, and tertiary stages. These three stages or strategies of prevention are summarized below.

- *Tertiary prevention* – encompasses all those strategies designed to keep persons who are already ill from becoming sicker. This is the classic "reactive" approach to social and health problems.
- *Secondary prevention* – involves the early identification of those who already have symptoms of some disease. At-risk profiles, generated from heightened surveillance of the target population, help to determine who are good candidates for early intervention. Secondary prevention represents a mix of reactive and proactive approaches.
- *Primary prevention* – focuses on stopping some problem behavior before it starts, the overall goal of which is to reduce health problems in the general population. Strategies may include educational and public information campaigns, changing the environment (or organization, or institution), immunizing potential hosts or victims, etc. These approaches are characterized as "proactive."

Is violence a disease?

Since the public health model views problems in society as diseases or disease-based, the three categories of prevention – primary, secondary, and tertiary – refer to the stage to which the disease has progressed at diagnosis or discovery. In this sense, tertiary prevention is the lowest level of prevention, in that it represents a state of affairs in which the disease has gone undiagnosed or unnoticed for quite some time, and has progressed to the point that the patient is seriously or chronically ill.[33] Proponents of public health argue that the typical criminal justice response represents merely a tertiary prevention effort, since most of its contacts are with core or repeat offenders who come to the attention of justice officials well after the fact.[34] At this stage in the progression of the disease, the best the criminal justice response can do is attempt to treat or rehabilitate. Often, however, among hardcore offenders the disease has progressed so far that the only viable option is either imprisonment or institutionalization, that is, the isolation of such people for their own, or others', good.[35]

It is important to point out here a serious problem in this attempt to treat violence as a disease. First of all, we must attempt to clear up some confusion over the concept of "disease" itself, for it has two distinct understandings or usages, namely, literal and metaphorical. As Thomas Szasz explains,

> Literally, the term *disease* denotes a demonstrable lesion of cells, tissues, or organs; metaphorically, it may be used to denote any kind of malfunctioning, of individuals, groups, economies, etc. (drug addiction, youth violence, economic depression, etc.).[36]

Hence, over the years social scientists, physicians, therapists, and even the lay public have become accustomed to extending the criteria of disease from malfunctions of the human body to malfunctions of the human mind (in the case of mental illness) or even of society (in this case, assuming that society is like an "organism" which can possess "diseased" states such as social disorganization, violence, and so forth). But conceptualizing society as an organism – otherwise known as organicism – is an ontological move, that is, a way of setting up an analytical strategy for simplifying the complexities of the human social world. Proponents of the public health model would be doing fine if they acknowledged they were using violence in the metaphorical sense to generate hypotheses or test theories about various aspects of inter-personal or school violence. However, many such proponents continue to insist that violence is in fact a literal disease. It will be shown upon closer examination, however, that this violence-as-a-literal-disease view cannot be sustained.

One of the first things we confront from the violence-as-literal-disease perspective is confusion over who the victim is, who the carrier of the disease is, and how the disease is acquired, as well as what the "risk" factors are for acquisition of the disease. As to the first point, we know that there are offenders perpetrating violence against others, and often innocent victims are injured or even killed as a result. So, in the case of violence, we have a diseased person (the violent offender) caus-ing harm to others. Fair enough. In the search for an analogy to a "real" disease that acts in a similar way, we are led to the communicable diseases. Here, a diseased person (whether infected with HIV, influenza, malaria, or what have you) wittingly or unwittingly causes harm to victims by passing on the disease to them. The disease is a biological or chemical agent – a pathogen – that insinuates itself into the tissues or blood of victims, slowly harming or killing them from the inside. The diseased state of the carrier (or offender) is replicated in the receiver (or victim). But does violence really act or unfold in this way?

There is one scenario to which proponents of the public health model might point in an effort to maintain the violence-as-disease analogy. They could point approvingly to the literature that suggests that violence is passed down from generation to generation, for exam-ple, the finding that children exposed to acts of violence in the home (or who are themselves victims of violence) are more likely to perpetrate violence against others. This theory of the intergenerational transmis-sion of violence also finds an ally in cultural theories of violence, namely, that America's violent popular culture instills a proneness toward violence and aggression among persons exposed to it. And as the amount of violent images one is exposed to increases, the more violent one is likely to become.[37]

The question that arises at this point, then, is this: If violence acts like a contagious disease, what is the pathogen? Certainly culture cannot be considered a proper pathogen, because everyone receives and is a bearer of culture, yet not everyone becomes violent (in fact, a very small minority do) as a result of being exposed to violent images in popular media and elsewhere.

David McDonald's take on violence from the framework of infectious disease epidemiology is instructive. From this perspective, the public health model focuses on the host (the victim of violence), the agent that creates the injury, the vector/vehicle that carries or conveys the agent, and the social context within which the violent incident occurs. As McDonald goes on to explain, from this perspective

> injury is best understood in terms of the agent of injury involved, and that the agent is energy. Accordingly, injury prevention and control turned its focus from assumed inadequacies of the victim (for instance, lazy, ignorant, and careless) to the injurious transfer of energy.[38]

The very odd implication of this is that energy or energy transfer is the pathogen impelling the disease of violence. But this again is simply logically untenable. A slap on the back for a job well done also involves energy transfer, yet by no stretch of the imagination could this act be considered violent.

James Gilligan has articulated another take on violence from the infectious disease epidemiology perspective. Gilligan argues that the violence pathogen is emotion, specifically, the experience of overwhelming shame and humiliation.[39] The author claims that violence-prone individuals lack the ego defenses that otherwise insulate "normal" persons from reacting violently whenever they are shamed or humiliated. In other words, for some reason violence-prone individuals are overwhelmingly vulnerable and sensitive to experiences of shame, and act upon these feelings inappropriately in the form of aggression and/or violence. Presumably, normal persons possess sufficient non-violent means by which to undo or deal with feelings of shame and humiliation. From this perspective, primary prevention would be targeted to stopping all forms of shaming and humiliation that persons might experience in their lives, especially as a result of social stratification, poverty, oppressive governments, and of course the innumerable -isms (e.g., racism, sexism, ageism, lookism). In addition, primary prevention could take the form of programs to enhance self-esteem or the feeling of self-worth.

But again, it seems bizarre to liken emotions to a pathogen. How did these violence-prone individuals acquire or contract these faulty emotions in the first place? If we are trying to stay true to infectious disease epidemiology, it appears that in no way, shape, or form could emotions serve as an appropriate pathogen regarding violence as a disease.

Community violence

Yet another approach to the violence-as-literal-disease argument is the notion that community violence causes both physical and psychological harm to those exposed to it, whether or not exposed persons then go on themselves to perpetrate violence. For example, Lorion argues that, by shifting from an individual to an ecological perspective, behavioral scientists can begin to understand that community violence is itself a community-based pathogen.[40] From this perspective, exposure to community violence is likened to an environmental toxin that has the potential to contaminate persons and their interpersonal relationships, thereby spreading the disease of violence even further.

But does this make sense? Lorion argues that community violence is similar to an airborne toxin that can act to disrupt the emotional, physical, behavioral, and interpersonal functioning of persons exposed to it.[41] Public health proponents argue that the causes and consequences of violence are broad and diverse, touching upon virtually every aspect of daily life. Various attempts to develop a prototype indicator set of the causes and consequences of violence typically come up with an exhaustive list of indicators, some of which are:

- impact on health and function (disease), which includes the direct effects of violence, namely physical injury, death, and psychological problems;
- impact on well-being, such as fear of crime and violence, as well as restricting activities or changing lifestyles as a result of such fear;
- individual responses to violence, which include suicide and attempted suicide, rape and attempted rape, prevalence of child maltreatment, prevalence of physical abuse of women by male partners, prevalence of elder abuse, and incidence of physical fighting, weapons carrying, and substance abuse among adolescents;
- costs of health care associated with intentional injuries (firearm or otherwise), the number of persons in substance abuse programs, and so forth;
- social environment factors, including the concentration of poor families in geographical areas; presence of gangs, illegal markets, and availability of firearms in communities; the number of hours of violence-related programming on television; the extent of gun control laws in an area, and the availability of shelters for battered women and their children.[42]

If indeed all these activities and settings – and many more not listed – are related to the etiology of violence or its consequence, then one would easily be led into the notion that community violence acts like a pathogen fueling other "pathologies" presumably connected to violence.[43] But how can violence be both itself a pathogen – as in the case of community violence – and something caused by pathogens – as is the case, for example, in our discussion of energy transfer or emotions as the pathogens underlying the "disease" of violence?

This appears to be where the logic of the violence-as-literal-disease approach breaks down. In light of this conceptual conundrum, public health proponents have shifted their focus somewhat, arguing that violence is like a social contagion that can spread across societies and from community to community. As Jeffrey Fagan and Garth Davies argue,

> we conceptualize the rise, spread, and decline in violence rates over time as a process akin to a contagious disease epidemic and test a theoretical framework of neighborhood risk as an engine of social contagion within and between these small social areas.[44]

The reasons violent crime rates vary from place to place is that certain communities possess features which make them more susceptible to the "disease" of violence. These community "risk" factors are the same problems discussed in chapter 6, namely a weakening or absence of informal controls and anemic levels of social capital. What purpose or purposes is served by the rephrasing of these issues into the language of medicine, pathology, or disease? Since the medical concepts and terminologies per se add no value to the explanation of problems in communities – whether violence or other issues – it must be the case that such concepts are invoked because of the social control functions they serve.

Conclusion: the disease metaphor in the schools

As discussed earlier, the rhetoric of disease and pathology has been applied with increasing regularity within the school context over the last few decades. Indeed, the modern public school system is shot through with the principles and operating assumptions of the psychotherapeutic ethos, whereby emotivism, developmentalism, an emphasis on feelings and subjectivity, and a confessional mode of problem-solving are emphasized (see chapter 4). Since many school teachers, administrators, and counselors are likely to have received the bulk of their training in educational psychology, they are apt to view schools as akin to mental health institutions – with teachers and parents acting as "co-therapists" along with school counselors – and students as fragile therapy clients.[45] This had led to the further expansion of mental health services provided in school, especially in light of the perception that school violence is increasing or more lethal than ever before.

Even when sociological perspectives are brought to bear on the problem of school violence, sociologists often acquiesce or consent to "psy complex" experts on this issue because the psychotherapeutic orientation is so deeply entrenched in school policy and organization.[46] Because the therapeutic orientation is so pervasive in schools, it is often treated as a taken-for-granted aspect of the organizational environment, and sociologists who have aspirations of working or conducting research in schools are more or less advised to respect this professional orientation and accommodate themselves to it, if for no other reason than to maintain and nurture political alliances with important gatekeepers within the school system.[47]

The following exchange between a junior high-school teacher and an anthropologist who was conducting school research provides an especially poignant illustration of the medicalized and therapeutic orientation prevalent in schools. The teacher is complaining to the researcher about the mid-semester arrival of another "troubled" teen to her classroom:

> TEACHER: She would just sit there, so sullen and non-responsive, like it was the last place she wanted to be. She had only been there a few days when one of the other kids said something to her, and the next thing I knew she picked up her textbook and threw it against the wall. She's a very sick little girl.
> RESEARCHER: Or maybe she was angry.
> TEACHER: Whatever . . . obviously the girl is very disturbed.

Researcher Janet Finn goes on to note that here the teacher has accepted a medicalized notion of troubling youth behaviors, one which promotes the view of adolescence itself as a pathology.[48] Persons outside of the professional school context also tend to accept the idea that children who perpetrate violence and other bad acts have somehow experienced trauma, abuse, or deprivation during their upbringing. And if these acting-out youth are their own children, parents are especially likely to accept the notion that violence is a disease because it excuses both them and their children, while the blame can be laid on the community for transmitting the disease of violence to them.[49]

The proliferation of the disease metaphor across Western societies is also consistent with recent community-based research which reports that growing numbers of Americans are suffering from a variety of mental disorders.[50] These surveys, often carried out by proponents of public health operating from the perspective of psychiatric epidemiology, tend to inflate the numbers of persons suffering from mental illnesses because mere symptoms of distress as reported by respondents – sadness, sexual dysfunction, loneliness, anxiety, and drug or alcohol abuse, for example – are counted as instances of *DSM* mental illnesses. The false high rates of mental illness are reported and perpetrated by a variety of groups, including advocacy groups – such as the National Alliance for the Mentally Ill – who have a vested interest in seeing that growing segments of the population are labeled mentally ill because it makes the mentally ill feel better about themselves, that they are not alone in their suffering. Finally, of course, pharmaceutical companies capitalize on surveys which find an "alarming" growth in mental illness because it expands markets for their products.

Suggestions for further reading

Armstrong, Thomas. 1995. *The Myth of the A.D.D. Child.* New York: Dutton.
Armstrong's book challenges many of the taken-for-granted assumptions of ADD or ADHD within the medical community, pointing out

how changing historical, cultural, and social conditions have made this disease not only plausible but also very "real."

Chriss, James J. (ed.) 1999. *Counseling and the Therapeutic State.* **New York: Aldine de Gruyter.**

This collection of essays examines the social organization of counseling and psychotherapeutic practice in modern Western society. The provision of counseling services by psychiatrists as well as a growing legion of non-physicians is testament to a psychotherapeutic culture which elevates to primacy the care of the individual and his or her psychic well-being.

Conrad, Peter. 1975. "The Discovery of Hyperkinesis: Notes on the Medicalization of Deviant Behavior." *Social Problems* **23 (1): 12–21.**

Many years before ADD/ADHD was officially diagnosed, problems associated with childhood fidgetiness were covered by the term "hyperkinesis." How hyperkinesis eventually became an official disorder of childhood and adolescence is chronicled in Conrad's article.

Prothrow-Stith, Deborah. 1993. *Deadly Consequences.* **New York: Harper Perennial.**

The author, a physician and public health advocate, lays out an agenda for conceptualizing violence as a disease which is particularly devastating with regard to children and teenagers. She also provides guidelines for reducing the incidence of violence and aggression in families and schools.

Wakefield, Jerome C. 2002. "Values and the Validity of Diagnostic Criteria: Disvalued versus Disordered Conditions of Childhood and Adolescence." Pp. 148–64 in *Descriptions and Prescriptions: Values, Mental Disorders, and the DSMs,* **ed. J. Z. Sadler. Baltimore: Johns Hopkins University Press.**

In this article Jerome Wakefield provides a well-reasoned and articulate argument for the possibility that many presumed mental illnesses of childhood and adolescence may simply be things society frowns upon, such as being shy, restless, aggressive, or fidgety, talking back to parents and or other authority figures, and so forth.

8 Legal Control: Racial Profiling, Hate Crimes, and the Growth in Imprisonment

Introduction

Although in chapter 5 we discussed some aspects of the "dark side" of legal control, in this chapter we will examine three critical issues in the modern criminal justice system in somewhat more detail. These three critical case studies – racial profiling, hate crimes, and the growth of the American prison population – respectively represent pressing concerns in policing, the courts, and corrections. We will begin with an overview and examination of racial profiling.

Racial profiling

Contrary to the dramatic depictions of police work in film and television, for the most part routine patrol work is a rather mundane affair which is far from glamorous or exciting. This is not to say that patrol work is not dangerous, however. Rather, rounds of random preventive patrol are typified by long stretches of "down time" which at any time can be punctuated by a dangerous or even life-threatening event.

Because of the uncertainties of police work, and the extreme danger that could be lurking just around the corner, the police have to be in a constant state of preparedness to deal with such contingencies. As part of this battle-readiness, police carry around in their heads an image of the kind of person that is particularly threatening. Jerome Skolnick has called this image the *symbolic assailant*, and persons who fit such a description warrant closer attention and circumspection from the police than do other individuals.[1]

As discussed in chapter 6, because of the concentration of poverty in urban inner-city areas and the perception or reality that these are high crime areas as well, police are apt to view all citizens living in these communities as symbolic assailants.[2] Because African-Americans and Hispanics tend to be overrepresented among the urban poor, it is unfortunately the case that, in urban America, the symbolic assailant is typically a young, black male. Although among urban American police symbolic assailants are young males – and specifically young *black* males – who are assumed to be the kind of persons that are especially likely to threaten the police with violence, among British police the characteristics of the symbolic assailant are expanded beyond the attributes of race and sex. Specifically, from the perspective of British police the symbolic assailant is not only one who is assumed to be dangerous (again young males), but also anyone who could challenge or disarm police authority, including lawyers, doctors, and social workers (as "challengers"), or even women and young children (as "disarmers").[3] Although the British case is certainly interesting and worthy of further discussion, in this section we will deal specifically with the symbolic assailant as conceptualized by urban American police.

According to Uniform Crime Reports data for 2004, although African-Americans comprise about 12 percent of the American population, they accounted for 27.1 percent of all arrests.[4] This means that African-Americans as a group are arrested at more than twice the rate that would be expected from their representation in the population. The incarceration statistics are grim as well. When considering the lifetime chances of a person serving time in prison, the chances for whites are 3.4 percent, for Hispanics 10 percent, and for blacks 18.6 percent. Further, "based on current rates of first incarceration, an estimated 32 percent of black males will enter state or federal prison during their lifetime, compared to 17 percent of Hispanics and 5.9 percent of whites."[5]

Now this in no way implies that African-Americans as a group are simply more criminally-prone than whites. There is plenty of evidence to suggest that the operation of the criminal justice system accounts for much of this discrepancy, based primarily on the fact that racial prejudice and discrimination are still very much alive in American, British, and other Western societies. Does this mean that police officers, judges, and district attorneys – the major players who select and process persons through the criminal justice system – are racist? Although an easy answer would be "yes," it is just not that simple. It is probably accurate to suggest that institutional racism certainly exists in the criminal justice system (as well as in most other major social institutions), but verifying to what extent, if at all, particular persons within the system act in ways that could be shown to be racist is often extremely difficult. In other words, although there are blatant and sometimes infamous cases of police misconduct or judicial malfeasance involving racist and/or discriminatory practices, ascertaining beyond the obvious cases how widespread such practices are throughout the system is not straightforward.

Nevertheless, one of the areas of routine police operations that has come under increased scrutiny is police stops of citizens, taking place either during routine traffic patrol or in some other context. There has been a long-acknowledged understanding among African-American men especially that police pay particularly close attention to them. Angela Davis provides the example of African-American men who can afford to do otherwise choosing to drive drab, nondescript cars instead of flashier or sportier ones so as to minimize the risk of being stopped by the police.[6] With the appearance of crack cocaine in the late 1970s and the subsequent full-scale launching of a "war on drugs," police began targeting much more vigorously the areas in which drug activities were alleged to be taking place. The focus of much of this police activity was the urban inner city and its predominantly minority (either racial or ethnic) population. A number of observers of police tactics in response to the problem of drugs in urban communities have argued that racial profiling started in earnest during the 1980s.[7] Specifically, Drug Enforcement Agency as well as local law-enforcement training empha-sized the importance of traffic stops of persons who fit the description of someone likely to be selling or transporting illicit drugs, especially on roads known as drug "pipelines."[8]

Racial profiling (sometimes referred to as "race-based policing") refers to the police practice of making enforcement decisions, such as making a stop, on the basis of a suspect's race.[9] *Hard* profiling uses race as the *only* factor in assessing criminal suspiciousness, while *soft* profil-ing uses race as one factor among others in determining police courses of action.[10] Critics of racial profiling, especially the "hard" version that, if proven or provable, is certainly illegal, facetiously refer to those who are stopped in this manner as committing the "crime" of "Driving While Black or Brown."[11]

The pretext stop and Whren v. United States (1996)

Since the 1980s a top priority among civil rights leaders has been to stop the blatant use of hard profiling by the police because of the way it disproportionately impacts black and Hispanic suspects. However, even many instances of soft profiling, whereby police use race as one but not the only factor, in pursuing suspects are considered by a number of observers as problematic as well. In some instances of course it is perfectly appropriate for police to take into consideration a person's race, especially in cases where the race of a crime suspect has been identified by a victim or witnesses. If, for example, a victim alleges that he was robbed at gunpoint and was able to describe the assailant as a black male, approximately 5 foot 8 with a heavy build, wearing a red shirt and blue jeans, who sped off in a light-colored, late-model Ford Mustang, the police would be expected to be on the lookout for the car and the person matching that description. To make a stop legitimate, the Fourth Amendment requires that police officers have *probable cause* or, at the very least, reasonable suspicion to detain a suspect. Continuing with the above example, if the police were to stop a black motorist driving a white Mustang who turned out not to be the true assailant, the police would be protected against charges of racial bias or other improprieties to the extent that they could prove that probable cause existed (based on the victim's description of the suspect and car as recorded in the police report).

Notice, however, that the question of what constitutes probable cause or reasonable suspicion is often an open one. To further compli-cate matters, the Supreme Court's ruling in *Whren* v. *United States* in 1996 upheld the use of pretext stops by the police. A *pretext stop* is the practice of stopping a driver for a minor violation for the primary purpose of searching for evidence of a more serious crime for which the officer lacked probable cause to make the stop.[12] Critics of *Whren* argue that police can use pretext stops as a way of harassing minority citizens, in that they can target these drivers whenever they witness a minor violation (such as a burned out taillight or a cracked windshield), even if they held no suspicion that the person being stopped committed a more serious crime.

The Supreme Court did, however, open the door for claims of racially biased law enforcement within the context of pretext stops under the Equal Protection Clause of the Fourteenth Amendment. Instead of holding officers accountable for violating the search and seizure provisions of the Fourth Amendment, which is a criminal violation if proven in a court of law, officers who are charged with a violation of the Fourteenth Amendment face only the possibility of a civil rights action, amounting to an allegation that the police officer denied the criminal defendant or suspect equal protection of the laws. Although there are a number of such cases awaiting adjudication stemming directly from charges of racial profiling, critics accuse the legal system of stacking the deck against criminal defendants and in favor of the police who engage in pretext stops that may often shade over into illegitimate forms of racial profiling.[13]

New issues in racial profiling since 9/11

Since the terrorist attacks against the United States on September 11, 2001, government responses have included the establishment of the Department of Homeland Security, which was authorized by sweeping anti-terrorism legislation signed into law by President Bush in late 2001.[14] Because the perpetrators were of Middle Eastern descent, counterterrorism measures have focused largely on monitoring the communications of alleged or known Middle Eastern terrorist organizations (such as al-Qaeda, Hamas, and Hezbollah); attempting to reduce or eliminate the flow into the United States of immigrants who may have ties with such organizations; and providing constant surveillance – including wiretaps and other law-enforcement tools as needed – at the federal, state, and municipal levels, of persons who match the socio-demographic characteristics of these terrorists.[15] This means that in many cities across the United States, in both urban and rural settings, there is a new symbolic assailant: the Middle Eastern or Muslim male.

A number of commentators have suggested that, immediately after the 9/11 attacks, a time in which anti-Arab sentiments were running particularly high, the newly legislated counterterrorism measures were adversely affecting especially those of Middle Eastern descent, including but not limited to racial profiling, scapegoating, mass detentions and mistreatments, governmental secrecy with respect to detainees, and a general decline of privacy and equal protection rights of both American citizens and visitors to the country.[16]

Even though there is evidence to suggest that racial profiling of blacks has been more acute, aggressive, and punitive in the United States than in Britain, problems of racial profiling as well as other types of racially biased law enforcement of Arabs and those of Middle Eastern descent since 9/11 appear to be at comparable levels in both countries.[17] Under the British Terrorism Act, first designed to deal with the history of terrorist activities of Northern Ireland extremists, a system of social profiling has developed in two stages, to be described below. It began during the early 1990s after London was bombed several times by the Provisional Irish Republican Army (IRA). In response to these bombings the city of London constructed a so-called *ring of steel*, which amounted to a series of high-level security measures such as roadblocks, armed checkpoints, a closed-circuit television (CCTV) security network, increased traffic restrictions, increased police presence and visibility, and the fortification of a number of buildings.[18] After the events of 9/11, because the security infrastructure of the ring of steel was already in place, London was able to apply the design already in place, along with improvements and modifications, to the new Middle Eastern terrorist threat.

In response to the threat of Middle Eastern terrorism specifically, British and more generally UK security services initially concentrated on suspected "enemy aliens," consisting primarily of foreign students and asylum seekers and refugees from Muslim regions of the world. This also included what Liz Fekete has described as "low-level police harassment around mosques."[19] The second stage moved into systematic and full-blown profiling, which could be described as a form of "religious profiling." As Fekete explains, "the intelligence services have moved on to profile Muslim communities wholesale, citizens and non-citizens alike."[20] The problem with this sort of "Islamophobia" is that it distorts the true nature of the threat potentially emanating from Muslim communities, since all persons – both political dissidents who may have genuine connections with terrorist groups and ordinary Muslims with no such connections or anti-Western ambitions or sentiments – are painted with the same broad brush.[21]

Hate crimes

Although criminal profiling is certainly a legitimate police practice, we have seen how other types of profiling, whether racial or religious, can be problematic with respect to imperiling the civil liberties of members of targeted groups, but also because of the confusion such profiling can generate for law enforcement, since true offenders are lumped in with a much larger group of innocent persons.

Whereas racial profiling has been treated as a critical case study of legal control specifically within the context of law enforcement, this next critical case study will focus on law and the courts, examining specifically the case of hate crime legislation. We shall first provide a

brief history of hate crime legislation, then look at exactly what constitutes a hate crime, that is, how it is defined. Finally, current controversies associated with hate crimes will be summarized, including the
Hate Crimes Sentencing Enhancement Act of 1994, which provides
more punitive penalties if it can be proven that a particular crime was
motivated by hate or bias toward a person merely because of his or her
membership in a particular group.

A brief history of hate crime legislation

Crimes motivated by hate are nothing new. In the book of Genesis from
the Bible, Cain killed his brother Abel in a premeditated act of rage
and jealousy because God favored Abel's sacrifice – a lamb from Abel's
flock – over his own. This first murder set a precedent for humankind,
and the problems of hate and rage have been an enduring part of our
human legacy, or so the story goes.

In America organized hate groups such as the Ku Klux Klan, which
has been operating since the 1920s, are some of the most visible
symbols of the continuing problem of hatred being perpetrated
against various groups. More recent incidents of hate-based crimes
include the murder in Jasper, Texas, of James Byrd,who was dragged
behind a pickup truck simply because he was black; the beating to
death of gay college student Matthew Shepard, who was tied to a fence
in the desert by his assailants and left to die; and the sad case of Abner
Louima, a black immigrant from Haiti, who was sodomized by a
broken broomstick at the hands of a New York City police officer.
(Louima survived.)[22]

With the march of modernity the idea arose that the worst aspects of
human living, especially the deliberate inflicting of pain by one human
being against another, could be reduced or even eliminated to the
extent that we continue to increase our knowledge of what makes
people "tick." The human and social sciences, such as psychology,
sociology, and criminology, very early on were dedicated in no
small measure to eliminating a variety of social pathologies, thereby
maximizing societal happiness and finally securing the long sought
after "good life."

The enactment of hate crime legislation is the story of a complicated
convergence of social movements and interest group politics, legislative and policymaking negotiations and initiative, interpretations by
courts of the earliest rounds of statute enactment, and the eventual
enactment of hate crime law, with uneven acceptance and application
as each state grappled with the pragmatics of policing and prosecuting
cases.[23] The first hate crimes law was the Hate Crimes Statistics Act
(HCSA), enacted in 1990.[24] President George H. W. Bush signed this into
law after more than a decade of growing concern over the seeming
spread of hate-motivated crimes being perpetrated not only against
persons of color, but also against homosexuals, women, those of a

particular national origin, the disabled, and those holding particular religious beliefs.

The HCSA initially was not meant to criminalize hate-based crime (that is, beyond the level of sanctions already in place for any particular criminal act), but rather to gather systematic data about the nature and extent of hate crimes. Although definitions vary based upon the kind of hate crime committed but also because of the unique language employed as various American states enacted versions of hate crime legislation, what makes a *hate crime* is "the existence of bias or prejudice of the perpetrator who committed the crime against an individual based on the victim's real or perceived social grouping."[25]

The reporting of hate crimes varies sometimes dramatically when comparing state data. For example, Illinois reported 133 hate crimes in 1991, 241 in 1992, a big jump to 724 in 1993, and then a precipitous decline to only 19 in 1994. Alabama reported only nine hate crimes *in total* for the eight-year period from 1991 to 1998. In 1992, both New Jersey and New York recorded their states' highest hate crime totals – 1,114 and 1,112 respectively – and both declined steadily over the next few years, with 1998 totals standing at 757 for New Jersey and 776 for New York.[26]

Based upon hate crime data for 2003 (reported in 2004), the FBI emphasized the following:

- The total number of hate crimes reported is holding steady at one of its lowest levels in the past decade. The 7,489 incidents in 2003 are just twenty-seven more than 2002. And the 2002 total was the lowest since 1994.
- Most of the 9,100 victims (or just over 52 percent) were targeted because of their race. Hate crimes based on religion and sexual orientation were a distant second, at 16 percent each.
- Hate-based murders are infrequent. In 2003, fourteen individuals were murdered, less than two-tenths of 1 percent of all victims.
- Vandalism and destruction are the preferred methods of attack. They represent 83 percent of hate-driven property crimes and 35 percent of all hate crimes.
- Intimidation was the most frequently reported hate crime. It accounted for nearly half of the total crimes against persons in 2003.
- Nearly one-third of all incidents in 2003 took place in or near a home or residence.[27]

Penalty enhancement law

An especially controversial area of hate crime legislation is the enactment of penalty enhancement laws in some jurisdictions. In order to illustrate what this is, consider the following situation. A white and a black male are arguing about something in a bar, and as the argument gets more heated the white person pulls out a knife and stabs the black person, seriously injuring him. Subsequent investigations revealed that the white person felt he had been cut off in traffic by the black person, and the two had exchanged unpleasantries out in the street before going into the bar. The black man seemed to be egging on the white man, calling him "punk" and "chicken," and inviting him to go settle the issue "like men." They did not know each other previous to this encounter, and there was no evidence of racial animosity on the part of the white person. The stabbing was simply the result of an escalation of mutual hostilities between these two persons precipitated by the traffic altercation.

Consider now the exact same event, namely, a white person stabbing a black person in that same bar after a heated argument. Immediately preceding the attack the white person had exhibited visible disgust over the fact that the black man was with a white woman, calling him the "n" word and saying he needed to "go back to the ghetto" and stay away from "our" women. The woman tried to restrain her friend and suggested they simply leave, but instead he confronted the white man, telling him that "we can take this outside and settle it like men." From that point on verbal hostilities escalated, the men moved toward each other in an aggressive and menacing manner, and the stabbing occurred.

In both cases we have the same event: a white man assaulting a black man with a knife and seriously injuring him. Yet because in the second case the white man's motivation for the attack flowed from his racist attitudes toward African-Americans, under the Hate Crime Sentencing Enhancement Act of 1994, not only could the white man be charged with assault with a deadly weapon (among other things), he could also be punished further for intentionally selecting this particular victim because of his race.[28] This seems to violate the spirit of the Fourteenth Amendment, which specifies equal treatment under the law. The law is set up to protect people from being treated differently, and in this case equal treatment under the law means that the same acts should receive the same punishments. Punishing the motivation in *addition* to punishing the act may be seen as an illegitimate attempt by the government to restrict unwanted speech or thoughts, which could be interpreted as a violation of free speech under the First Amendment.

Yet, as Brian Levin has pointed out, the law frequently takes into account the motivations for a criminal act and establishes severity of punishments based upon such considerations.[29] For example, if a person enters a building with the intent of taking something of value from the premises, it is *burglary*. But if the person enters the building for some other reason – for example, the person may have checked the doorknob and discovered it was unlocked, and slipped inside without specifically planning a burglary – then it is *criminal trespass*, which is typically a less serious offense. Another example is the statute operating in many jurisdictions that provides for harsher punishments for those persons who carry a gun or other deadly weapon during the commissioning of a crime than for those who commit the same act without carrying a weapon.

In short, the law punishes crimes motivated by racial hatred or other forms of bias more severely than crimes not motivated by such attitudes because the former are considered to cause more social harm than the latter.

America's imprisonment binge

Crime rates in both the United States and Canada began increasing in the mid-1960s, peaked in the early 1990s, and have fallen or leveled off ever since. Even with this upturn in the crime rate beginning in the 1960s, however, incarceration rates had remained relatively stable for nearly fifty years during the period 1925 to the early 1970s.[30] During this time both the Canadian and the American incarceration rate hovered between 100 and 110 prisoners per 100,000 population. However, after 1973 they diverged markedly: whereas the Canadian rate remained at approximately the same level it had been since the 1920s, the American incarceration rate grew dramatically. Today the United States has the highest incarceration rate in the world, exceeding 700 prisoners per 100,000 population.[31]

As of 2004, there were over two million Americans incarcerated in state or federal prisons, local jails, and juvenile detention facilities.[32] Along with over four million Americans either on probation or on parole, this means that nearly seven million Americans are either imprisoned or in some other way involved with the criminal or juvenile justice systems. This "mass incarceration" has affected some groups disproportionately: "Nine out of ten prison inmates are male, most are under the age of forty, African Americans are seven times more likely than whites to be in prison, and nearly all prisoners lack any education beyond high school."[33] In the next section we will discuss some of the factors that have caused America's "imprisonment binge."[34]

Factors in the imprisonment binge

A variety of factors have contributed to America's current high rate of incarceration. First, the previously mentioned *war on drugs*, launched in earnest during the Reagan administration and expanded under the next three presidents (George H. W. Bush, Bill Clinton, and George W. Bush), sent an unprecedented number of persons to prison, the majority of whom were poor and/or ethnic and racial minorities. The war on drugs and its aftermath almost single-handedly created the problem of prison overcrowding that wreaked havoc on the American correctional system during the 1980s and 1990s. For example, between 1980 and 1997 drug arrests tripled, and the number of people going to prison for a drug offense went up 1,040 percent, compared to only 82 percent for a violent crime and 207 percent for a non-violent crime.[35]

Indeed, newer hybrid courts, such as the drug treatment court, mental health court, and teen and family court, which appeared beginning in the late 1980s, have arisen largely through the efforts of judges who became frustrated with the backlog of drug-related cases and who were seeking alternatives to traditional sanctions which otherwise would have landed these defendants back into the overburdened prison and jail system.[36]

Second, *partisan politics* have played an increasingly important role in the public discourse concerning imprisonment and the viability and necessity of its use and even expansion for dealing with the real or perceived problems of crime. Michael Tonry explains the way that crime became a wedge issue in American politics, especially after the 1960s:

> On crime control, conservatives blamed rising crime rates on lenient judges and soft punishments, and demanded toughness. On welfare, conservatives blamed rising welfare rolls on welfare cheats and laziness, and demanded budget cuts. On affirmative action, conservatives blamed White unemployment and underemployment on quotas, and urged elimination of affirmative action.[37]

A third and related factor is the *loss of confidence* in the government and the concomitant rise of single-issue voter sentiment. This loss of confidence arose largely through citizen perceptions, especially emerging after the 1970s, that government programs have done little to solve such pressing issues as health care, education, welfare, crime, consumer protection, and infant and childcare, to name a few.[38] There has been a general perception not only of government failure and incompetence in these areas, but also that this incompetence has come at a high price. Between 1970 and 1995, for example, government expenditures for health care have outpaced inflation by a 5 to 1 margin, for education by 3.5 to 1, and for criminal justice by 6 to 1.[39]

In a 1958 survey of Americans conducted by the National Elections Studies, Center for Political Studies, at the University of Michigan, one question that was asked measured citizen trust of government. The question was: "How much of the time do you trust government in Washington to do what is right – just about always, most of the time, or only some of the time?" In 1958, 73 percent of those polled responded either "just about always" or "most of the time" to the question, while only 23 percent responded "only some of the time." In 1970, the total percentage of persons that trusted government "just about always" or "most of the time" dropped to 53 percent. And in 1995, only 25 percent of those polled trusted the federal government "just about always" or "most of the time."

It is interesting to note that this long-term decline in trust in government was reversed briefly in 2001 following the terrorist attacks of 9/11. In the 2001 poll, conducted by ABC News and the *Washington Post*, 64 percent of those polled responded that they trusted the government "just about always" or "most of the time." By 2005, however, the level of trust had decline once again, with the figure standing at 31 percent.[40]

This collapse in government confidence has meant that citizen sentiment regarding the "good life" has fragmented into numerous single-
issue or "hot button" agendas which produce rancorous partisan bick-
ering among private citizens and at all levels of government as
portrayed through the media. Single-issue political agendas – whether
abortion, the death penalty, getting tough on crime, funding and taxing
issues, education, and victims rights – tend to break down into an "us
versus them" struggle, with one side claiming righteousness and virtuousness on the issue while portraying the other side as not only wrong
or misguided but perhaps even as evil. Crime as a single-issue agenda
is subject to this rancorous discourse, and tends to be emotion-driven
and in essence hijacked by a "moral majority" of concerned citizens
who claim that politicians are "too soft" on crime and who thereby seek
more retributive and punitive approaches toward offenders.

An example of such grassroots populism was the "three strikes and
you're out" legislation that emerged out of Washington and then
California, which mandated life in prison without the possibility of
parole on a defendant's third felony conviction, regardless of how serious that third offense actually was. Critics of three strikes legislation
argued that penal policy ought not to be decided in such a knee-jerk
and emotional way, and that such legislation might likely send the
California court and corrections systems into fiscal emergency because
of the backlog of cases it will produce (for example, defendants will
have less incentive or be given no opportunity to plea bargain for a
lesser charge), as well as a growth in the prison population because
offenders will be given longer sentences.[41]

A fourth broad factor contributing to high incarceration rates is the
decline of the rehabilitative ideal. Whereas the goal of retribution is to
punish offenders because they *deserve* to be punished ("just deserts"),
since the assumption is made that they willfully violated the criminal
law, the idea of rehabilitation is to discover *why* offenders break the law
and to instill prosocial adjustments in these persons so that they will
not offend again. Whereas retribution or just deserts favors determi-
nate sentencing (equal sentences for similar crimes), rehabilitation
favors *indeterminate sentences*, which means that an offender is kept in
prison for treatment or other ameliorative measures only so long as it
takes him or her to get "well." Once "cured," the prisoner is released
back to the community so he or she can become a productive member
of society, rather than sitting in a jail or prison cell wasting taxpayers'
dollars.

The rehabilitative ideal, a prominent feature of the criminal justice
system from the 1890s through the early 1970s, was considered during
this period to be both a laudable and an attainable goal of the system.
But for many of the reasons discussed above, by the early 1970s there
was a loss of confidence in the ability actually to rehabilitate offenders
within correctional facilities, and in light of this many urged a return to
incarceration, not only because it was perceived to be more harsh and

punitive, but also because it was fairer. How could incarceration be viewed as both fairer *and* harsher than rehabilitation?

The rehabilitative model of justice had always adopted a medical case model for handling and processing clients. That is to say, under the auspices of the rehabilitative ideal, offenders who were earmarked for a treatment program upon the recommendations or mandate of the court would be given a thorough assessment upon entry into the facility ("intake and assessment"), and a unique treatment plan would be drawn up to meet the particular needs of the offender. During his or her period of incarceration, parole board members would be given reports as to the progress of the offender through the program, and at any point a determination could be made that the person no longer poses a threat to the community and could thereby be released.

Although, for purposes of determining if and when a prisoner should be released, putting this sort of discretion into the hands of health professionals would appear to meet the general spirit of the rehabilitative model and its therapeutic mode of sanctioning, the reality was that correctional discretion was often being used in a biased and prejudicial manner. For example, studies clearly show that indigent persons and members of ethnic and racial minorities are less likely to be considered viable candidates for rehabilitation, and even when they are placed into these programs they are less likely to be granted parole in a timely manner when compared with their white counterparts. Indeed, the report of the Working Party of the American Friends Service Committee entitled *Struggle for Justice*, published in 1971, fundamentally challenged the use of indeterminate sentencing within the criminal justice system. As David Garland notes, the authors of the report claimed that the criminal justice system's discriminatory use of the power to punish, particularly its use of imprisonment, was simply "a tool to repress blacks, the poor, the young and various cultural minorities."[42] Because of its hypocrisy and paternalism, and because of its naïve faith that rehabilitation could be both therapeutic and effective (which it was rarely shown to be), proponents of "progressive penology" were dealt a severe blow by a growing number of critics, and the rehabilitative ideal withered on the vine while the goals of retribution, deterrence, and incapacitation once again attained prominence.[43]

A fifth factor fueling the reemergence of punitive sanctions is the *return of the victim*, which is itself part of a broader trend toward what David Garland calls expressive justice. As discussed in earlier chapters, with the professionalization of policing and the promulgation of constitutional protection of criminal defendants in Britain, the United States, and other constitutional democracies, punishments were taken out of the hands of the members of the community and made the responsibility of the state. This meant that for the most part victims of crime were left on the sidelines while a specialized, professional coterie of formal control agents – police, district attorneys, lawyers, judges, treatment professionals, and correctional administrators – worked toward the collective goal of securing justice for crime victims. Over the last three decades, however, crime victims have become more visible with regard to both criminal court proceedings and media portrayals of especially poignant or compelling cases of victimization. In an interesting twist, therapeutic efforts have shifted away from perpetrators and are now focused more squarely on victims. This therapeutic ethos has now been translated into the new political imperative that "victims must be protected, their voices must be heard, their memory honoured, their anger expressed, their fears addressed."[44]

As Garland further notes, up until recently openly avowed expressions of vengeful sentiment were virtually taboo. Public officials connected with the district attorney's office and the courts were expected to go about their business in a professional and sober manner, allowing procedural law to take its course and hopefully winning a conviction on the basis of the evidence presented. Now more than ever, however, public officials are openly expressing public anger and resentment over the plight of "helpless" victims and vowing to extract whatever vengeance is legally available. A new kind of *expressive justice* has emerged, reflected in the explicitly retributive discourse of victims' rights, which in turn provides impetus for politicians to support and lawmakers to enact increasingly draconian laws. [45]

Suggestions for further reading

Blomberg, Thomas G. and Stanley Cohen (eds). 2003. *Punishment and Social Control*, enlarged 2nd edn.   New York: Aldine de Gruyter.
This is an edited volume on current issues and controversies in social control, with special emphasis on trends in punishment in both the United States and Western Europe.

Garland, David. 2001. *The Culture of Control: Crime and Social Order in Contemporary Society*. Chicago: University of Chicago Press.
Garland argues that profound changes in the nature of punishment in modern society – where among other things incarceration rates continue to increase even as crime rates are decreasing – are the result of the distinct social organization of late modernity (or postmodernity) as well as conservative political agendas that came into vogue beginning in the 1980s in both the United States and Britain.

Graham, Stephen (ed.) 2004. *Cities, War, and Terrorism: Towards an Urban Geopolitics*. Oxford: Blackwell.
A collection of essays which examines the ways cities are becoming sites for global contestation, for example, social movements in the arenas of identity politics, gay rights, anti-globalization, and of course terrorism.

Nolan, James L., Jr. 2001. *Reinventing Justice: The American Drug Court.* Princeton, NJ: Princeton University Press.
A study in the rise of one kind of hybrid or "problem-solving" court, namely the drug treatment court, which first appeared in America in 1989 and which has since proliferated across the globe. In applying Goffman's dramaturgical model of self- and team-presentations, Nolan argues that the drug court finds its impetus in America's therapeutic culture.

Skolnick, Jerome H. 1966. *Justice without Trial: Law Enforcement in Democratic Society.* New York: Wiley.
A now classic study in the field of police sociology. Among many of Skolnick's enduring contributions to the field, perhaps the greatest is his concept of the symbolic assailant, namely, the image of the typical offender that police officers carry around in their head.

9 Terrorism and Social Control

Introduction ▰▰▰▰▰▰▰▰▰▰▰▰▰▰

This book began with the recounting of the terrorist attacks against the London public transit system in 2005, and established the groundwork for understanding and explaining the nature of social control in modern society more generally. Although concerns about order and control are on the minds of most us at some level – whether reflected in worries over crime, the quality of our schools, or who our neighbors are and what they are up to – the relatively recent threat of terrorism ratchets up these concerns tenfold. This chapter, then, provides a comprehensive overview of the nature of terrorism, the kinds of threats terrorist acts pose to citizens and governments, and the sorts of control and counterterrorism measures that nation-states have implemented in response to these threats.

The topics covered in this chapter are the ways in which terrorists employ stealth and deception in carrying out their attacks; the proliferation of new laws and new government agencies in the United States and elsewhere, especially those that have emerged since September 11, 2001; a brief discussion of the role Osama bin Laden has played in fomenting terrorism worldwide, chiefly as leader of the terrorist organization al-Qaeda; an analysis of the especially deadly strategy of suicide attacks and related martyrdom operations; and an overview of sociologist Donald Black's theory of terrorism, which views terrorism as a form of self-help which seeks to cause as much mayhem and destruction as possible against citizens and other national assets in order to gain concessions from target governments. We will begin, however, with an eerie series of events that involved the actor James Woods.

Terrorism, deception, and public trust ▰▰▰▰▰▰▰▰▰▰

In an interview broadcast on the Fox network program *The O'Reilly Factor* on February 14, 2002, actor James Woods recounted an incident that had transpired about a month before the horrific events of September 11.[1] In early August Woods was traveling from Boston to Los Angeles, and surrounding him in first class were four men who appeared to be of Middle Eastern descent. Although he could not go into details about what made him suspicious of the men (because of ongoing FBI investigations), Woods believed they were preparing to

162

hijack the plane, and he asked to speak to the pilot to convey his concerns.

Woods's suspicions concerning the men were noted, and a report was summarily filed with the FAA about the incident. A month later, when the terrorist attacks on the World Trade Center and Pentagon occurred, Woods was reminded once again of the incident on the plane, and he was urged by friends to contact the FBI, which he did. The next morning an FBI agent was at Woods's home to interview him about the incident. As it turned out, two of the four men Woods identified from the earlier incident were among the nineteen suicide hijackers involved in 9/11. In essence, Woods had witnessed on that earlier flight a rehearsal run of the fateful 9/11 attacks.

At the prodding of interviewer Bill O'Reilly, Woods was asked to go into more detail about the things that made these four men stand out in his mind. Besides the fact that the men were taking a transcontinental flight without any hand luggage, Woods suggested that subtle aspects of their behavior gave them away. Woods said he was attuned to something being amiss, and that he noticed their behavior "because I guess I'm an actor and it's kind of what I [do for a living]. I just kind of observe people." The four men simply did not fit well into the scene. As Woods continued:

> And there were four guys. When the flight attendant, who was a woman, came up to them, they literally ignored her like she didn't exist, which is sort of a kind of Taliban, you know, idea of womanhood, as you know, not even a human being. I mean, it seems their disrespect for women is so extraordinary. And they didn't order alcohol. And they just – and – I can't go into the details, but it just – it was – as I explained to the FBI, as if you were at a nightclub and everybody's enjoying an act on the stage. And the camera behind that act on the stage and sort of panning the audience. And everybody's focused on the singer, except four people sort of in the room kind of doing something else [motioning his head as if looking around] and connected to each other. . . . I thought they were either law enforcement officers or four terrorists in that they had that thing that – guys who are undercover or on a mission have between each other. And it's impossible to explain.

Here, we see Woods explaining that his particular line of work – acting – put him in a position to notice subtle goings-on around him that other people had missed. And it would probably not be unreasonable to take him at his word on this point. Actors are indeed students of social behavior, as are presumably certain social scientists trained in the vagaries of face-to-face interaction and small-group behavior (Erving Goffman being a case in point). Oftentimes the carrying out of nefarious activities requires deception on the part of perpetrators. The ability to dissemble and blend into a scene as if all is normal is the art of *fabricating frames*. As Goffman describes it, fabrication is

> the intentional effort of one or more individuals to manage activity so that a party of one or more others will be induced to have a false belief about what it is that is going on. A nefarious design is involved, a plot

or treacherous plan leading – when realized – to a falsification of some part of the world.[2]

Jack Gibbs defines terrorism as "illegal violence or threatened violence against human or nonhuman objects," and one of the key provisions of his definition is that the terrorist act "had secretive, furtive, and/or clandestine features that were expected by the participants to conceal their personal identity and/or their future location."[3] Obviously the four terrorists on the dry run witnessed by Woods did not completely mask their intentions, but since no one in law enforcement responded they blended into the background of everyday life well enough for their purposes. Clearly, suicide bombing plots require this sort of stealth and fabrication. Suicide bombers attempt to infiltrate public places where a number of persons are gathered – markets, public squares, outdoor events – and blow themselves up, hoping to maximize casualties in the process.[4] Suicide bombing is particularly nefarious because the targets are most often not military but civilian, and the aim is to cause as much chaos and destruction as possible to force governments to cede to their demands, whether religious, political, economic, or ideological.

With regard to strategic operations against the United States and the European Community, the major aim of suicide terrorism is to erode confidence in public places, thereby leading ultimately to the collapse or hollowing out of civil society. The transit system is an especially vulnerable target for this because in modern industrial economies mobility is essential. People go to where the jobs are, and as a consequence a large percentage of the gross domestic product of the United States is tied to transportation, be it planes, trains, automobiles, buses, subway systems, or rental cars. One of the immediate and still lasting effects of the 9/11 attacks has been the crippling of the airline industry, as riderships fell to a record low immediately after the event; meanwhile increasing oil prices have contributed to a long-term economic downturn for the industry, which began before 9/11. Bankruptcy filings will continue to be a prominent operating reality for the airline industry, and even commercial airlines in better health have little hope of paying off their long-term debt.

Ontological security and global terrorism

The interesting thing about terrorism, especially the specific strategy of suicide bombing, is that it is a particularly poignant example of a postmodern form of warfare which seeks to engage the enemy not out on the battlefield, but within the cozy confines of everyday life. This upsetting of the standard ideas concerning how to engage in "proper" or "traditional" forms of warfare has fundamentally altered our understanding of the taken-for-granted world of everyday life. Modern industrial societies thrive on the taken-for-grantedness of the stability and security of everyday life, that is, of public society. This is the concept of

[Handwritten margin notes: Terrorism; Suicide Bombers; Transit Systems ↓ Vulnerable Targets ↓ Mobility is Essential]

ontological security, namely, the trust that human beings develop in their dealings with others in the everyday world.[5] For example, most persons walking around in public places are not constantly worried about someone coming up from behind and smashing them on the head with a brick. To the extent that ontological security is diminished, persons will retreat from public places and not partake in the activities of civil society. With an absence of a vibrant public sphere, more authoritarian and repressive regimes of control may emerge. This is one of the goals of Islamic terrorism. The examination of suicide terrorism, then, sheds light on why modern society is continuing toward the "carceral society" of Foucault, and why systems of informal control continue to fall into disrepair in our postmodern surveillance society where appearances are assumed to be deceptive and where no one can be trusted. This is the "new penology" of postmodern society where constant surveillance of the population is emphasized (consistent with public health principles).[6]

The new era of globalization has also ushered in what Ulrich Beck has described as the *world risk society*.[7] In early modernity, especially with the rise of the human sciences, it was believed that risk could be controlled and the future could be predicted with some certainty. But this unbridled optimism concerning the eradication of contingency in all areas of life may simply have been an artifact of the Enlightenment impulse toward the perfectibility and predictability of human life, using reason and scientific method as guides toward its accomplishment. There was also the assumption made that risks could be understood and controlled within the boundaries of sovereign nations, each dedicated to ensuring the maximization of life chances of its citizenry. Yet, technological and human progress has shown us that there is still much that cannot be adequately predicted, and that new risks are appearing on the scene in increasing numbers – examples include mad cow disease, nuclear proliferation, environment hazard and degradation, the HIV virus, infectious diseases increasingly resistant to antibiotic treatment, the continuing escalation of mental "illnesses" as documented in *DSM*, and of course terrorism – many of which are not confined to the borders of nation-states but instead implicate the entire globe. It is within this context that terrorism may contribute to new formal regimes of control and surveillance.[8]

The most spectacular and devastating suicide terrorist attack to date was of course the September 11, 2001, attacks against the United States perpetrated by the global terrorist organization al-Qaeda, led by Osama bin Laden. Almost immediately as the first images were aired of the crashing of airplanes into New York City's World Trade Center towers, Americans perhaps for the first time gained a sense that the world had changed in a fundamental way, and certainly not for the better. The devastation was indeed massive, as close to 3,000 persons were killed and billions upon billions of dollars of financial losses were suffered in those areas hardest hit, notably New York City, the Pentagon, the airline

al-Qaeda
↓
Global Terrorist Org.

and transportation industries, the insurance industry, and the financial markets.

The law-enforcement and legislative responses to the terrorist attacks were startlingly swift, much of the urgency prodded on by the belief, certainly not totally misplaced, that Americans needed rapid and visible reassurances that they were safe and secure in their homes, their neighborhoods, their communities, and their workplaces. These symbols of rapid response appeared most readily in the forms of the USA PATRIOT Act, which authorized the establishment of the Department of Homeland Security, and the Air Transportation Safety and System Stabilization Act, both signed into law by President Bush in 2001.

Since 9/11 there have been no major terrorist incidents in the United States, even as terrorist activities continued worldwide with no apparent end in sight. In July 2005, for example, terrorist attacks in London and the Red Sea resort of Sharm el-Sheik, Egypt, served to illustrate the resolve of al-Qaeda and other terrorist groups to cause as much destruction and mayhem as possible. The question on the minds of many is, are the policies, strategies, and counterterrorism measures currently in place in the United States sufficient to avoid a repeat of a catastrophic 9/11-type event?

It could be argued that, in some areas of the response to terrorism, certain "target-hardening" strategies have made such an attack less likely. By target-hardening strategies I mean primarily new or expanded federal law-enforcement responses such as the establishment of the Department of Homeland Security, an expansion of routine public surveillance, extended wiretap authority, shoring up security at border checkpoints, legislation aimed at facilitating tracking and monitoring of persons in terms of both migration and immigration, and a greater commitment to human assets in espionage. Many have decried that a number of these target-hardening strategies – especially those associated with changes in immigration and border policies – have contributed to the erosion of civil liberties and due process.[9] The USA PATRIOT Act has pushed to the limit the fragile balancing act between assuring citizens' freedom and civil liberties, on the one hand, and maintaining order, public safety, and national security on the other. In the next section a summary of some of the more important changes in the law that have taken place since the passage of the Act will be provided.

To Wear Down

Changes in the law since 9/11

On October 26, 2001, President George W. Bush signed into law the USA PATRIOT Act (H.R. 3162), the full title of which is "Uniting and Strengthening America by Providing Appropriate Tools Required to Intercept and Obstruct Terrorism." The Act was pushed through without much legislative debate, passing the House easily on a vote of 357 to

66 and the Senate on a vote of 98 to 1. (Democratic senator Russ Feingold of Wisconsin cast the only dissenting vote.) Several sections of the Act are especially controversial, and these will be discussed briefly.[10]

Section 215, under the title "Access to records and other items under the Foreign Intelligence Surveillance Act," authorizes the government to seize personal records such as video rentals, books checked out from the library, medical and phone records, and information on the church, mosque, or synagogue one attends. Previous to the Act the government was required to produce a warrant and show probable cause to access private information of this sort. Indeed, under section 215 the government can now force third-party holders of personal records – such as libraries, schools, churches, or hospitals – to turn over this information. Even further, the holders of these records are barred from informing persons whose records have been obtained that such a search of records ever took place. Just so long as the Department of Justice states that the investigation is needed to protect against "international terror," the record keepers are forced to comply with the request.

Another controversial part of the Act is section 802, titled "Definition of domestic terrorism." Domestic terrorism becomes a new category of crime, and is defined as "acts dangerous to human life that are a violation of the criminal laws of the United States," just so long as the actor's intent is to "influence the policy of a government by intimidation or coercion."[11] According to this definition domestic terrorism could include various forms of protest that previously were not crimes in and of themselves, such as environmental activism, abortion clinic protests, or even protests against the government staged, for example, in front of the White House, the Pentagon, or other government buildings.

Sections 411 and 412 are titled respectively "Definitions relating to terrorism" and "Mandatory detention of suspected terrorists; habeas corpus; judicial review." Section 411 makes association with terrorist organizations a crime, even if the person who it is claimed is associated with the terror organization did not know about its terror activities. This is a dangerous form of "guilt by association" that is now codified into law for purposes of combating terrorism. Section 412 allows the Attorney General to detain aliens suspected of terrorist activities or association with terrorist organizations for a period of time without any prior showing or court ruling that the person is actually a threat. The effect of sections 411 and 412 is that aliens accused of terrorist actions or associations can either be deported or detained without judicial review (except for habeas corpus, which is not likely to be used in such cases).

The PATRIOT Act has effectively shifted great discretionary powers to the president, more so than at any time in American history.[12] This is reflected as well in the way 9/11 changed the police response to terrorism. For example, in the months following the attacks the FBI assigned 4,000 of its 11,500 special agents to counterterrorist activities.[13] And of course the passage of the USA PATRIOT Act and the creation of the Department of Homeland Security shortly after 9/11 meant that counterterrorist police work became more bureaucratized – that is, subject to administrative oversight, control, and regulation at the federal level, with the president acting as chief law-enforcement officer – and as a consequence policing was placed more firmly under political scrutiny as well. In effect, 9/11 accelerated the militarization of the police, a trend that began in the late 1970s with the "war on drugs" and the continuing growth of an urban "underclass" which requires policing (see chapter 6).[14]

Even so, potential checks on the newly expanded discretionary powers of the executive branch, written into the PATRIOT Act itself, consisted of a number of *sunset* provisions which had to be reauthorized by Congress if they were to continue as law after December 31, 2005. The controversial sections of the PATRIOT Act discussed here (215, 411, 412, and 802) for example, are all sunset provisions, that is, they were due to expire at the beginning of 2006 unless reauthorized by Congress. Organizations such as the ACLU had been actively fighting against real or perceived civil rights abuses built into these and other sunset provisions, and as of late 2005 the sentiment among Washington politicians and legislators seemed to be that many of them would indeed be allowed to expire.[15]

After a protracted period of bitter and often heated legislative wrangling over the issue, President Bush signed into law a renewal of the PATRIOT ACT on March 9, 2006. Many of the disputed sunset provisions were retained, but with some modifications. For example, section 215 clarifies that most libraries are not subject to demands for information about suspected terrorists. It also gives libraries and other entities that receive subpoenas for information on terror suspects or terrorist organizations the right to challenge the requirement that they not inform anyone of the inquiry.[16]

The rise of Osama bin Laden and al-Qaeda: a brief history[17]

The Koran insists that a Muslim's primary duty is the creation of an egalitarian society in which all people – rich and poor alike – are treated with respect. In order to achieve this, true believers of the faith should engage in jihad (literally translated as "effort," not "war," as often assumed) in all areas of life, including secular, spiritual, personal, and political.[18] There are two broad traditions of jihad: the greater jihad (*al-jihad al-akbar*) and the lesser jihad (*al-jihad al-asghar*). The *greater jihad* involves struggle against one's own weaknesses, sins, and vices; it is a program for self-betterment according to the dictates of Islamic law and custom. The *lesser jihad*, on the other hand, is about self-preservation and self-defense. Self-defense can of course manifest itself as confrontation, conflict, and outright war when interpreted by a collectivity of believers who perceive the justness of such a spiritual effort. The notion of "holy war" within radical Islam derives from the

lesser jihad, and lies behind much of the worldwide terrorism perpetrated by various Islamic groups.[19]

Up until 1980 the use of open warfare in the service of the lesser jihad
was isolated and sporadic. Militant Islam, that ideology linked to
modern terrorist activities including suicide bombings, finds its beginnings in 1979, the year the Soviet Union invaded Afghanistan. In order to
combat communist expansionism, President Ronald Reagan decided to
send arms and money to the leaders of the Afghan mujahideen (literally
"strugglers" but now often interpreted as "holy warriors"), whom
Reagan described as "the moral equivalents of America's founding
fathers."[20] One of those "freedom fighters" was Osama bin Laden, a
Saudi Arabian with great family wealth who earned a civil engineering
degree from Jeddah University in 1979. Bin Laden and his mujahideen
received backing from both the Saudi and United States governments to
repel the Soviet incursion into Afghanistan, and the CIA even put bin
Laden on their payroll for a while, helping with training and financial
support of his troops.

Why did bin Laden eventually turn against the United States to
become the most notorious and feared terrorist mastermind ever?
The short answer was the 1991 Gulf War, an armed conflict between the
United States and Iraq precipitated by Iraq's earlier invasion of oil-rich
Kuwait. A few years earlier, in 1988, the Soviets withdrew from
Afghanistan, and as a result bin Laden's standing among militant
Muslims grew. There were disagreements among various factions over
what to do with the mujahideen since the Soviet threat had ended.
Their hardcore leaders agreed to establish a base (or *al-qaeda*) to carry
out a worldwide jihad. Some among the incipient al-Qaeda leadership
wanted to concentrate on areas of the world – the Philippines, Kashmir,
central Asia, and Palestine, for example – where "infidels" had gained a
foothold and were distorting the teachings of Islam or threatening
Muslim lands. Others wanted to take on Muslim governments directly
and rid them of their "Westernized" or otherwise offensive secular
elements. By this time, though, bin Laden was back in Saudi Arabia, not
sure which direction to go in the struggle to establish al-Qaeda.

Saddam Hussein's invasion of Kuwait in 1990 solved bin Laden's
quandary, since he and other Salafi mujahideen hated everything
Hussein stood for. For bin Laden, Hussein was a secularist tyrant whose
actions were antithetical to the teachings of Islam, especially with
regard to the latter's passion for amassing great personal wealth at the
expense of the majority of Iraqi citizens. At one point bin Laden actually offered the services of his mujahideen to help expel Hussein's forces
from Kuwait. Instead, the Saudi royal family requested that the United
States step in to defend the kingdom. Bin Laden became openly critical
of the Saudi government, and as a result he was expelled from the country and his Saudi passport was revoked.[21]

When the American "infidels" arrived on Arabic sacred soil, it was too
much for bin Laden and the Salafists to bear, and now bin Laden had to

choose between the lesser of two evils: the apostate Hussein or the infidel United States. He grudgingly chose Hussein, al-Qaeda's resolve to combat the "great Satan" of the United States was strengthened, and the modern era of global terrorism was born.

After his expulsion from Saudi Arabia, bin Laden moved to Khartoum, Sudan, where he parlayed his wealth and influence in the establishment of global terrorist operations against the "distant enemy," namely, the United States, Israel, and all allies and sympathizers. By 1998, bin Laden had been evicted from Sudan as well, and at this point became a nomad, a man without a country. CIA intelligence reported in that year that he had relocated to the inaccessible mountain region near the border of Pakistan and Afghanistan, orchestrating a loose network of al-Qaeda and Taliban operatives across the region as well as contacts sympathetic to the cause of jihad in virtually all corners of the globe.

In 1998, at the same time as he was facing the unfolding Monica Lewinsky scandal, President Clinton decided to strike the infrastructures that bin Laden had built and was continuing to build in both Sudan and Afghanistan. This was in retaliation for two simultaneous suicide bombings of American embassies in Nairobi and Tanzania carried out by al-Qaeda; 213 people were killed in the Nairobi attack, while eleven were killed in Tanzania, with thousands injured. Because of intelligence reports which suggested that bin Laden would be at the site, on August 20, 1998, Clinton ordered cruise missile strikes into the Zawhar Kili rock gorges in eastern Afghanistan. Simultaneous to this attack, thirteen cruise missiles were fired at the al Shifa chemical plant in Khartoum, a plant which purportedly was owned in part by bin Laden and which was suspected of producing precursor substances associated with chemical weapons.[22] The missile strikes backfired. As Steve Coll explains,

> bin Laden's reputation in the Islamic world had been enhanced. He had been shot at by a high-tech superpower and the superpower missed. Two instant celebrity biographies of bin Laden appeared in Pakistani stores. Without seeming to work very hard at it, bin Laden had crafted one of the era's most successful terrorist media strategies. The missile strikes were his biggest publicity payoff to date.[23]

Martyrdom and suicide attacks

Over the next three years bin Laden escalated al-Qaeda's global jihad, culminating in the suicide attacks of 9/11. After the 9/11 attack bin Laden sent occasional audio and video messages to the media (most frequently the al-Jazeera network in Qatar) explaining various aspects of al-Qaeda's mission. His discussion of "martyrdom operations" is especially insightful.

> We stress the importance of the martyrdom operations against the enemy – operations that inflict harm on the United States and Israel that have been unprecedented in their history, thanks to Almighty

God. We also point out that whoever supported the United States, including the hypocrites of Iraq or the rulers of Arab countries, those who approved their actions and followed them in this crusade war by fighting with them or providing bases and administrative support, or any form of support, even by words, to kill the Muslims in Iraq, should know that they are apostates and outside the community of Muslims. It is permissible to spill their blood and take their property. God says: "O ye who believe! Take not the Jews and the Christians for your friends and protectors: they are but friends and protectors to each other." And he amongst you that turns to them [for friendship] is of them. Verily, Allah guideth not a people unjust.[24]

Obviously bin Laden places great emphasis on martyrdom operations (otherwise known as suicide terrorism or suicide attacks) as perhaps the most effective strategy for realizing al-Qaeda's major political objectives. Although it appears to be a highly irrational act, suicide terrorism possesses a strategic logic containing five major elements. *First*, suicide terrorism is typically not random or idiosyncratic, but carefully planned and executed. Rather than being the random acts of desperate or depraved individuals, suicide attacks are orchestrated by an organized group to achieve specific political goals. *Second*, "the strategic logic of suicide terrorism is specifically designed to coerce modern democracies to make significant concessions to national self-determination."[25] The specific goal is often the withdrawal of the target state's military forces from a perceived national homeland (as typified in the Palestinian–Israeli conflict). *Third*, since 1980 the use of suicide terrorism has increased worldwide ostensibly because *it pays*. Some examples of government concessions to terrorist organizations following suicide bombing campaigns are:

- the retreat by American and French military forces from Lebanon in 1983;
- the retreat of Israeli forces from Lebanon in 1985;
- Israeli forces abandoning the Gaza Strip and the West Bank in 1994 and 1995;
- the Sri Lankan government's creation of an independent Tamil state beginning in 1990;
- the Turkish government's granting of autonomy to the Kurds in the late 1990s; and
- the forced evacuation by the Israeli government of Israeli settlers from the Gaza Strip in 2005.[26]

Suicide bombings are much more lethal than other types of attacks. For example, between 1980 and 2001 suicide attacks accounted for only 3 percent of all terrorist attacks but 48 percent of total deaths from terrorism.[27]

Fourth, although terrorist organizations have forced concessions from governments, as indicated by the above list, the strategy of suicide terror may be approaching a point of diminishing returns. The exacting of moderate damage against a civilian population to force moderate concessions from governments may indeed work, but increasing the intensity of attacks and death counts will likely not lead to increased concessions on the part of target governments. Although many observers decry the potential civil rights abuses arising from the USA PATRIOT Act in response to the loss of close to 3,000 lives at the hands of al-Qaeda, the reality is that the United States has not yet become the tyrannical, repressive regime that al-Qaeda had hoped to produce. *Fifth*, although the strategy of suicide attacks poses a dilemma for modern democratic governments, perhaps the more effective response to such attacks is not heightened offensive military operations or the granting of more concessions, but investing in significant resources in border defenses and homeland security, just as the United States has done.

Granted also that, unlike the state of Israel or other countries that have been recent targets of suicide attacks (such as Great Britain and Spain), the United States is geographically large and spread out. Even a devastating attack on the United States that claims thousands of lives, such as what happened on September 11 in New York, Pennsylvania, and Washington, DC, may not significantly impact other major American cities, at least not directly. For example, if a suicide bomber walked into a fruit market in Seattle, Washington, and managed to detonate explosives strapped to his body and kill fifty civilians, it would certainly be tragic and a major media event for the next several weeks, but life as most Americans know it would not be altered significantly. To be sure, for a while at least people even far away from the event would likely be more careful about being out and about in public places and may change their short-term travel plans, and municipal and state governments may change certain operating procedures (for example, more careful checking of packages or backpacks in public places and transportation venues).

Even with more emphasis placed on homeland security and border defense, it is hard to tell exactly how effective such "target-hardening" strategies really are. One could make the argument that, since no major attacks have occurred since 9/11, the new operating policies in place since the enactment of the USA PATRIOT Act have made a decisive difference. But one should also consider that in all the years previous to 9/11 there were no attacks close to that magnitude perpetrated, and of course also during that time there was no Department of Homeland Security. In October of 2005 President Bush announced that since 9/11 ten serious al-Qaeda plots had been foiled, three of them targeting the United States.[28] But, again, it is difficult to determine whether the new safety procedures in place led to the foiling of these plots, or whether they would have likely be averted anyway with the old counterterrorism measures.

From the perspective of militant Islam suicide is distinguished from martyrdom operations. A suicide puts their life to an end for selfish reasons, and is therefore condemned, but martyrdom is a heroic act that has no connection to suicide. Therefore, from the perspective of militant Islam it is a misnomer to refer to "suicide missions"; they are instead martyrdom missions.

Those who give themselves up for the greater goal of defeating the enemy, whether infidels or apostates, and who carry out the missions successfully (rather than making it out alive or being captured) are referred to as shahids. The *shahid* (or martyr) who gives up his life in the jihad against a sworn enemy is promised grace or salvation in the afterlife.[29] The family of a shahid may also be compensated for the martyr's services. In Iraq while Saddam Hussein was in power, for example, families of shahids who successfully completed their suicide missions received $25,000, along with a personally worded "certificate of esteem."[30]

Donald Black's theory of terrorism

Sociologist Donald Black's theory of social control was briefly considered in chapter 2, and here we illustrate how it can be applied to the specific case of terrorism. To reiterate, Black defines social control as "how people define and respond to deviant behavior."[31] This allows a broad conceptualization of social control, one which encompasses not only legal prohibitions or regulations (legal control), but also informal sanctions such as frowns, gossip, scolding, or shows of disapproval (informal control). In addition the conceptualization allows for a wide range of third-party interventions, and of course medical interventions of this sort are compatible with medical control. For Black, then, "social control is present whenever and wherever people express grievances against their fellows."[32] Since terrorism is a form of grievance, for Black terrorism is a type of social control.[33] Up to this point we have discussed social control within the context of the response to terrorism by governments and other entities. But it is not inconsistent with the threefold typology of social control developed here that terrorism could, following Black, be considered a type of social control as well. If so, which type of social control is it?

Black states that "Terrorism in its purest form is self-help by organized civilians who covertly inflict mass violence on other civilians."[34] This means that terrorism is informal control, in that it is extra-legal and certainly not therapeutic. To fill in the details of this theory of terrorism, we must first briefly summarize the more general theory from which it derives, namely pure sociology.

Eliminating the person from sociological analysis

Black's *pure sociology* attempts to purge all psychologism and subjectivism from sociological explanation. Black also seeks to eliminate from consideration all explanations that posit underlying motives as the engine of social behavior. Such explanations are teleological, and they are incompatible with a pure sociology which need never reference such underlying psychological dispositions or traits. As Black argues,

> Classical sociology is the model of sociology itself. Moreover, the classical conception of social reality is psychological (a matter of subjectivity), the classical logic of explanation is largely teleological (a matter of means and ends), and the classical subject is largely the person (including a number or group of persons). Social action is individual action.[35]

Pure sociology is different in that it completely rejects the classical and now contemporary assumptions of subjectivism, individualism, and teleology (explaining human behavior as a means to an end). Pure sociology is what normal sociology is not. The main problem with normal sociology is that it is teleological, imputing that social actors – whether individuals or collectivities – do what they do in order to attain desired ends. But this is unscientific, because goals or purposes are not observable.

Another problem with normal sociology is that it is ideological, to the extent that sociologists are apt to study topics of deep and abiding interest to them. Because of this, sociologists have remained and continue to remain too close to their subject matter, and may even hold aspirations as to the preferred outcomes of their own research. For example, women study women, Americans study American society, homosexuals study homosexuals, members of minority groups study their own minority groups, and so forth. This makes for bad science, because researchers who are too close to their subject matter, rather than acting dispassionately and objectively toward the objects of their inquiry, are apt to view their "scientific" work as a personal or political matter.

There is a tendency to "psychologize" scientific explanation because, as individuals in our everyday lives, we think, we have feelings and emotions, and we assume that our minds and internal mental states are experienced and understood in basically the same way by other human beings. Since it is difficult if not impossible to think of the human social world apart from the conscious agents who populate it, perhaps the only way to excise the contaminating effects of subjectivity from sociological analysis is to do away with persons entirely. And this is what Black has done. Rather than talking about the behavior of persons, Black talks about the behavior of science, or art, or law, or even terrorism. This is profoundly counterintuitive because we have all come to know, understand, and expect that it is *people*, after all, who are involved in law, science, art, terrorism, etc. As Black explains, "Because social life such as law or science or art has no psychology of its own – no mind, no thoughts, no subjectivity – psychology totally disappears from sociology."[36]

Pure sociology and social space

For Black, social life – not people – inhabits a universe of its own, which is social space. *Social space*, which is created by human interaction, consists of five dimensions. These dimensions are *vertical space* (social stratification or vertical hierarchy); *horizontal space*, or the distribution of persons across time and space in relation to one another (social morphology); *symbolic space* (culture); *corporate space* (the organizational or corporate level); and *normative space* (which is equivalent to social control).[37]

Each of these dimensions may vary by location, direction, and distance. For example, in the vertical dimension of social space a society may be characterized by an uneven distribution of wealth: those higher up have far more valued resources than those below. Beginning with these simple concepts, hypotheses can be generated covering an almost endless array of substantive areas. For example, is there more crime in higher or lower locations in social space? How about religion, friendship, or sport?[38] The direction may be pertinent as well: crimes may be upward or downward (higher-ups victimizing those in lower locations or vice versa), but so may be gifts, complaints, therapy,[39] or other aspects of social life. As for distance, does law increase or decrease with relational distance? Research clearly shows that intimates are far less likely to use law to resolve conflict than are those who are less familiar to one another.

We are now in a position to summarize how terrorism is explained with reference to the five dimensions of social space.[40] First of all, Black conceptualizes violence as a strategy for handling grievances, or as a form of social control more generally. This is the normative dimension of social space. To be specific, all forms of violence, including terrorism, may be understood as a form of self-help which acts moralistically to inflict pain on another. Whereas normal crimes such as robbery or assault, or even vigilantism, tend to target individuals, terrorism targets collectivities, and its victims are chosen indiscriminately. And unlike other forms of mass violence such as lynchings or riots, terrorism is well organized and frequently often organizationally based (such as, for example, the global terror network of al-Qaeda). In terms of the vertical dimension of social space, terrorism acts upward, that is, it is initiated by those of lower status, who seek to inflict mass violence against those of higher status (civilian populations of target governments).

Terrorism resembles warfare but is at best merely quasi-warfare. This is because traditional warfare is overt and bilateral, meaning that hostilities are openly acknowledged and declared, and the violence is reciprocal or perpetrated by both sides of the dispute against each other. Terrorism, on the other hand, is more likely to be covert and unilateral. Also unlike pure warfare, which adheres to a set of rules regarding how to conduct "proper" warfare according to international rules of engagement, terrorism plays by no such set of rules. Because of this, innocent civilians are just as appropriate a target for terrorist actions as military personnel.[41] And unlike conventional warfare, with its sustained, brute force, terrorism is more apt to be hit and run and utilize its own members in direct suicide attacks. Rather than the highly sophisticated missile technology of smart bombs, terrorist organizations may opt for the smartest bombs of all, using as delivery systems humans, who can choose the exact location and time for self-detonation for purposes of maximizing casualties.[42]

Terrorism is "social control from below," a type of grievance in which relationally and culturally distant status subordinates attempt to inflict mass casualties against status superiors, namely, target governments.[43] The grievances tend to be chronic and politically charged, often over the return of disputed lands or the right to self-governance or political autonomy. In order to injure a militarily superior enemy, terrorist organizations attempt to get their members to blend in with the citizenry of the target government, living day to day among the "enemy" as normally as possible while scheming to unleash an attack when the time is right. It is a parasitic strategy. Hence, in relation to target governments terrorism tends to be physically close but socially (or culturally) distant in social space. (This cultural distance tipped off James Woods to the intentions of the would-be hijackers on the plane.) The targets tend to be selected wherever large groups of people congregate, hence transportation systems, markets and shopping malls, sports stadiums, and commercial or government buildings are especially likely to be singled out for attack.

The parasitic strategy of terrorism has become particularly visible in the open warfare between Israel and the terrorist organization Hezbollah which began in July of 2006. Although terrorist organizations have become part of the legitimate government of a few sovereign nations (for example, Hamas in Palestine), for the most part they operate without the official sanction of local or regional governments. In the case of Lebanon, Hezbollah simply set up camp in the southern region of the country, just across its border with Israel, and with funding from both Iran and Syria slowly built up a weapons arsenal that far surpassed the ability of Lebanese police or military to challenge their presence there. In effect, Hezbollah had become parasitic on the host Lebanese nation, with dire consequences for Lebanon and Israel, and imperiling the stability of the entire region.

Conclusion

Black's theory – that terrorism is a type of grievance in which moralistic revenge in the form of collective violence is pursued against target governments – although a good starting point, may be deficient in some respects. Richard Rosenfeld, for example, has argued that terrorism is not only a grievance against target governments, it is also a grievance against modernity. As much as anything, terrorists hope to damage or destroy key features of modern Western constitutional democracies, including their free markets, religious tolerance, liberalism, secular humanism, openness and mobility, and even globalization.[44] The Islamic terrorists who hijacked airplanes on September 11 and crashed them into the Twin Towers and the Pentagon did so because they stood as icons of the United States' greed, arrogance, and impiety.[45]

Of course, since Black is not interested in theorizing the intentions of particular actors in social space, including terrorists, holding him to task for not finding a place for such motivating factors as militant Islam's hatred for Western societies' openness, liberalism, materialism, and perceived "godlessness" may not be particularly damaging to the integrity of his theoretical system. This represents a disagreement on how far theorists want to go in politicizing the power differentials that exist between terrorists and the governments they seek to destroy. Black finds a place for this in his theory by way of the vertical and normative dimensions of social space, but he is not much interested in making normative judgments concerning the "criminal" nature of terrorism's response to powerlessness. On this point I agree with him.

A number of alternative theories do, however, explicitly include this normative or ideological dimension. One example is the theory of David Boyns and James David Ballard, which begins with the assertion that "terrorism is a powerful response to powerlessness." This leads to their basic definition of terrorism, which is "a violent response to hegemonic dominance and may represent an attempt to overcome the dominant hegemony by the creation of an alternative, a counterhegemonic movement."[46]

In any event, terrorism and counterterrorism activities have reduced societal reliance on informal control, to the extent that public trust has diminished. With that has followed a greater reliance on general surveillance of the population, which assumes that everyone is at risk either for victimization or offending.[47] As discussed more fully in the final chapter, legal control in the wake of 9/11 has effectively blurred the boundaries between the military and the police, but has also prodded the expansion of municipal and federal police forces. (Or, if not actual expansion, municipal governments are being tasked with such federal mandates as the development of comprehensive evacuation plans, while police are expected to comply with federal guidelines regarding local law-enforcement preparedness and response to terrorist threats.)

The terrorist emphasis on mass disruption and destruction of civil society means that not only are transportation and business enterprises targeted for attack, but also mass delivery systems such as mail and package, water, and energy. (Indeed, the first reaction of a number of observers upon news of the massive blackout that occurred in the northeastern United States in 2003 was that it was caused by terrorists.) For example, more and more municipal sewer districts are making the transition from a reliance on private security firms to the establishment of their own sworn police forces. In essence, municipal water and sewage districts are keen to turn their around-the-clock security guards into sworn police officers. State representative Jim Trakas of Independence, Ohio, who introduced a bill in 2005 to allow the formation of sewer district police forces, said, "If you would have asked me on Sept. 10, 2001, I would have said that the sewer district does not need a police force. But in light of what we've learned, it's a matter of public safety and health."[48]

Finally, because terrorism operates without official or explicit state sponsorship, terrorists are everywhere and nowhere. Since terrorists are for the most part not bound together by geography, their social solidarity is assured by non-traditional means, through global networks of communication and media. This means that fighting terrorism will achieve only partial success if based on localized logics of target hardening, border defense, and homeland security, and this returns us once again to Beck's notion of the world risk society. Since terrorism is a global phenomenon that transcends traditional understandings of time and place, successful counterterrorism measures must be global in nature as well.[49] As Karin Knorr Cetina explains,

> Countering terrorism will have to become a truly global effort involving a coalition of governments, extending to remote regions of the world, engaging the global struggle of ideas, and translating short-term concerns into long-term internal and external commitments.[50]

Suggestions for further reading

Coll, Steve. 2004. *Ghost Wars: The Secret History of the CIA, Afghanistan, and bin Laden, from the Soviet Invasion to September 10, 2001.* New York: Penguin.
An authoritative overview and summary of the United States' involvement with terrorists and terror organizations since the mid-1970s.
Deflem, Mathieu (ed.) 2004. *Terrorism and Counter-Terrorism: Criminological Perspectives.* Amsterdam: Elsevier.
This edited volume illustrates the utility of sociological and criminological perspectives on the problem of terrorism. Contributors include Donald Black, Richard Rosenfeld, Gary LaFree, Gregg Barak, and Victor and Aaron Kappeler.
Mythen, Gabe and Sandra Walklate. 2006. "Criminology and Terrorism: Which Thesis? Risk Society or Governmentality?" *British Journal of Criminology* 46: 379–98.
The authors describe the "new terrorism" which is posing challenges to Britain, the United States, and other Western countries. This new terrorism, fueled largely by Islamic fundamentalism, is deadlier and more unpredictable than the "old" terrorism represented by the activities of such groups as the Irish Republican Army (IRA). The authors

contemplate the utility of explanations based in the risk society (Beck) and governmentality (Foucault) for explaining the new terrorism.

Sageman, Marc. 2004. *Understanding Terror Networks.* **Philadelphia: University of Pennsylvania Press.**

Utilizing concepts from social network theory, Sageman provides a thorough explanation of the history and organization of terrorism, as well as sociodemographic characteristics of those involved in terror organizations.

Shay, Shaul. 2004. *The Shahids: Islam and Suicide Attacks,* **trans. R. Lieberman. New Brunswick, NJ: Transaction.**

A piercing examination of the process by which individuals are recruited into terrorist organizations for the ultimate purpose of carrying out suicide bombings.

10 Conclusion: The Future of Social Control?

Introduction

Based upon recent trends, especially as these have been heavily influenced by the reality of global terrorism, it is hard to perceive a future that is not at least in some measure impacted by the distortions to the social fabric which terrorism has wrought. As discussed in the last chapter, informal social control appears to have waned significantly as a result not only of the threat of terrorism, but also of other long-term changes characteristic of the advent of the postmodern or postindustrial society. This has paved the way for the ascendancy of legal and medical control, and in some instances the boundaries between the three forms of control have become blurred. For example, British sociologist Anthony Giddens, an advocate of communitarianism and trusted advisor to Prime Minister Tony Blair and the Third Way politics of his New Labour party, argues that the police should work closely with citizens and take on roles of community advocacy, counseling, and family preservation in addition to their traditional law-enforcement roles.[1] This policy perspective is also represented at the Home Office, the government department responsible for internal affairs in England and Wales, which has recently promulgated an assortment of anti-social behavior ordinances and policies.

This concluding chapter will contemplate the future of social control in light of these and other factors which, taken together, are creating hybrid or interlocking systems of control. We will begin with an examination of Home Office policies with regard to the problem of anti-social behavior.

The anti-social behaviour orders

According to information provided on the Home Office website, the purpose of the Anti-Social Behaviour Orders (or ASBOs) is to "provide the tools for practitioners and agencies to effectively tackle anti-social behaviour."[2] ASBOs are "statutory measures that aim to protect the public from behaviour that causes or is likely to cause harassment, alarm or distress."[3] These are civil orders made in court, and can be applied by local authorities such as the police (including transit police) and registered social landlords, but not by everyday citizens.

In effect, the ASBO places more power in the hands of municipal police and other functionaries to act aggressively against behaviors and conduct that by all rights traditionally have been handled informally by individuals within the context of their communities. The Act received Royal Assent on November 20, 2003, and some of the new police powers are:

- widening the use of fixed-penalty notices against such things as noise nuisances, truancy, and graffiti, targeting especially sixteen- and seventeen-year-olds;
- increased ability to disperse groups in areas designated as suffering from serious and persistent anti-social behaviors;
- new mechanisms for enforcing parental responsibility for children who act in anti-social ways in school or in the community; and
- extending power to landlords to take action against anti-social tenants, including quicker evictions and removing the right to buy homes. [4]

As discussed in chapter 5, by making pertinent to the police a whole host of events and activities that were previously understood as neighborhood problems to be solved by residents of the community, ASBOs are an example of net-widening. The parenting orders are an especially telling aspect of the ASBO, insofar as a growing concern with the lawlessness of children in particular since the 1980s has led to something of a moral panic about the status of children in modern society. The precursor to the ASBO was the Home Office's Crime and Disorder Act of 1998, which was an explicit attempt to address youth crime by focusing on the linkages between schools, families, and the community in the production of delinquency. This act, along with the more recent ASBO, has linked the police and the local community more tightly together in the attempt to assure community safety at levels never before imagined. In effect, the net of control over children especially has tightened considerably.[5]

Indeed, with the launching in late 2005 of the "Respect Task Force," the New Labour government continues to show an especially keen interest – some would say obsession – with the behavior of young people. The Respect Task Force targets parents whose alleged inadequacies in the areas of socialization, monitoring, and supervision of their children has contributed to a growing number of youth who have little or no respect for authority and traditional social institutions (especially the schools, the courts, and law enforcement). Under responsibilization (to be discussed below), decency and respect are now viewed as reciprocal obligations between parents, children, and the community, and a growing number of parent orders deal specifically with this issue.[6]

The ASBO in Great Britain is consistent with a more general policy orientation among Western European nations to expand the traditional conceptualization of crime to include disorder, incivilities, and even bad or merely unpleasant behavior. For example, in a document published in 2000 by the European Commission, crime was defined not only as offenses that clearly violate national laws, but also as "anti-social conduct which, without necessarily being a criminal offence, can by its cumulative effect generate a climate of tension and insecurity."[7]

This sentiment in turn was clearly influenced by a group of American writers who, beginning in the early 1980s, argued that crime and other social evils result from inattention to seemingly small and insignificant features of everyday life. The most famous of these writings is the *broken windows* thesis of James Q. Wilson and George L. Kelling.[8] According to Wilson and Kelling, a broken window left unrepaired for several days or longer may signal to others an absence of capable guardians in the area. This in turn may lead to the general sentiment that "no one cares," and disreputable persons are more likely to be drawn to the area, igniting a downward spiral into further deviance, incivility, and crime. Wilson and Kelling further argued that, in their preferred roles as professional crime fighters, police were overlooking seemingly trivial events and activities in neighborhoods – such as arguments or scuffles, public drinking, hanging out at street corners, bus stops, and other public places, and generally mischievous or threatening behaviors – because they were deemed to fall outside their crime control mandate. In order to address the perception or reality of rising crime rates, the authors recommended that police departments get officers out of their patrol cars and back onto foot patrols.

The broken windows thesis appeared at about the same time that community policing was gaining momentum in many American cities. As discussed in previous chapters, community policing attempts to integrate citizens and police in a more meaningful way, including increasing the visibility of officers in the community by way of foot patrols and the establishment of a number of community programs staffed by police personnel (such as DARE and GREAT). Community-oriented policing (COP) adopts a customer service model, in that police are overtly concerned with citizen perspectives toward the police and toward crime and other issues in their community. The idea is that, with meaningful collaboration between police and citizens, informal social control can be restored and strengthened, because citizens are no longer antagonistic toward the police but instead form partnerships with them to reduce levels of disorder, anti-social behavior, and crime in local communities.

In the UK and other Western European nations, rather than talk of community policing per se, governments have been more prone to adopt the rhetoric and language of social capital (see chapter 6). For example, in London the Office of National Statistics (ONS) is concerned with measuring and monitoring the level of social capital in various communities. The main aspects of social capital identified by ONS are "citizenship, neighbourliness, trust and shared values, community involvement, volunteering, social networks, and civil and political participation."[9]

Responsibilization

It should be understood that within this nexus of community policing, social capital, and Third Way/communitarian ideals, the UK anti-social behaviour orders represent one method by which governments are attempting to place more of the responsibility for community maintenance and order in the hands of citizens.[10] David Garland has referred to this as the *responsibilization* strategy, and, as he further explains,

> Instead of addressing crime in a direct fashion by means of the police, the courts and the prisons, this [responsibilization] approach promotes a new kind of indirect action, in which state agencies activate action by non-state organizations and actors. The intended result is an enhanced network of more or less directed, more or less informal crime control, complementing and extending the formal controls of the criminal justice state.[11]

The equivalent in the United States is *third-party policing*, which is defined as "police efforts to persuade or coerce non-offending persons to take actions which are outside the scope of their routine activities, and which are designed to indirectly minimize disorder caused by other persons or to reduce the possibility that crime may occur."[12] Shop owners, landlords, and neighborhood associations are the kinds of persons and groups on whom police are most likely to put pressure to promote "collective responsibility" in targeted areas.

Under community policing, police departments inform local citizens that the crime problem is too vast and complex to be managed by the police alone, and it is within this context that they feel emboldened to ask for the help of citizens to be that extra set of eyes and ears which was largely muted and deemed to be irrelevant during the second era of municipal policing (namely, professionalization and early reform). In some ways, this is consistent with Foucault's notion of governmentality and the process of fanning out disciplinary mechanisms more broadly across the community. It is the condition of "the many watching the many."

This also represents the postmodern problem of boundary blurring: if everyone is responsible for crime control and disorder, meaningful distinctions between the police, government personnel, and nongovernmental actors and organizations become harder and harder to draw. The blurring of boundaries also appears in the guise of the court's growing reliance on alternative or intermediate sanctions, including a whole host of community-based sanctions. Indeed, if punishments or treatments can be carried out successfully within communities rather than in prisons or asylums, or if a person's home can serve as a prison as effectively as traditional correctional facilities, the strategy of social control shifts to an examination of how best to mix and merge informal, formal, and medical control resources. And, of course, the enormous growth of privatization in both policing and corrections further blurs the boundaries between the roles of public and private organizations in social control.

Actuarial justice and the new penology

Another indication of changes in the relationship between formal, informal, and medical control is the emergence of what Jonathan Simon and Malcolm Feeley refer to as the *new penology*.[13] The authors argue that key changes since the Progressive Era (1890s through about 1910) have produced a new, "postmodern" way of thinking about crime and crime policy.

One of these key changes is in the realm of *discourses*. Under modernity the way to talk about and understand criminality was the relationship between individuals and their communities (whether religious, economic, or psychological, or in terms of the helping professions). In contrast, under postmodernity crimes are talked about as a technical problem to be dealt with on a systems or operations level. In particular, crimes now tend to be viewed as a problem of actuarial risk management.

Another key change concerns the *objectives* or goals of punishment. In modernity punishment was envisioned as being "rational" (proportional to the crime), and the goal was changing persons on a case-by-case basis (rehabilitation or reform) so they wouldn't offend again (deterrence). Under postmodernity, however, the primary objective is no longer the transformation of individuals. The new objectives that rise to prominence are risk management and the management of the system itself, or "convenience over conscience," as argued by David Rothman.[14]

A third key change is in the area of *techniques*. Here, postmodern approaches for dealing with crime and disorder are mixed with recycled or repackaged modernist techniques. Once introduced as a way of improving administrative knowledge of defendants or suspects (such as through profiling, auditing, screening, and so forth), these now have become endpoints in the operation of the system. The operation of the criminal justice system has become more reflexive and self-referential, as actors both within the system and without (such as criminologists and other experts in the community) monitor the activities of key personnel such as the police, judges, and corrections officials under the guise of "research," "continuous improvement," "quality control," and "best practices."

In addition, the gap between professional and public (or lay) discourses about crime has grown wider. There appears to be a declining consensus about what to do about crime and disorder, which is consistent with the theorized loss of certitude about the world that persons are experiencing under the postmodern condition. Consistent with this is the proliferation of a growing legion of "experts" – whether used in court to bolster a case, "talking heads" in the media, or policy think-tanks servicing government and industry – ready to defend numerous positions about the nature of criminality. For example: "three strikes and you're out" was a grassroots movement, but professional discourses within criminology, law, and the social sciences have been highly critical. The same can be said of boot camps, lie detectors, random drug testing, and so forth.

Under modernity we had faith in the "scientific" approach to the problem of crime, especially during the Progressive Era (the heyday of the social sciences, where the birth of sociology and social work took place). In contrast, the new penology is content to conduct surveillance on whole populations because intervention at the individual level is now viewed as ineffective. This is of course consistent with the loss of faith in rehabilitation and the general position that "nothing works." In effect, there is no compelling vision with which to come to terms with the problems of crime and disorder. According to Simon and Feeley, it is now an administrative problem to be "managed." As a consequence expediency runs rampant (for example, judges tacking on drug testing as part of a probationary sentence when drugs were not part of the criminal complaint).

In sum, the major operational logic of the new penology is *actuarial justice*. Feeley and Simon describe its major characteristics as follows.

- Actuarial justice relies on accounting procedures, such as the traditional measures of risk previously utilized in industry, finance, and medicine.
- It is concerned with techniques for identifying, classifying, and managing groups assorted by levels of dangerousness.
- It takes crime for granted.
- It accepts deviance as normal.
- It is skeptical that liberal interventionist crime control strategies do or can make a difference.
- Its aim is not to intervene in individuals' lives for the purpose of changing them (rehabilitation) or punishing them (retribution). Rather it seeks to regulate groups as part of a strategy of managing danger.[15]

Dangerization

Hence, from the perspective of Simon and Feeley as well as a number of other scholars, Western governments are now primarily concerned with the management of risk and danger. By concentrating on risk in this way, governments are contributing to yet another "postmodern" blurring of boundaries. The most important boundary that has become blurred, according to Michalis Lianos, is the distinction between the normal and the deviant.[16] Under the traditional view, those who violated the community's norms deserved to be punished, and were identified and set aside for processing through the justice and penal systems.

However, under the new condition to which Lianos refers as *dangerization*, individuals are not necessarily identified and responded to on the basis of their deviant acts. Instead, groups of persons, places, or events are identified as actually or potentially dangerous. In the postmodern condition, as more and more categories of persons, places, and events are identified as risky or dangerous, the entire society becomes identified as a risk society (see chapter 9), hence the notion of the "normal" as opposed to the occasionally deviant no longer makes sense.

Even within the condition of dangerization, social and economic exchanges continue to be facilitated by a growing reliance on constant and routine surveillance (such as the use of closed-circuit television in urban areas). Rather than relying on the fallible perceptions of human beings, automated systems of surveillance can allow access to places and events through circuits of exclusion and inclusion.[17] In other words, rather than reacting to deviant acts that may take place, the goal is to manage environments by allowing or denying access to persons based on selected group factors, often facilitated through the use of searchable databases. Examples of this type of *social sorting* include loyalty cards at grocery stores and pharmacies; codes, passwords, and biometric scanning devices for electronic or physical access to buildings, products, or services; routine use of identification cards not only in business and government establishments but also increasingly in the schools; and physical alteration and modification of space, such as the erection of barriers, checkpoints, or other engineering designs which seek to allow access to persons who possess certain characteristics while keeping out those who do not possess the desired traits (as in the case of gated communities).[18]

The colonization of the lifeworld

The current ascendancy of concepts such as social capital, broken windows, and communitarianism, as well as policies such as community policing, third-party policing, and anti-social behaviour orders, is reflective of the recognition that the "invisible hand" of the market cannot solve persistent and chronic social problems such as crime, joblessness and unemployment, social isolation and marginalization of some groups, racism and sexism, or environmental degradation. When market forces can no longer be relied on to bond persons to conventional society, there is a tendency for these formal systems to encroach further into the realm of everyday life or the lifeworld. This attempt to steer lifeworld (or informal) activities by infusing them with oversight and directives from the formal realm (of law, medicine, the courts and the police) is what Jürgen Habermas has described as the *colonization of the lifeworld*. This is the problem of rationalization as discussed in chapter 1, but it goes even beyond Weber's original position.

In order to understand this, we must briefly cover the distinction Habermas makes between system and lifeworld.[19] Drawing from standard phenomenology, the *lifeworld* simply represents that part of society which is concerned with socialization, with face-to-face behavior, with family and other primary group relations, and with the development of self through close and ongoing contact with significant others. In this sense, the lifeworld is synonymous with everyday life (as discussed in chapter 3), and the primary form of control operating here is informal.

By *system*, on the other hand, Habermas is referring to more formalized institutional settings, where other aspects of one's status-set become salient, such as worker, citizen, student, professor, customer, or patient. For example, when I am moving through anonymous public space I am identified and dealt with by others, at least initially, only on the basis of my being "male." Likewise, when I am at home with my family, I am "father" to my children and "husband" to my wife. The norms operating within these lifeworld settings are informal and tacitly understood. But when I step into other more formal settings, I experience what might be called *institutional capture*. For example, when I leave my home and family and begin my day at the university, my status as "professor" becomes most salient, and a whole array of formal norms attach to my actions. Within this and other formal institutional settings, systems imperatives guide much of my conduct and choices for action. In other words, within formal institutional settings what will transpire regarding my actions is largely decided for me, and there is not the same level of negotiation over definitions of the situation typical of the lifeworld. In formalized settings, scripts are already written. (Think, for example, how tightly regulated and scripted our behaviors are in the courtroom, perhaps the most heavily formalized of all social settings.)

Whereas the lifeworld is integrated through tacit understandings of one's obligations toward significant others such as family and friends, the system is integrated on the basis of functional "needs" of the system. For example, in order for economic activity to work smoothly and efficiently, workers' actions have to be coordinated with others' actions with much greater precision than is the case for actions taking place in informal settings (such as between family members or friends). This means that formal guidelines tend to be promulgated for all members of a work group, and time pressures will be brought to bear to maximize the efficiency of workers' activities but also to minimize mutual interference. As a crucial aspect of modern social systems, norms of punctuality seek to ensure that vital actions will be dispersed across space and time in a predictable manner.

According to Habermas, however, with continuing societal rationalization systems imperatives of efficiency and predictability tend to become parasitic on everyday lifeworld activities, thereby producing a variety of distortions. Instead of negotiating the conditions of their existence voluntarily within the context of shared lifeworlds, actors increasingly find more and a greater variety of "experts" ready and willing to step in to provide guidance about their everyday activities, be it dating, raising children, discussing and interpreting news of the day, how to do a wedding reception, or even how to throw a surprise birth-day party. The colonization of the lifeworld by the system serves to mute everyday communicative action, and more than ever actors find themselves at the mercy of broader systems imperatives shaping and guiding – through either "strong" suggestions or outright coercion – their thoughts and actions.

Conclusion: shoring up informal control

What are we to do about this increasing encroachment of systems imperatives into previously informally regulated areas of life? Are we fated to live in what Habermas has called an "expertocracy," where collective understandings of everyday life are replaced by the formal-ized rulings and recommendations of lawyers, bureaucrats, and the cost–benefit analyses of economists and organizational consultants?[20] Enlightenment and Progressive thinkers such as Lester Ward believed that science and reason would usher in an era of universal education where the errors of past thought would be corrected, thereby leading to the general improvement of society.[21] But it appears now that instru-mental reason is being used more narrowly, as a technology to control various persons and groups that are seen as persistently incorrigible, disorderly, criminal, strange, or unpredictable.[22] Indeed, with the advent of more expansive and continuous surveillance technologies, we have moved from concentrating efforts on a relatively visible group of offenders or misfits to assuming that all persons within the camera's gaze are "bad." Since everyone is now potentially an offender, the police cannot hope to do the work of legal control alone, and hence everyone is asked to do their fair share.

Agents of legal control are faced with a peculiar juggling act: they must break the bad news that everyone is bad, but also ask these very same persons to watch over everyone else, in effect expecting citizens to act as auxiliary police officers in the service of their community. One way of dealing with this dilemma is for agents of control to cajole citizens, for example, by selling the notion that today's police are not only excellent communicators, but also more sensitive and compassionate toward citi-zens because of their training in soft skills and multiculturalism.[23] In addition, because they are better educated, police should be trusted to take greater initiative, to solve problems, and to be a proactive rather than merely a reactive force. In effect, the police are boundary-spanning multitaskers, their new hybrid role being required in the postmodern metropolis where, sadly, nobody can be trusted, and where traditional measures have failed to distinguish the normal from the deviant.

Ultimately, then, citizens – who of course cannot be trusted – are being asked to take on more responsibility for the maintenance of the social system. Responsibilization takes many forms: traditional welfare programs have been transformed into welfare-to-work programs where the state divests its financial burden by using the social capital of families and the local community; municipal police are asking persons to draw upon neighborhood funds of information capital to assure social control; and the public school system, facing shrinking budgets and enrollments, is asking PTAs, social services (especially the public health wing), the police, and even families (for example, through home schooling) to pick up the slack.[24]

It appears that, at least for the short term, local governance will continue to pursue strategies of responsibilization, and will continue to find ways to steer informal activities via the rhetoric of social capital, communitarianism, and community policing. Yet, however well intentioned these programs and policies may be, from this author's perspective there remain grave reservations about the formal sector's supervision and oversight of the informal realm because of the problems of the colonization of the lifeworld already discussed. In other words, there is an attempt to combine coercion with compassion in these varied hybrid undertakings – for example, community policing, intermediate sanctions, anti-social behaviour and parenting orders, third-party policing, and a variety of so-called problem-solving courts such as drug courts, youth and family courts, mental health courts, and community courts – but the two simply do not mix very well.[25]

It is my opinion that the formal realm poisons and taints the informal realm whenever the former attempts to steer the activities of the latter. But there is no going back to a golden era of mechanical solidarity, of tight-knit communities where everyone knew everyone else, and where individuals were held in check by the awesome and awe-inspiring presence of a collective conscience. For example, instead of trying to make the police more user-friendly as they take on a variety of roles including social worker, therapist, social scientist, and community activist, we should be satisfied in recognizing, along with Egon Bittner, that the core of the police role is the non-negotiable distribution of coercive force in society.[26] Any further attributes we attempt to assign to the police amount to little more than circumlocutions, or rhetorical flourishes, which seek to soften the harsh reality that, even in an era of progress where peaceful means are presumably more widely available to handle disputes and disturbances, the police are there as an embarrassing reminder that outright coercion is needed and still wins the day in many instances.[27]

Hence, the police should be allowed to fulfill their mandate in as pure and unadulterated fashion as possible. They are specialists in crime control and order maintenance. Under the community policing model, however, police are conceptualized more as generalists, hearkening back to the roles they originally occupied during the earliest, political spoils era. In order to understand what playing the role of generalist means now in comparison to what it meant then, one must understand the changing nature of society and community over the three broad eras of policing. This contrast and comparison is summarized in table 10.1. The vast array of service functions assigned to the police under community policing

Table 10.1 *The three eras of policing and changes in community and police roles*

	Policing eras		
	Political spoils	Early professionalization and reform	Community policing
Police as:	*Generalists,* attending to broad needs of citizens and political leadership	*Specialists,* primarily in crime control	*Generalists,* boundary-spanning multitaskers serving a diverse citizenry
Nature of community:	*Homogeneity* but appearance of incipient levels of heterogeneity and increasing social disorder	Increasing *heterogeneity* and crime rates achieving historic highs beginning in the 1960s	*Heterogeneity* and diversity of community at historically high levels; crime rates decline while incarceration rates increase
Prevailing conditions:	Structural transformation in the division of labor: the transition from self-help to sworn police force means police are beholden to political machinery and and local ward leaders	Attempts to professionalize and reform police in light of previous era's corruption (close citizen contact) and political patronage abuses	The return of police generalization, but this time in the context of community diversity and shrinking municipal budgets, where local governance seeks to extract greatest "bang for the buck" from safety forces
Direction of control emphasis:	Informal to formal	Increasingly formal	Formal to informal (or, rather, attempts to combine various forms of control under the condition of police–community reciprocity)

gives them entrée into the informal realm where they are simply not needed and, indeed, where they may do more harm than good. On this point I agree with Steve Herbert, who argues that "The police's coercive role means that they are not good community builders, and thus we fool ourselves – and harm communities – by holding onto the more elaborate rhetoric of community policing."[28]

Likewise, judges ought to oversee their courts narrowly focused on issues of procedural law, and should not be overly concerned with taking on or embracing other roles such as therapist, child advocate, or community activist. And with regard to the practice and rhetoric of medicine, it is now likely that the interventions of medical or medically informed practitioners have penetrated the informal realm so deeply that no amount of wishful thinking will undo it. The therapeutic ethos is one of the staples of modern or postmodern culture. One of the important functions of critical scholarly analysis, then, is to point out where and in what form the therapeutic ethos operates to distort life-world activities.

Suggestions for further reading

Burney, Elizabeth. 2005. *Making People Behave: Anti-Social Behaviour, Politics and Policy.* Cullompton, Devon: Willan.
An excellent overview of New Labour policies in the UK, especially with regard to Home Office anti-social behaviour ordinances which seek to hold people accountable for their bad, but not necessarily criminal, behavior.

Habermas, Jürgen. 1984/1987. *Theory of Communicative Action,* 2 vols., trans. T. McCarthy. Boston: Beacon Press.
A landmark study in general theory. It is here that Habermas formulates his important concepts of distorted communication and the colonization of the lifeworld.

Herbert, Steve. 2006. *Citizens, Cops, and Power: Recognizing the Limits of Community.* Chicago: University of Chicago Press.
An empirical investigation of citizen attitudes toward community policing. Although on the one hand citizens welcome some of the initiatives connected with community policing, citizens also like to be left alone, to their own devices. Problems associated with conceptualizing "community" in light of the American cultural emphasis on individualism are highlighted.

Lianos, Michalis. 2000. "Dangerization and the End of Deviance." *British Journal of Criminology* 40: 261–78.
Lianos argues that one of the primary results of the societal loss of faith in the criminal justice goal of rehabilitation is that we now treat all persons as potentially evil – facilitated through constant surveillance of public places – and hence no meaningful distinctions exist between the normal and the deviant. This trend toward "dangerization"

has effectively turned the concept "deviance" into an empty signifier devoid of meaning.

Rose, Nikolas. 2000. "Government and Control." *British Journal of Criminology* **40: 321–39.**

Rose examines claims made of the rise of a post-disciplinary society characterized by electronic surveillance, Panopticism, the risk society, and actuarial justice, among other things. Although there are many different approaches being tried in government and elsewhere with regard to the governing of conduct, there is no single coherent strategy holding these disparate efforts together. Rose concludes that control programs are more ad hoc and pragmatic than carefully orchestrated by master planners (i.e., "big brother").

Notes

INTRODUCTION

1 Cohen (1985, p. 3).
2 Nadel (1953, p. 265).
3 MacIver and Page (1949, p. 137).
4 Nye (1958). For a summary of Nye's work as well as other control theories, see Paternoster and Bachman (2001).
5 Katovich (1996). For a discussion of the limitations of the "control as evil" perspective, see Gibbs (1994, pp. 32–4).
6 Beniger (1986).
7 This theory of control is summarized in Gibbs (1989a, 1994).
8 These examples are taken from Gibbs (1994, p. 44).
9 Gibbs (1989a, pp. 58–9).
10 This example is from Gibbs (1994, pp. 51–2).

CHAPTER 1   WHAT IS SOCIAL CONTROL?

1 Information on the London bombings of July 7 and July 21 was collected from *Time* magazine, *US News and World Report*, the *Cleveland Plain Dealer*, and AP wire reports as summarized at www.yahoo.com and www.msnbc.com.
2 Two of the bombers, Mohammed Siddique Khan and Shazad Tanweer, were in Pakistan between November 2004 and February 2005 and could have been in contact with al-Qaeda operatives during this time. Yet the precise nature of this trip remains unclear (see Phythian 2005).
3 Armitage (2002), cited in Farrington and Jolliffe (2005, p. 65).
4 Welsh and Farrington (2004) and Farrington and Jolliffe (2005).
5 By July 30, all four suspects in the failed bombing attempt had been arrested as a result of police raids in London and in Rome. They could best be described as "copycatters" who had no direct ties to al-Qaeda.
6 Ross (1896). This and other articles on social control are collected in Ross (1901).
7 Ward (1883, 1893).
8 Harp (1995, p. 174).
9 See, e.g., Rafter (2004).
10 See Ward (1893).
11 See Simmel (1950).
12 See Ross (1896, pp. 519–20).
13 For more on this point, see Sumner (1997). Although I agree with Sumner's assessment of the uniquely American beginnings of the study of social control, I would argue that he neglects the writings of Ward (see, e.g., 1893, 1903, 1906), Giddings (1896, 1899, 1909), and other early American sociologists whose work on general sociology either preceded or were coterminous with Ross's writings on social control. Because of this neglect, Sumner jumps right from Ross to Robert Park, and although Park's work on social control was important, by no means was this the whole story. In America, Ward and Giddings beat Park to the punch by some two decades.
14 See especially Janowitz (1975).
15 Parts of this section have appeared in Chriss (2004).

16 During the modern era restitutive law – which Durkheim understood to mean civil law – emerged and operated alongside the longer-standing criminal law. Due to space constraints, civil law (or the law of torts) will not be covered in this book.

17 On postmodernity see, e.g., Agger (2002), Lyotard (1984), and Staples (2000).

18 See, e.g., Freud (1927) and Parsons (1964).

19 A more thorough discussion of agents of socialization will be provided in chapter 3.

20 For a good discussion of social control as socialization and the internalization of moral codes, see Ellwood (1925, pp. 157–87).

21 See, e.g., Best (1999), Chriss (1999b), Elliott et al. (1998), and Putnam (2000).

22 Weber (1968, p. 31).

23 Ibid., p. 53.

24 Ibid., pp. 215–16.

25 Ibid., p. 231.

26 Ibid., p. 241.

27 Weber (1978 [1922], p. 39).

28 Giddings (1899, p. 203).

29 See especially Habermas (1996).

30 See Habermas (1975).

31 For more on the concept of the state as moral regulator, see Corrigan and Sayer (1985), Melossi (2004), and Ruonavaara (1997).

32 These points are taken from Novak (1999, pp. 25–31).

33 See, for example, Wong (2006).

34 This discussion is taken from Scott (1998, pp. 64–71).

35 Ibid., p. 66.

36 Ibid., p. 69.

CHAPTER 2   A TYPOLOGY OF SOCIAL CONTROL

1 See Black (1998).

2 For the classic statement of the important ways external third parties alter dyadic (or two-person) social relations, see Simmel (1950). Donald Black (1998) has also made extensive use of this idea.

3 This issue regarding the medicalization of everyday troubles and how offenders are increasingly forced into therapy, or choose to undertake therapy voluntarily, points to the rise and persistence of a modern "therapeutic state" (see, e.g., Chriss 1999a; Furedi 2004a; Moskowitz 2001; Nolan 1998; and Ward 2002). This will be returned to in greater detail in chapter 4.

4 This summary draws from the *Cincinnati Post* online edition as well as from www.yahoo.com.

5 See Bittner (1970).

6 Ibid., p. 37.

7 Ibid.

8 Horne (2001, p. 4).

9 Sumner (1906, p. 2).

10 Ibid., p. 3.

11 Ibid., p. 13.

12 Ibid., p. 30.

13 Ibid., p. 55.

14 Ibid., p. 34.

15 This discussion is taken from Coleman (1990, pp. 241–65).

16 Ibid., p. 243.

17 It is unlikely that such a situation would escalate beyond the verbal level, but with the rate of childhood allergies to peanuts on the rise (see Grundy et al. 2002), skittish parents sitting with peanut-allergic children may feel emboldened toward higher levels of confrontation.

18 See Ellwood (1925, p. 454).
19 See Lloyd (1901).
20 Roth and Mehta (2002, p. 132).
21 See Mead (1925).
22 See Heckathorn (1990).
23 For a definitive statement on social control as backward-looking, see Macy (1993).
24 For a discussion of meat eaters and grass eaters as applied to the problem of police corruption, see Nas et al. (1986).
25 Hirschi and Gottfredson (2005, pp. 215–17).
26 Ibid., pp. 217–19.
27 For a useful summary of the labeling perspective, see Herman-Kinney (2003).
28 Ditton (1979).
29 Ibid., p. 102.
30 See especially Black (1983).
31 Ibid., p. 34.
32 For discussions of how anti-social norms, as well as various forms of anti-social control, emerge out of formal or informal control (or their combination), see Heckathorn (1990) and Kitts (2006).

CHAPTER 3   INFORMAL CONTROL

1   The concept of the "natural surrounding world" is taken from Gurwitsch (1979).
2   For a summary of the sociology of everyday life, or what is sometimes referred to as existential sociology, see Adler et al. (1987) and Gouldner (1975).
3   Ellwood (1925, pp. 193–4).
4   Gumplowicz (1899, p. 157).
5   For discussions of reference groups, see for example Eisenstadt (1954) and Shibutani (1962).
6   This discussion of the seven basic sources of socialization is a modification of the topic covered in Arnett (1995, pp. 619–24).
7   See Giddings (1899), Sumner (1906), and Ward (1903).
8   Hillery (1968, p. 245).
9   Clinton (1995).
10 For examples, see Arnett (1995, pp. 621–2).
11 See Hirschi (1969).
12 Harris (1998).
13 See Gouldner (1979).
14 This discussion is taken from Chao et al. (1994).
15 Ibid., p. 732.
16 This discussion owes in part to Hervieu-Léger (1998).
17 L'Engle et al. (2006).
18 See, e.g., Sariolghalam (2003) and Tsui (2005).
19 This summary of Lewin, Sherif, and Whyte is informed by Harrington and Fine (2006, pp. 8–9).
20 See Asch (1951, 1952).
21 See especially Milgram (1963, 1965). These and other obedience experiments are summarized in Milgram (1974).
22 See Centola, Willer, and Macy (2005).
23 There are many versions of Andersen's story "The Emperor's New Clothes," which was originally published in 1837. The version I am referring to is from Andersen (1959).
24 Centola, Willer, and Macy (2005, p. 1012).
25 Ibid., pp. 1036–7.
26 Back (1981, p. 331).
27 Simmel (1950).
28 Ibid., p. 9.

29 These five points are a summary and extension of Harrington and Fine (2000).
30 For a discussion of weak and strong ties from the perspective of network theory, see Granovetter (1973).
31 Results of this survey are cited in Putnam (2000, p. 274).
32 Goffman served as president of the American Sociological Association in 1982, and his presidential address appropriately was titled "The Interaction Order" (Goffman 1983). However, Goffman was too ill to attend and did not deliver the paper himself.
33 Goffman (1983, p. 4).
34 Goffman (1959).
35 On the various elements comprising a competent lecture, see "The Lecture" in Goffman (1981).
36 On the concept of interaction ritual, see Goffman (1967). On the concept of normal appearances, see Goffman (1971).
37 Civil inattention is discussed in Goffman (1963a, pp. 83–8).
38 Role distance is discussed most explicitly in Goffman (1961b).
39 For more on virtual versus authentic selves or identities, see Goffman (1963b, pp. 2–40).
40 An abridged version of this example of role distance was previously reported in Chriss (1999c).
41 A number of critics (see, e.g., Gouldner 1970; Habermas 1984; Wilshire 1982; Young 1990) have accused Goffman of having an overly cynical view of human behavior, one that amounts to a "con man" theory of everyday life. For a summary of these and other criticisms, see Chriss (1999c, 2003).
42 For the concept of fabricated frames, see Goffman (1974). For a brilliant discussion of secrecy, see Goffman (1959, pp. 141–66).

CHAPTER 4   MEDICAL CONTROL

1 The story of Cartwright and his drapetomania diagnosis is summarized in Armstrong (2003).
2 Conrad and Schneider (1980, p. 242).
3 See Fox (1959).
4 For more on the notion of normalizing discourses, see Foucault (1978).
5 Williams and Arrigo (2006, p. 6).
6 Foucault (1977).
7 Ellwood (1912, pp. 356–7).
8 See, e.g., Foucault (1965, 1973), Ward (2002), and Wingerter (2003).
9 Zola (1972, p. 487).
10 Weisheit and Klofas (1998, p. 198).
11 The term "hygienization" is from Somers (1995), while "public healthification" is from Meyer and Schwartz (2000).
12 This information is taken from the story "Singer Wilson Asked to Not Glamorize Chewing Tobacco," the *Plain Dealer*, Friday, August 26, 2005, p. A13.
13 See Adler and Adler (2006, p. 139).
14 See, e.g., Ballard and Elston (2005).
15 See Conrad and Schneider (1980, pp. 172–214), Conrad (1992), and Kutchins and Kirk (1997, pp. 55–99) for discussions of homosexuality in relation to both medicalization and demedicalization.
16 These recommendations of the APA nomenclature committee are quoted in Robertson (2004, p. 164).
17 For the concept of remedicalization, see Conrad and Angell (2004).
18 Ibid., p. 39.
19 See Starr (1982).
20 Chriss (1999a).
21 See Clarke et al. (2003).
22 See Moynihan and Cassels (2005).

23 Furedi (2006).

24 On the concept of disease mongering, see Moynihan et al. (2002).

25 See Warner (1984) for a discussion of the yellow plague of 1878–84.

26 Eskin (2002, pp. 6–7).

27 Short (2006, pp. 204–5).

28 See Cutler and Miller (2005).

29 On the issue of medical expansionism or imperialism, see Schissel (1997), Strong (1979), and Williams (2001).

30 See Chriss (1999a) and Illich (1976, p. 244).

31 For a case study of one such EAP, see Tucker (1999).

32 See, e.g., Chriss (2002).

33 For more on these issues, see Chriss (2002), Fishbein (1991), Menninger (1968), Raine (1993), and Skodal (1998).

34 For discussions of the psychotherapeutic ethos and its relation to the therapeutic state, see Foucault (1976), Furedi (2004a), Moskowitz (2001), Nolan (1998, 1999), Rose (2003), and White (1998).

35 Information on the Marv Albert incident is taken from a CNN report located at http://www.cnn.com/SHOWBIZ/TV/9807/16/marv.albert.

36 From "Sales Limps her Way to UConn Mark," the *Wichita Eagle*, Wednesday, February 25, 1998, p. 4c.

37 As Docheff and Conn (2004) explain, more recently some of the non-scoring policies have been implemented to keep increasingly aggressive parents and spectators from getting out of hand. Keeping the scoreboard blank means no angry parents, the pressure is taken off the kids to perform, and everyone walks away happy.

38 Chriss (1999a, pp. 5–6).

39 See Oliverio and Lauderdale (1996).

40 The innovator of therapeutic jurisprudence is David Wexler, a professor of law and psychology at the University of Arizona. For several key readings in therapeutic jurisprudence, see Wexler and Winick (1996) and Winick and Wexler (2003).

41 Chriss (2002, pp. 205–6).

42 This example is taken, with modifications, from Hora et al. (1999).

43 For an excellent discussion of the growth of emotionalism in the criminal law, see Karstedt (2002).

44 See Schram (2000, p. 88).

45 See, e.g., Modell and Haggerty (1991).

46 Furedi (2004b, p. 20).

47 The National Center for PTSD's psychological first aid manual, as well as other disaster handouts and information, is available at http://www.ncptsd.va.gov/pfa/PFA.html.

48 Furedi (2004b, p. 21).

49 See Riska (2003).

50 Ibid., p. 74.

51 Ibid., p. 72.

52 Conrad and Schneider (1980, p. 248).

53 Illich (1976).

54 Schneiderman (2003, p. 191).

55 This and some of the other points to be discussed pertaining to the dark side of medicalization are taken from Conrad and Schneider (1980, pp. 248–60).

56 See Toby (1998).

57 For more on the abuse excuse, see Dershowitz (1994).

58 The classic statement on this problem is found in Scheff (1966). For later discussions see Brown (1987) and Kirk and Kutchins (1992). For application of the Type II error to the specific problem of depression, see Dworkin (2001).

59 On this point see Coreil et al. (2001, p. 176).

60 For more on the typical set of pattern variables associated with the role performance of professionals, see Parsons (1951).
61 Conrad and Schneider (1980, p. 249).
62 For a discussion of the problem of distorted communication in modern society,
see Habermas (1984, 1987).
63 Conrad and Schneider (1980, p. 251).
64 See Armstrong (2003).
65 There are the occasional scientific treatments of crime and deviance that still take
evil seriously. See for example Katz (1988).
66 This information was found at the website http://www.crimelibrary.com/news/
ap/08052/2002_btk_starts_sentence.html.

CHAPTER 5   LEGAL CONTROL

1 This information was found on the Bureau of Justice Statistics website,
http://www.ojp.usdoj.gov/bjs/eande.htm.
2 For information on medieval England and the later history of the criminal justice
system in England and the United States, I am drawing primarily from Johnson
and Wolfe (1996).
3 As Müller (2005) reports, the hue and cry was used not only against perpetrators,
but often by victims as well.
4 For more on collective responsibility, the frankpledge system, and related
systems of personal pledging that appeared in medieval England, see Feinberg
(1968), Pimsler (1977), and Postles (1996).
5 McIntosh (1998, pp. 2–45).
6 Ibid., pp. 54–107.
7 See Warden (1978).
8 Siebert (1990, p. 8).
9 Ibid., p. 12.
10 Ibid., p. 21.
11 This section of the discussion of colonial America draws from Walker (1980,
pp. 11–34).
12 Ibid., pp. 14–15.
13 See Friedman (1993, pp. 62–5).
14 Ibid., pp. 20–7.
15 For useful discussions of the Enlightenment as it relates to political, legal, and
social changes beginning in the eighteenth century, see Lasch (1991), Meyer
(1976), and Scott (1998).
16 Garland (1997, p. 24).
17 For a summary of Beccaria's thought, see Maestro (1973).
18 Cooper (1981, p. 678).
19 Sutherland and Cressey (1955, p. 274).
20 These points are summarized in Cooper (1976, pp. 78–80).
21 For an informative discussion of the history and ultimate passage of the
Penitentiary Act, see Devereaux (1999).
22 Rothman (2002b, p. 57).
23 Reid (1997).
24 Grimsted (1972, p. 372).
25 Broeker (1961).
26 Ibid., p. 372.
27 See Blomberg and Lucken (2000, pp. 48–61).
28 For a detailed exposition of this argument, see Rothman (2002b).
29 Monkonnen (1983, p. 126).
30 For this discussion of the three eras of policing I draw from Bittner (2003) and
Kelling and Moore (1988).
31 These examples are taken from the community policing program of Cleveland,
Ohio.

32 This is taken from a document titled "New Community Policing Operating Model for Dayton Police," p. 2, located at http://www.ci.dayton.oh.us/download/ cope2.pdf.
33 Lee (2001).
34 Rose and Clear (2004, p. 232).
35 See Cohen (1985) for a useful treatment of net-widening.
36 Reiman (1996, p. 165).
37 See Shelden (2001).
38 Blume et al. (2004, p. 167).
39 See, e.g., Hagan et al. (1979).
40 See Chesney-Lind (1997).
41 Foucault (1977, p. 204).
42 Ibid., p. 205.
43 Ibid., p. 298.
44 Garland (1999).
45 For useful discussions of the goals of punishment, see Ashworth (1997) and Nolan (2001, pp. 156–64).
46 Garland (1991, p. 158).
47 For more on the "family crisis" thesis and its implications for informal social control, see Chriss (1999b), Garland (2001, pp. 82–4), Liska (1997), Meier (1982), and van Krieken (1986).

CHAPTER 6 INFORMAL CONTROL: THE URBAN UNDERCLASS, HOUSING SEGREGATION, AND THE CODE OF THE STREET

1 This section's discussion of the shifting bases of informal social control over the life course is informed by Sampson and Laub (1993, pp. 17–23).
2 Wang et al. (2005, pp. 307–9).
3 Durkheim (1984, p. 238).
4 Thomson (2005, p. 422).
5 See Simmel (1950).
6 Musolf (2003).
7 Reiss (1951, p. 197).
8 Ibid., p. 198.
9 Ibid., p. 200.
10 See Wiatrowski et al. (1981).
11 This summary of Hobbes's thought is provided by Ellwood (1938, pp. 116–27).
12 Durkheim (1951).
13 Hirschi (1969, p. 16). The quote is from Durkheim (1951, p. 209).
14 See especially Parsons (1951).
15 Hirschi (1969, p. 30).
16 Ibid., p. 23.
17 Ibid., p. 26.
18 Ibid., p. 20.
19 Ibid., pp. 83–109.
20 Ibid., p. 83.
21 Ibid., p. 92.
22 Ibid., p. 94.
23 See Simons et al. (2004).
24 Gottfredson and Hirschi (1990).
25 See, e.g., Taylor (2001).
26 Hirschi (2004, p. 540).
27 Hirschi and Gottfredson (1983).
28 Hirschi (2004, p. 541).
29 See, for example, Geis (2000) and Taylor (2001).
30 Gottfredson and Hirschi (1990, p. 89).
31 The research I am referring to here is the study by Unnever et al. (2006).
32 Portes (1998, p. 6).

33 Putnam (2000, p. 19).
34 Putnam (1995, p. 66).
35 See "Public Giving Government, Business Lower Marks," AP news story from October 25, 2005, available at www.yahoo.com.
36 Putnam (1995, p. 71).
37 Wilson and Aponte (1985, p. 239).
38 Ibid., p. 247.
39 Cohen (1998, p. 224).
40 See, e.g., Boxill (1991), Crowther (2000, p. 151), and Heisler (1991).
41 Marks (1991, p. 455).
42 This is the argument of Wilson (1987). Since 1991 Wilson has used the term "ghetto poor" instead of the underclass.
43 Wilson (1991, p. 594).
44 See Greene (1991, p. 240).
45 Massey and Lundy (2001).
46 This sort of "linguistic profiling" has also been shown to operate within the housing insurance industry. For a summary, see Squires and Chadwick (2006).
47 See Anderson (1994, 1999).
48 Anderson (1999, p. 33).
49 See Parsons (1967).
50 Ibid., p. 342.
51 See Peterson and Krivo (2005) and Weiss and Reid (2005).
52 The following discussion is based on Anderson's (1999, pp. 66–106) chapter 2, titled "Campaigning for Respect."
53 Kubrin (2005).
54 Anderson (1999, pp. 35–65).
55 Silver and Miller (2004, p. 553).
56 On this point, see especially Halpern (2005, pp. 10–13).
57 Fagan and Tyler (2005, p. 219).
58 Ibid., p. 236.
59 See MacDonald and Stokes (2006) and Sampson and Bartusch (1998).
60 See Anderson (1999) and Rose and Clear (1998).
61 Rose and Clear (2004).
62 Ibid., p. 236.
63 Ibid., p. 242.
64 See Lynch and Sabol (2004).
65 Coleman (1990, p. 300).
66 For recent validation research on Anderson's theory, see Brezina et al. (2004).
67 See Bellair (1997).
68 Smith (2005, p. 3).
69 Ibid., p. 45.

CHAPTER 7   MEDICAL CONTROL: ADHD, SELECTIVE MUTISM, AND VIOLENCE AS A DISEASE

1 For representative works by these authors, see Foucault (1965), Goffman (1961a), Scheff (1966), and Szasz (1961, 1963). For an overview of the anti-psychiatry movement, see Chriss (1999a).
2 Skene (2002, p. 115).
3 For discussions of selective mutism, see Anstendig (1999), Gordon (2001), Kehle et al. (1998), Kumpulainen et al. (1998), Moldan (2005), and Rye and Ullman (1999).
4 See, e.g., Gordon (2001, p. 83).
5 American Psychiatric Association (2000, p. 127).
6 See Anstendig (1999, pp. 418–19).
7 For a general discussion of the medicalization of shyness beyond the specific case of selective mutism, see Scott (2006).
8 See Chriss (1999b, 2007).

9 See, e.g., Kehle et al. (1998), Kumpulainen et al. (1998), Moldan (2005), and Rye and Ullman (1999).
10 This is from Gordon (2001, p. 86). The work cited in the quotation is Kolvin and Fundudis (1981).
11 Anstendig (1999) and Moldan (2005).
12 This case is discussed in Rye and Ullman (1999, pp. 314–21).
13 Wakefield (2002).
14 Ibid., pp. 154–5.
15 Ibid., p. 161.
16 See Tuchman (1996).
17 Oliverio and Lauderdale (1996, p. 359).
18 Conrad (1975, p. 13).
19 Ibid., p. 14.
20 See Gureasko-Moore et al. (2005), Livingston (1997), Oliverio and Lauderdale (1996), and Searight and McLaren (1998).
21 For several recent studies, see Hjörne (2005) and Rafalovich (2005a, 2005b).
22 This argument has been made by Wakefield (2002, pp. 155–6).
23 See Armstrong (1995, pp. 26–7).
24 See, e.g., Beresh-Taylor (2000) and Gable and Van Acker (2000).
25 Weisheit and Klofas (1998, p. 198).
26 See, e.g., Guetzloe (1992) and McMahon (2000).
27 Dahlberg (1998).
28 Mercy et al. (2003, p. 256).
29 Dulmus and Hilarski (2002, p. 129).
30 Durch et al. (1997, p. 345).
31 Lutzker and Wyatt (2006, p. 3).
32 Prothrow-Stith (1993, p. 138).
33 Guetzloe (1992).
34 McMahon (2000).
35 Guetzloe (1992, p. 8).
36 Szasz (2000, p. 4).
37 See, e.g., Cantor (2000), Montgomery (2000), and Pollack (2000).
38 McDonald (2000, p. 4).
39 Gilligan (2000, p. 1802). See also Hartling and Luchetta (1999).
40 Lorion (2001, pp. 97–8).
41 Ibid., p. 103.
42 See Durch et al. (1997, pp. 345–57).
43 See Dulmus and Hilarski (2002).
44 Fagan and Davies (2004, p. 129).
45 Chriss (1999a, p. 22) and Kramer (1991).
46 Ingleby (1985).
47 See Epstein (1996) and Ward (2002).
48 Finn (2001, p. 167).
49 Willert and Willert (2000, p. 27).
50 This research is reported in Horwitz and Wakefield (2006).

CHAPTER 8   LEGAL CONTROL: RACIAL PROFILING, HATE CRIMES, AND THE GROWTH IN IMPRISONMENT

1 Skolnick (1966).
2 Ibid., pp. 217–18.
3 See Holdaway (1983), as cited in Norris et al. (1992, pp. 217–18).
4 These data are from a document titled "Crime in the United States," located at the Federal Bureau of Investigation and Department of Justice website (http://www.fbi.gov/ucr/cius_04).
5 These data are from the Bureau of Justice Statistics website (http://www.ojp.usdoj.gov/bjs/crimoff.htm#lifetime).

6 Davis (2003).

7 See, e.g., Bouza (2001), Eldredge (1998), Harris (2003), and Tonry (1996).

8 Batton and Kadleck (2004, p. 33).

9 Withrow (2004, p. 224).

10 Mac Donald (2003, p. 10).

11 See, e.g., Fredrickson and Siljander (2002) and Harris (2003).

12 See Holbert and Rose (2004, p. 7).

13 See Davis (2003, pp. 238–42) and Fredrickson and Siljander (2002).

14 The major portion of this legislation is the USA PATRIOT Act, which will be discussed more fully in the next chapter.

15 For discussions of these and other counterterrorism measures, see Deflem (2004) and Thomas (2004).

16 See, e.g., Newman (2003, p. 222) and Welch (2003, p. 332).

17 See, e.g., Norris et al. (1992).

18 For more on London's ring of steel, see Coaffee (2004).

19 Fekete (2004, p. 8).

20 Ibid., p. 9.

21 Ibid., pp. 9–10.

22 These incidents are reported in Levin and McDevitt (2002, pp. 5–6).

23 See Jenness and Grattet (2001).

24 Cogan (2002, p. 174).

25 Ibid.

26 These data are summarized in Perry (2001, pp. 252–3).

27 These are UCR data for the 2004 reporting period from the website http://www.fbi.gov/ucr/cius_04.

28 Levin (1999, p. 11).

29 See ibid., pp. 12–19.

30 See Blumstein (2003).

31 Tonry and Farrington (2005).

32 These data are from "Prisoners in 2004," a Bureau of Justice Statistics Bulletin available at http://www.ojp.usdoj.gov/bjs/pubalp2.htm#Prisoners.

33 Western et al. (2004, p. 1).

34 The term "imprisonment binge" to describe recent American penal philosophy and practice has been used by Austin et al. (2003).

35 Shelden (2004, p. 6).

36 For more on the drug treatment court, see Chriss (2002) and Nolan (2001).

37 Tonry (1999, p. 427).

38 See especially Caplow and Simon (1999).

39 Tonry (1999, p. 429).

40 These survey data were summarized in Study#6056, and the 2005 data were gathered via interviews of 1,013 Americans that took place between September 9 and 12, 2005, conducted by NBC News and the *Wall Street Journal.* The full document may be found at http://online.wsj.com/public/resources/documents/poll20050914.pdf.

41 For examples of critical analyses of three strikes laws, see Austin et al. (1999) and Schmertmann et al. (1998).

42 Garland (2001, p. 55).

43 Ibid., p. 56.

44 Ibid., p. 11. See also Garland (2003, pp. 64–9). Although the rehabilitative ideal is in deep decline, there are still aspects of the therapeutic ethos evident within the operation of the criminal justice system, especially for those crimes that many consider to be illnesses, such as drug use, excessive gambling, and other so-called addictions. For discussions of therapeutic justice as applied to the conceptualization and operation of drug courts, see Nolan (2001).

45 Garland (2001, p. 9).

CHAPTER 9   TERRORISM AND SOCIAL CONTROL

1 A transcript of this interview may be found at http://www.foxnews.com.
2 Goffman (1974, p. 83).
3 Gibbs (1989b, p. 330).
4 See Weigert (2003).
5 See, e.g., Giddens (1984) and Zaretsky (2002).
6 The implications of the new penology and actuarial justice (Feeley and Simon 1994) for the future of social control will be explored further in the last chapter.
7 Beck (2002).
8 For more on the rise of the surveillance society, referred to variously as the "security society" or the "maximum security society," see Cohen (1985), Fekete (2004), Horwitz (1990), Innes (2003), Lyon (2001), Marx (1995), and Staples (2000).
9 See, e.g., Baker (2002), Eland (2003), Hardin (2004), Mythen and Walklate (2006), and Welch (2003).
10 This discussion of controversial sections of the USA PATRIOT Act is informed by Krislov (2004) and Lithwick and Turner (2004).
11 Lithwick and Turner (2004, p. 100).
12 Crotty (2004, p. 199).
13 Deflem (2004, p. 80).
14 See Crowther (2000).
15 For a summary of these sunset provisions, see "USA PATRIOT Act Sunset: Provisions that Expire on December 31, 2005," CRS Report for Congress. Document available at www.fas.org/sgp/crs/intel/RL32186.pdf.
16 Information from "Bush Signs Tempered USA Patriot Act," *Plain Dealer*, March 10, 2006, p. A8.
17 Much of this section's discussion of Osama bin Laden and the rise of al-Qaeda is drawn from Coll (2004) and Sageman (2004, pp. 34–9).
18 This section of the discussion draws from Mamdani (2004, pp. 50–62).
19 This is not to imply that most terrorism occurring worldwide is Islamic or religion-based. Indeed, the world's leader in suicide terrorism is the Liberation Tigers of Tamil Eelam, a group that follows a secular ideology with Marxist-Leninist elements (Pape 2003, p. 343).
20 Mamdani (2004, p. 119).
21 Shay (2004, pp. 173–4).
22 Coll (2004, p. 411).
23 Ibid., p. 412.
24 Bin Laden (2006, pp. 6–7).
25 Pape (2003, p. 344).
26 Ibid.
27 Nunn (2004, p. 2). In Iraq, so-called improvised explosive devices (or IEDs) have been the leading killer of American troops. IEDs are roadside bombs hidden in various ways, such as buried just below the ground's surface or placed inside the carcass of a dead animal. (This information is taken from the story "IEDs Remain Top Killer of Troops in Iraq," located at the website http://news.yahoo.com/s/ap/20060310/ap_on_go_ca_st_pe/roadside_bombs_1).
28 "Bush Says 10 al-Qaida Plots Foiled since Sept. 11," *Plain Dealer*, October 7, 2005, p. A12.
29 Shay (2004, pp. 1–33).
30 Ibid., p. 257.
31 Black (1998, p. 4).
32 Ibid.
33 See Black (2004a, 2004b).
34 Black (2004b, p. 14).
35 Black (2000, p. 344).
36 Ibid., p. 347.

37 See Black (1995).
38 Black (1998, p. 159).
39 See Tucker (1999).
40 Black cites Senechal de la Roche (1996) as a significant influence on his own theory of terrorism.
41 Black (2004a, p. 11).
42 See Nunn (2004) and Pellicani (2004).
43 Baumgartner (1984) and Black (2004a, p. 13).
44 Rosenfeld (2004).
45 Zaretsky (2002, p. 98). It should be noted that, in citing Zaretsky here and referring to the "greed, arrogance, and impiety" of the United States, this does not necessarily reflect my own sentiments or position on the matter. Rather, this is an articulation of how some Islamic fundamentalists involved in terrorist activities typically view the United States and other "distant enemies." On this and other issues covered throughout the book I have attempted, following Max Weber, to remain as value-neutral as possible.
46 Boyns and Ballard (2004, p. 10).
47 Haggerty and Gazso (2005).
48 "Sewer District Wants Option of Armed Police," *Plain Dealer*, June 29, 2005, p. B1.
49 See Beck (2002) and Spence (2005).
50 Knorr Cetina (2005, p. 213).

CHAPTER 10   CONCLUSION

1 See Giddens (1998, pp. 87–8). This is also discussed in James and James (2001, p. 213).
2 The website is http://old.homeoffice.gov.uk/crime/antisocialbehaviour/-legislation/asbact.html.
3 This is found at http://old.homeoffice.gov.uk/crime/antisocialbehaviour/orders/index.html.
4 Brown (2004, p. 203).
5 See, e.g., James and James (2001).
6 See Jamieson (2005).
7 Commission of the European Communities (2000, p. 4). This was cited in Burney (2005, pp. 143–4).
8 See Wilson and Kelling (1982).
9 Faulkner (2003, p. 290).
10 See, e.g., Brown (2004), Burney (2005), Faulkner (2003).
11 Garland (2001, p. 124).
12 Buerger and Mazerolle (1999, p. 402).
13 See Feeley and Simon (1994) and Simon and Feeley (2003).
14 See Rothman (2002a [1980]).
15 Feeley and Simon (1994, p. 173).
16 This discussion is taken from Lianos (2000).
17 See Rose (2000).
18 For further discussions of social sorting through the use of automated socio-technical environments, see Lianos (2000), Lyon (2003, 2004), Marx (1995), and Staples (2000).
19 For more on system versus lifeworld, see Chriss (1995) and Habermas (1984).
20 See Chriss (1999b, p. 195), Crossley (2003), and Habermas (1984).
21 See Ward (1903, 1906).
22 See Levin (2000, p. 17).
23 As opposed to earlier times when police for the most part relied on coercive force whenever engaging citizens during routine patrol, under community policing officers presumably act with more sensitivity and compassion. To what extent this is actually occurring has been investigated in Meliala (2001).

24 See Somers (2005) for an excellent discussion of how the concept of social capital smuggles in aspects of responsibilization, such as the examples given in this paragraph.
25 For discussions of hybrid courts and similar undertakings which seek to combine compassion and coercion, see Chriss (2002), Dorf and Fagan (2003), and Nolan (2003). Squires (2006, p. 162) uses language similar to my own when he refers to the anti-social behaviour ordinances as "the blurring of care and control processes."
26 Bittner (1970).
27 See Klockars (1999) for more on the circumlocutions of community policing.
28 Herbert (2006, p. 139).

References

Adler, Patricia A. and Peter Adler. 2006. "The Deviance Society." *Deviant Behavior* 27 (2): 129–48.

Adler, Patricia A., Peter Adler, and Andrea Fontana. 1987. "Everyday Life Sociology." *Annual Review of Sociology* 13: 217–35.

Agger, Ben. 2002. *Postponing the Postmodern: Sociological Practices, Selves and Theories.* Boulder, CO: Rowman & Littlefield.

American Psychiatric Association. 2000. *Diagnostic and Statistical Manual of Mental Disorders*, 4th edn, text revision. Washington, DC: American Psychiatric Association.

Andersen, Hans Christian. 1959. *The Emperor's New Clothes.* New York: Harcourt.

Anderson, Elijah. 1994. "The Code of the Streets." *Atlantic Monthly* 273: 81–94.

Anderson, Elijah. 1999. *Code of the Street: Decency, Violence, and the Moral Life of the Inner City.* New York: Norton.

Anstendig, Karin D. 1999. "Is Selective Mutism an Anxiety Disorder? Rethinking its *DSM-IV* Classification." *Journal of Anxiety Disorders* 13 (4): 417–34.

Armitage, Rachel. 2002. *To CCTV or Not? A Review of Current Research into the Effectiveness of CCTV Systems in Reducing Crime.* London: Association for the Care and Resettlement of Offenders.

Armstrong, Thomas. 1995. *The Myth of the A.D.D. Child.* New York: Dutton.

Armstrong, Thomas. 2003. "Attention Deficit Hyperactivity Disorder in Children: One Consequence of the Rise of Technologies and Demise of Play." Pp. 161–75 in *All Work and No Play: How Education Reforms Are Harming our Preschoolers*, ed. S. Olfman. Westport, CT: Praeger.

Arnett, Jeffrey Jensen. 1995. "Broad and Narrow Socialization: The Family in the Context of a Cultural Theory." *Journal of Marriage and the Family* 57 (3): 617–28.

Asch, Solomon E. 1951. "Effects of Group Pressure upon the Modification and Distortion of Judgments." Pp. 177–90 in *Groups, Leadership and Men: Research in Human Relations*, ed. H. Guetzkow. Pittsburgh: Carnegie Press.

Asch, Solomon E. 1952. *Social Psychology.* Englewood Cliffs, NJ: Prentice-Hall.

Ashworth, Andrew. 1997. "Sentencing." Pp. 1095–135 in *Oxford Handbook of Criminology*, 2nd edn, ed. M. Maguire, R. Morgan, and R. Reiner. Oxford: Oxford University Press.

Austin, James, John Clark, Patricia Hardyman, and Henry D. Alan. 1999. "The Impact of 'Three Strikes and You're Out.' " *Punishment and Society* 1 (2): 131–62.

Austin, James, John Irwin, and Charles Kubrin. 2003. "It's About Time: America's Imprisonment Binge." Pp. 433–69 in *Punishment and Social Control*, enlarged 2nd edn, ed. T. G. Blomberg and S. Cohen. New York: Aldine de Gruyter.

Back, Kurt W. 1981. "Small Groups." Pp. 320–43 in *Social Psychology: Sociological Perspectives*, ed. M. Rosenberg and R. H. Turner. New York: Basic Books.

Baker, Nancy V. 2002. "*The Law*: The Impact of Antiterrorism Policies on Separation of Powers: Assessing John Ashcroft's Role." *Presidential Studies Quarterly* 32 (4): 765–78.

Ballard, Karen and Mary Ann Elston. 2005. "Medicalisation: A Multi-dimensional Concept." *Social Theory and Health* 3 (3): 228–41.

Batton, Candice and Colleen Kadleck. 2004. "Theoretical and Methodological Issues in Racial Profiling Research." *Police Quarterly* 7 (1): 30–64.

Baumgartner, Mary P. 1984. "Social Control from Below." Pp. 303–45 in *Toward a General Theory of Social Control*, vol. 1: *Fundamentals*, ed. D. Black. Orlando: Academic Press.

Beck, Ulrich. 2002. "The Terrorist Threat: World Risk Society Revisited." *Theory, Culture and Society* 19 (4): 39–55.

Bellair, Paul E. 1997. "Social Interaction and Community Crime: Examining the Importance of Neighbor Networks." *Criminology* 35 (4): 677–703.

Beniger, James R. 1986. *The Control Revolution: Technological and Economic Origins of the Information Society.* Cambridge, MA: Harvard University Press.

Beresh-Taylor, Laura. 2000. "Preventing Violence in Ohio's Schools." *Akron Law Review* 33 (2): 311–49.

Best, Joel. 1999. *Random Violence: How We Talk about New Crimes and New Victims.* Berkeley: University of California Press.

bin Laden, Osama. 2006. "In his Own Words: Excerpts from Osama bin Laden's Messages." Pp. 1–8 in *Current Perspectives: Readings from InfoTrac College Edition: Terrorism and Homeland Security*, ed. D. K. Gupta. Belmont, CA: Wadsworth.

Bittner, Egon. 1970. *The Functions of the Police in Modern Society.* Chevy Chase, MD: National Institute of Mental Health.

Bittner, Egon. 2003. "Staffing and Training Problem-Oriented Police." Pp. 151–8 in *Punishment and Social Control*, 2nd edn, ed. T. G. Blomberg and S. Cohen. Hawthorne, NY: Aldine de Grutyer.

Black, Donald. 1983. "Crime as Social Control." *American Sociological Review* 48 (1): 34–45.

Black, Donald. 1995. "The Epistemology of Pure Sociology." *Law and Social Inquiry* 20: 829–70.

Black, Donald. 1998. *The Social Structure of Right and Wrong*, rev. edn San Diego: Academic Press.

Black, Donald. 2000. "Dreams of Pure Sociology." *Sociological Theory* 18 (3): 343–67.

Black, Donald. 2004a. "Terrorism as Social Control." Pp. 9–18 in *Terrorism and Counter-Terrorism: Criminological Perspectives*, ed. M. Deflem. Amsterdam: Elsevier.

Black, Donald. 2004b. "The Geometry of Terrorism." *Sociological Theory* 22 (1): 14–25.

Blomberg, Thomas G. and Karol Lucken. 2000. *American Penology: A History of Control.* Hawthorne, NY: Aldine de Gruyter.

Blume, John, Theodore Eisenberg, and Martin T. Wells. 2004. "Explaining Death Row's Population and Racial Composition." *Journal of Empirical Legal Studies* 1 (1): 165–207.

Blumstein, Alfred. 2003. "Stability of Punishment: What Happened and What Next?" Pp. 255–69 in *Punishment and Social Control*, enlarged 2nd edn, ed. T. G. Blomberg and S. Cohen. New York: Aldine de Gruyter.

Bouza, Anthony V. 2001. *Police Unbound: Corruption, Abuse, and Heroism by the Boys in Blue.* Amherst, NY: Prometheus Books.

Boxill, Bernard R. 1991. "Wilson on the Truly Disadvantaged." *Ethics* 101 (3): 579–92.

Boyns, David and James David Ballard. 2004. "Developing a Sociological Theory for the Empirical Understanding of Terrorism." *American Sociologist* 35 (2): 5–25.

Brezina, Timothy, Robert Agnew, Francis T. Cullen, and John Paul Wright. 2004. "The Code of the Street: A Quantitative Assessment of Elijah Anderson's Subculture of Violence Thesis and its Contribution to Youth Violence Research." *Youth Violence and Juvenile Justice* 2 (4): 303–28.

Broeker, Galen. 1961. "Robert Peel and the Peace Preservation Force." *Journal of Modern History* 33 (4): 363–73.

Brown, Alison P. 2004. "Anti-Social Behaviour, Crime Control and Social Control." *Howard Journal* 43 (2): 203–11.

Brown, Phil. 1987. "Diagnostic Conflict and Contradiction in Psychiatry." *Journal of Health and Social Behavior* 28 (1): 37–50.

Buerger, Michael E. and Lorraine Green Mazerolle. 1999. "Third-Party Policing: Theoretical Analysis of an Emerging Trend." Pp. 402–26 in *The Police and Society: Touchstone Readings*, 2nd. edn, ed. V. E. Kappeler. Prospect Heights, IL: Waveland Press.

Burney, Elizabeth. 2005. *Making People Behave: Anti-Social Behaviour, Politics and Policy.* Cullompton, Devon: Willan.

Cantor, Joanne. 2000. "Media Violence." *Journal of Adolescent Health* 27 (2): 30–4.

Caplow, Theodore and Jonathan Simon. 1999. "Understanding Prison Policy and Population Trends." Pp. 63–120 in *Prisons*, ed. M. Tonry and J. Petersilia, vol. 26, *Crime and Justice: A Review of Research*, ed. M. Tonry. Chicago, IL: University of Chicago Press.

Centola, Damon, Robb Willer, and Michael Macy. 2005. "The Emperor's Dilemma: A Computational Model of Self-Enforcing Norms." *American Journal of Sociology* 110 (4): 1009–40.

Chao, Georgia T., Anne M. O'Leary-Kelly, Samantha Wolf, Howard J. Klein, and Philip D. Gardner. 1994. "Organizational Socialization: Its Content and Consequences." *Journal of Applied Psychology* 79 (5): 730–43.

Chesney-Lind, Meda. 1997. *The Female Offender: Girls, Women, and Crime.* Thousand Oaks, CA: Sage.

Chriss, James J. 1995. "Habermas, Goffman, and Communicative Action: Implications for Professional Practice." *American Sociological Review* 60 (4): 545–65.

Chriss, James J. 1999a. "Introduction." Pp. 1–29 in *Counseling and the Therapeutic State*, ed. J. J. Chriss. New York: Aldine de Gruyter.

Chriss, James J. 1999b. "The Family under Siege." Pp. 187–98 in *Counseling and the Therapeutic State*, ed. J. J. Chriss. New York: Aldine de Gruyter.

Chriss, James J. 1999c. "Role Distance and the Negational Self." Pp. 64–80 in *Goffman and Social Organization*, ed. by G. W. H. Smith. London: Routledge.

Chriss, James J. 2002. "The Drug Court Movement: An Analysis of Tacit Assumptions." Pp. 189–213 in *Drug Courts in Theory and in Practice*, ed. J. L. Nolan, Jr. New York: Aldine de Gruyter.

Chriss, James J. 2003. "Goffman as Microfunctionalist." Pp. 181–96 in *Goffman's Legacy*, ed. A. J. Treviño. Lanham, MD: Rowman & Littlefield.

Chriss, James J. 2004. "The Perils of Risk Assessment." *Society* 41 (4): 52–6.

Chriss, James J. 2007. "Preface: Issues in the Juvenile Justice System." Pp. vii–xii in *Current Perspectives – Readings from InfoTrac College Edition: Juvenile Justice*, ed. J. J. Chriss. Belmont, CA: Wadsworth.

Clarke, Adele E., Laura Mamo, Jennifer R. Fishman, Janet K. Shim, and Jennifer Ruth Fosket. 2003. "Biomedicalization: Technoscientific Transformations of Health, Illness, and U.S. Biomedicine." *American Sociological Review* 68 (2): 161–94.

Clinton, Hillary Rodham. 1995. *It Takes a Village and Other Lessons Children Teach Us.* New York: Simon & Schuster.

Coaffee, Jon. 2004. "Recasting the 'Ring of Steel': Designing Out Terrorism in the City of London?" Pp. 276–96 in *Cities, War, and Terrorism: Towards an Urban Geopolitics*, ed. S. Graham. Oxford: Blackwell.

Cogan, Jeanine C. 2002. "Hate Crime as a Crime Category Worthy of Policy Attention." *American Behavioral Scientist* 46 (1): 173–85.

Cohen, Philip N. 1998. "Black Concentration Effects on Black–White and Gender Inequality: Multilevel Analysis for U.S. Metropolitan Areas." *Social Forces* 77 (1): 207–29.

Cohen, Stanley. 1985. *Visions of Social Control: Crime, Punishment and Classification*. Cambridge: Polity.

Coleman, James S. 1990. *Foundations of Social Theory*. Cambridge, MA: Belknap Press.

Coll, Steve. 2004. *Ghost Wars: The Secret History of the CIA, Afghanistan, and bin Laden, from the Soviet Invasion to September 10, 2001*. New York: Penguin.

Commission of the European Communities. 2000. *The Prevention of Crime in the European Union: Reflection on Common Guidelines and Proposals for Community Financial Support*. COM/2000/0786.

Conrad, Peter. 1975. "The Discovery of Hyperkinesis: Notes on the Medicalization of Deviant Behavior." *Social Problems* 23 (1): 12–21.

Conrad, Peter. 1992. "Medicalization and Social Control." *Annual Review of Sociology* 18: 209–32.

Conrad, Peter and Alison Angell. 2004. "Homosexuality and Remedicalization." *Society* 41 (5): 32–9.

Conrad, Peter and Joseph W. Schneider. 1980. *Deviance and Medicalization: From Badness to Sickness*. St Louis: C. V. Mosby.

Cooper, Robert Alan. 1976. "Ideas and their Execution: English Prison Reform." *Eighteenth-Century Studies* 10 (1): 73–93.

Cooper, Robert Alan. 1981. "Jeremy Bentham, Elizabeth Fry, and English Prison Reform." *Journal of the History of Ideas* 42 (4): 675–90.

Coreil, Jeannine, Carol A. Bryant, and J. Neil Henderson. 2001. *Social and Behavioral Foundations of Public Health*. Thousand Oaks, CA: Sage.

Corrigan, Philip and Derek Sayer. 1985. *The Great Arch: English State Formation as Cultural Revolution*. Oxford: Blackwell.

Crossley, Nick. 2003. "Even Newer Social Movements? Anti-Corporate Protests, Capitalist Crises and the Remoralization of Society." *Organization* 10 (2): 287–305.

Crotty, William. 2004. "On the Home Front: Institutional Mobilization to Fight the Threat of International Terrorism." Pp. 191–234 in *The Politics of Terror: The U.S. Response to 9/11*, ed. W. Crotty. Boston: Northeastern University Press.

Crowther, Chris. 2000. "Thinking about the 'Underclass': Towards a Political Economy of Policing." *Theoretical Criminology* 4 (2): 149–67.

Cutler, David and Grant Miller. 2005. "The Role of Public Health Improvements in Health Advances: The Twentieth-Century United States." *Demography* 42 (1): 1–22.

Dahlberg, Linda L. 1998. "Youth Violence in the United States: Major Trends, Risk Factors, and Prevention Approaches." *American Journal of Preventive Medicine* 14 (4): 259–72.

Davis, Angela J. 2003. "Race, Cops, and Traffic Stops." Pp. 233–50 in *Crime Control and Social Justice: The Delicate Balance*, ed. D. F. Hawkins, S. L. Myers, Jr., and R. N. Stone. Westport, CT: Greenwood Press.

Deflem, Mathieu. 2004. "Social Control and the Policing of Terrorism: Foundations for a Sociology of Counterterrorism." *American Sociologist* 35 (2): 75–92.

Dershowitz, Alan. 1994. *The Abuse Excuse and Other Cop-Outs, Sob Stories and Evasions of Responsibility*. Boston: Little, Brown.

Devereaux, Simon. 1999. "The Making of the Penitentiary Act, 1775–1779." *Historical Journal* 42 (2): 405–33.

Ditton, Jason. 1979. *Controlology: Beyond the New Criminology*. London: Macmillan.

Docheff, Dennis M. and James H. Conn. 2004. "It's No Longer a Spectator Sport: Eight Ways to Get Involved and Help Fight Parental Violence in Youth Sports." *Parks and Recreation* 39 (3): 62–70.

Dorf, Michael C. and Jeffrey A. Fagan. 2003. "Problem-Solving Courts: From Innovation to Institutionalization." *American Criminal Law Review* 40: 1501–11.

Dulmus, Catherine N. and Carolyn Hilarski. 2002. "Children and Adolescents Exposed to Community Violence." Pp. 129–47 in *Handbook of Violence*, ed. L. A. Rapp-Paglicci, A. R. Roberts, and J. S. Wodarski. New York: Wiley.

Durch, J. S., L. A. Bailey, and M. A. Stoto (eds) 1997. *Improving Health in the Community*. Washington, DC: National Academy Press.

Durkheim, Emile. 1951 [1897]. *Suicide*, trans. J. Spaulding and G. Simpson. Glencoe, IL: Free Press.

Durkheim, Emile. 1984 [1893]. *The Division of Labor in Society*, trans. W. D. Halls. New York: Free Press.

Dworkin, Ronald E. 2001. "The Medicalization of Unhappiness." *Public Interest* 144: 85–99.

Eisenstadt, S. M. 1954. "Reference Group Behavior and Social Integration: An Explorative Study." *American Sociological Review* 19 (2): 175–85.

Eland, Ivan. 2003. "Bush's War and the State of Civil Liberties." *Mediterranean Quarterly* 14 (4): 158–75.

Eldredge, Dirk C. 1998. *Ending the War on Drugs: A Solution for America*. Bridgehampton, NY: Bridge Works Publishing.

Elliott, Delbert S., Beatrix A. Hamburg, and Kirk R. Williams (eds) 1998. *Violence in American Schools: A New Perspective*. Cambridge: Cambridge University Press.

Ellwood, Charles A. 1912. *Sociology in its Psychological Aspects*. New York: Appleton.

Ellwood, Charles A. 1925. *The Psychology of Human Society: An Introduction to Sociological Theory*. New York: Appleton.

Ellwood, Charles A. 1938. *A History of Social Philosophy*. New York: Prentice-Hall.

Epstein, Joyce L. 1996. "New Connections for Sociology and Education: Contributing to School Reform." *Sociology of Education* (extra issue): 6–23.

Eskin, Frada. 2002. "Public Health Medicine: The Constant Dilemma." *Journal of Public Health Medicine* 24 (1): 6–10.

Fagan, Jeffrey and Garth Davies. 2004. "The Natural History of Neighborhood Violence." *Journal of Contemporary Criminal Justice* 20 (2): 127–47.

Fagan, Jeffrey and Tom R. Tyler. 2005. "Legal Socialization of Children and Adolescents." *Social Justice Research* 18 (3): 217–42.

Farrington, David P. and Darrick Jolliffe. 2005. "Crime and Justice in England and Wales, 1981–1999." Pp. 41–81 in *Crime and Punishment in Western Countries, 1980–1999*, ed. M. Tonry and D. P. Farrington. Chicago: University of Chicago Press.

Faulkner, David. 2003. "Taking Citizenship Seriously: Social Capital and Criminal Justice in a Changing World." *Criminal Justice* 3 (3): 287–315.

Feeley, Malcolm M. and Jonathan Simon. 1994. "Actuarial Justice: The Emerging New Criminal Law." Pp. 173–201 in *The Futures of Criminology*, ed. D. Nelken. London: Sage.

Feinberg, Joel. 1968. "Collective Responsibility." *Journal of Philosophy* 65 (21): 674–88.

Fekete, Liz. 2004. "Anti-Muslim Racism and the European Security State." *Race and Class* 46 (1): 3–29.

Finn, Janet L. 2001. "Text and Turbulence: Representing Adolescence as Pathology in the Human Services." *Childhood* 8: 167–91.

Fishbein, Diana H. 1991. "Medicalizing the Drug War." *Behavioral Sciences and the Law* 9: 323–44.

Foucault, Michel. 1965. *Madness and Civilization*, trans. R. Howard. New York: Pantheon.

Foucault, Michel. 1973. *The Birth of the Clinic: An Archaeology of Medical Perception*, trans. A. M. Sheridan Smith. London: Tavistock.

Foucault, Michel. 1976. *Mental Illness and Psychology*. New York: Harper & Row.

Foucault, Michel. 1977. *Discipline and Punish: The Birth of the Prison*, trans. A. Sheridan. New York: Vintage Books.

Foucault, Michel. 1978. *The History of Sexuality*, trans. R. Hurley. New York: Pantheon.

Fox, Renée C. 1959. *Experiment Perilous: Physicians and Patients Facing the Unknown*. Glencoe, IL: Free Press.

Fredrickson, Darin D. and Raymond P. Siljander. 2002. *Racial Profiling: Eliminating the Confusion between Racial and Criminal Profiling and Clarifying What Constitutes Unfair Discrimination and Persecution*. Springfield, IL: Charles C. Thomas.

Freud, Sigmund. 1927. *The Ego and the Id*, trans. J. Riviere. London: Hogarth Press.

Friedman, Lawrence M. 1993. *Crime and Punishment in American History*. New York: Basic Books.

Furedi, Frank. 2004a. *Therapy Culture: Cultivating Vulnerability in an Uncertain Age*. London: Routledge.

Furedi, Frank. 2004b. "The Silent Ascendancy of Therapeutic Culture in Britain." Pp. 19–50 in *Therapeutic Culture: Triumph and Defeat*, ed. J. B. Imber. New Brunswick, NJ: Transaction.

Furedi, Frank. 2006. "The End of Professional Dominance." *Society* 43 (6): 14–18.

Gable, Robert A. and Richard Van Acker. 2000. "The Challenge to Make Schools Safe: Preparing Education Personnel to Curb Student Aggression and Violence." *Teacher Educator* 35 (3): 1–18.

Garland, David. 1991. "Sociological Perspectives on Punishment." Pp. 115–65 in *Crime and Justice: A Review of Research*, vol. 14, ed. M. Tonry. Chicago: University of Chicago Press.

Garland, David. 1997. "Of Crimes and Criminals: The Development of Criminology in Britain." Pp. 11–56 in *Oxford Handbook of Criminology*, 2nd edn, ed. M. Maguire, R. Morgan, and R. Reiner. Oxford: Oxford University Press.

Garland, David. 1999. " 'Governmentality' and the Problem of Crime." Pp. 15–43 in *Governable Places: Readings on Governmentality and Crime Control*. ed. R. Smandych. Aldershot: Ashgate.

Garland, David. 2001. *The Culture of Control: Crime and Social Order in Contemporary Society*. Chicago: University of Chicago Press.

Garland, David. 2003. "Penal Modernism and Postmodernism." Pp. 45–73 in *Punishment and Social Control*, enlarged 2nd edn, ed. T. G. Blomberg and S. Cohen. New York: Aldine de Gruyter.

Geis, Gilbert. 2000. "On the Absence of Self-Control as the Basis for a General Theory of Crime." *Theoretical Criminology* 4 (1): 35–53.

Gibbs, Jack P. 1989a. *Control: Sociology's Central Notion*. Urbana: University of Illinois Press.

Gibbs, Jack P. 1989b. "Conceptualization of Terrorism." *American Sociological Review* 54 (3): 329–40.

Gibbs, Jack P. 1994. *A Theory about Control*. Boulder, CO: Westview Press.

Giddens, Anthony. 1984. *The Constitution of Society: Outline of the Theory of Structuration*. Cambridge: Polity.

Giddens, Anthony. 1998. *The Third Way: The Renewal of Social Democracy*. Cambridge: Polity.

Giddings, Franklin H. 1896. *Principles of Sociology*. New York: Macmillan.

Giddings, Franklin H. 1899. *The Elements of Sociology*. New York: Macmillan.

Giddings, Franklin H. 1909. "Social Self-Control." *Political Science Quarterly* 24: 569–88.

Gilligan, James. 2000. "Violence In Public Health and Preventive Medicine." *The Lancet* 355: 1802–4.

Goffman, Erving. 1959. *The Presentation of Self in Everyday Life*. New York: Anchor Doubleday.

Goffman, Erving. 1961a. *Asylums: Essays on the Social Situation of Mental Patients and Other Inmates*. Garden City, NY: Anchor.

Goffman, Erving. 1961b. *Encounters: Two Studies in the Sociology of Interaction*. Indianapolis: Bobbs-Merrill.

Goffman, Erving. 1963a. *Behavior in Public Places: Notes on the Social Organization of Gatherings*. New York: Free Press.

Goffman, Erving. 1963b. *Stigma: Notes on the Management of Spoiled Identity*. Englewood Cliffs, NJ: Prentice-Hall.

Goffman, Erving. 1967. *Interaction Ritual: Essays on Face-to-Face Behavior*. Chicago: Aldine.

Goffman, Erving. 1971. *Relations in Public: Microstudies of the Public Order*. New York: Harper Torchbooks.

Goffman, Erving. 1974. *Frame Analysis: An Essay on the Organization of Experience*. Boston: Northeastern University Press.

Goffman, Erving. 1981. *Forms of Talk*. Philadelphia: University of Pennsylvania Press.

Goffman, Erving. 1983. "The Interaction Order." *American Sociological Review* 48: 1–17.

Gordon, Neil. 2001. "Mutism: Elective or Selective, and Acquired." *Brain and Development* 23: 83–7.

Gottfredson, Michael R. and Travis Hirschi. 1990. *A General Theory of Crime*. Stanford, CA: Stanford University Press.

Gouldner, Alvin W. 1970. *The Coming Crisis of Western Sociology*. New York: Basic Books.

Gouldner, Alvin W. 1975. "Sociology and the Everyday Life." Pp. 417–32 in *The Idea of Social Structure*, ed. L. A. Coser. New York: Harcourt Brace Jovanovich.

Gouldner, Alvin W. 1979. *The Future of Intellectuals and the Rise of the New Class*. New York: Seabury Press.

Granovetter, Mark. 1973. "The Strength of Weak Ties." *American Journal of Sociology* 78 (6): 1360–80.

Greene, Richard. 1991. "Poverty Concentration Measures and the Urban Underclass." *Economic Geography* 67 (3): 240–52.

Grimsted, David. 1972. "Rioting in its Jacksonian Setting." *American Historical Review* 77 (2): 361–97.

Grundy, Jane, Sharon Matthews, Belinda Bateman, Taraneh Dean, and Syed Hasan Arshad. 2002. "Rising Prevalence of Allergy to Peanut in Children: Data from 2 Sequential Cohorts." *Journal of Allergy and Clinical Immunology* 110 (5): 784–9.

Guetzloe, Eleanor. 1992. "Violent, Aggressive, and Antisocial Students: What Are We Going to Do with Them?" *Preventing School Failure* 36 (3): 4–9.

Gumplowicz, Ludwig. 1899. *The Outlines of Sociology*, trans. F. W. Moore. Philadelphia: American Academy of Political and Social Science.

Gureasko-Moore, David P., George J. DuPaul, and Thomas J. Power. 2005. "Stimulant Treatment for Attention-Deficit/Hyperactivity Disorder: Medication Monitoring Practices of School Psychologists." *School Psychology Review* 34 (2): 232–45.

Gurwitsch, Aron. 1979. *Human Encounters in the Social World*, trans. F. Kersten. Pittsburgh: Duquesne University Press.

Habermas, Jürgen. 1975. *Legitimation Crisis*, trans. T. McCarthy. Boston: Beacon Press.

Habermas, Jürgen. 1984. *Theory of Communicative Action*, vol. 1, trans. T. McCarthy. Boston: Beacon Press.

Habermas, Jürgen. 1987. *Theory of Communicative Action*, vol. 2, trans. T. McCarthy. Boston: Beacon Press.

Habermas, Jürgen. 1996. *Between Facts and Norms: Contributions to a Discourse Theory of Law and Democracy*, trans. W. Rehg. Cambridge, MA: MIT Press.

Hagan, John, John H. Simpson, and A. R. Gillis. 1979. "The Sexual Stratification of Social Control: A Gender-Based Perspective on Crime and Delinquency." *British Journal of Sociology* 30 (1): 25–38.

Haggerty, Kevin D. and Amber Gazso. 2005. "Seeing beyond the Ruins: Surveillance as a Response to Terrorist Threats." *Canadian Journal of Sociology* 30 (2): 169–87.

Halpern, David. 2005. *Social Capital.* Cambridge: Polity.

Hardin, Russell. 2004. "Civil Liberties in the Era of Mass Terrorism." *Journal of Ethics* 8 (1): 77–95.

Harp, Gillis J. 1995. *Positivist Republic: Auguste Comte and the Reconstruction of American Liberalism, 1865–1920.* University Park: Pennsylvania State University Press.

Harrington, Brooke and Gary Alan Fine. 2000. "Opening the 'Black Box': Small Groups and Twenty-First-Century Sociology." *Social Psychology Quarterly* 63 (4): 312–23.

Harrington, Brooke and Gary Alan Fine. 2006. "Where the Action Is: Small Groups and Recent Developments in Sociological Theory." *Small Group Research* 37 (1): 4–19.

Harris, David A. 2003. *Profiles in Injustice: Why Racial Profiling Cannot Work.* New York: New Press.

Harris, Judith R. 1998. *The Nurture Assumption.* New York: Free Press.

Hartling, Linda M. and Tracy Luchetta. 1999. "Humiliation: Assessing the Impact of Derision, Degradation, and Debasement." *Journal of Primary Prevention* 19 (4): 259–78.

Heckathorn, Douglas D. 1990. "Collective Sanctions and Compliance Norms: A Formal Theory of Group-Mediated Social Control." *American Sociological Review* 55: 366–84.

Heisler, Barbara Schmitter. 1991. "A Comparative Perspective on the Underclass: Questions of Urban Poverty, Race, and Citizenship." *Theory and Society* 20 (4): 455–83.

Herbert, Steve. 2006. *Citizens, Cops, and Power: Recognizing the Limits of Community.* Chicago: University of Chicago Press.

Herman-Kinney, Nancy J. 2003. "Deviance." Pp. 695–720 in *Handbook of Symbolic Interactionism*, ed. L. T. Reynolds and N. J. Herman-Kinney. Lanham, MD: Altamira Press.

Hervieu-Léger, Danièle. 1998. "The Transmission and Formation of Socioreligious Identities in Modernity: An Analytical Essay on the Trajectories of Identification." *International Sociology* 13 (2): 213–28.

Hillery, George A., Jr. 1968. *Communal Organizations: A Study of Local Societies.* Chicago: University of Chicago Press.

Hirschi, Travis. 1969. *Causes of Delinquency.* Berkeley: University of California Press.

Hirschi, Travis. 2004. "Self-Control and Crime." Pp. 537–52 in *Handbook of Self-Regulation: Research, Theory, and Applications*, ed. R. F. Baumeister and K. D. Vohs. New York: Guilford Press.

Hirschi, Travis and Michael R. Gottfredson. 1983. "Age and the Explanation of Crime." *American Journal of Sociology* 89: 552–84.

Hirschi, Travis and Michael R. Gottfredson. 2005. "Punishment of Children from the Perspective of Control Theory." Pp. 214–22 in *Corporal Punishment of Children in Theoretical Perspective*, ed. M. Donnelly and M. A. Straus. New Haven, CT: Yale University Press.

Hjörne, Eva. 2005. "Negotiating the 'Problem-Child' in School: Child Identity, Parenting and Institutional Agendas." *Qualitative Social Work* 4 (4): 489–507.

Holbert, Steve and Lisa Rose. 2004. *The Color of Guilt and Innocence: Racial Profiling and Police Practices in America.* San Ramon, CA: Page Marque Press.

Holdaway, Simon. 1983. *Inside the British Police: A Force at Work*. Oxford: Blackwell.

Hora, Peggy F., William G. Schma, and John T. A. Rosenthal. 1999. "Therapeutic Jurisprudence and the Drug Court Movement: Revolutionizing the Criminal Justice System's Response to Drug Abuse and Crime in America." *Notre Dame Law Review* 74 (2): 439–537.

Horne, Christine. 2001. "Sociological Perspectives on the Emergence of Norms." Pp. 3–34 in *Social Norms*, ed. M. Hechter and K. OPp. New York: Russell Sage Foundation.

Horwitz, Allan V. 1990. *The Logic of Social Control*. New York: Plenum Press.

Horwitz, Allan V. and Jerome C. Wakefield. 2006. "The Epidemic in Mental Illness: Clinical Fact or Survey Artifact?" *Contexts* 5 (1): 19–23.

Illich, Ivan. 1976. *Medical Nemesis: The Expropriation of Health*. New York: Random House.

Ingleby, D. 1985. "Professionals as Socializers: The 'Psy Complex.'" In *Research in Law, Deviance and Social Control*, ed. A. Scull and S. Spritzer. New York: JAI Press.

Innes, Martin. 2003. *Understanding Social Control: Deviance, Crime and Social Order*. Buckingham: Open University Press.

James, Adrian and Allison James. 2001. "Tightening the Net: Children, Community, and Control." *British Journal of Sociology* 52 (2): 211–28.

Jamieson, Janet. 2005. "New Labour, Youth Justice and the Question of 'Respect.'" *Youth Justice* 5 (3): 180–93.

Janowitz, Morris. 1975. "Sociological Theory and Social Control." *American Journal of Sociology* 81 (1): 82–108.

Jenness, Valerie and Ryken Grattet. 2001. *Making Hate a Crime: From Social Movement to Law Enforcement*. New York: Russell Sage Foundation.

Johnson, Herbert A. and Nancy Travis Wolfe. 1996. *History of Criminal Justice*. Cincinnati: Anderson.

Karstedt, Susanne. 2002. "Emotions and Criminal Justice." *Theoretical Criminology* 6 (3): 299–317.

Katovich, Michael A. 1996. "Cooperative Bases of Control: Toward an Interactionist Conceptualization." *Social Science Journal* 33 (3): 257–71.

Katz, Jack. 1988. *Seductions of Crime: Moral and Sensual Attraction in Doing Evil*. New York: Basic Books.

Kehle, Thomas J., Melissa R. Madaus, Victoria S. Baratta, and Melissa A. Bray. 1998. "Augmented Self-Modeling as a Treatment for Children with Selective Mutism." *Journal of School Psychology* 36 (3): 247–60.

Kelling, George L. and Mark H. Moore. 1988. "The Evolving Strategies of Policing," in *Perspectives on Policing*, no. 1. Washington, DC: National Institute of Justice.

Kirk, Stuart A. and Herb Kutchins. 1992. *The Selling of DSM: The Rhetoric of Science in Psychiatry*. New York: Aldine de Gruyter.

Kitts, James A. 2006. "Collective Action, Rival Incentives, and the Emergence of Antisocial Norms." *American Sociological Review* 71: 235–59.

Klockars, Carl B. 1999. "The Rhetoric of Community Policing." Pp. 427–45 in *The Police and Society*, 2nd edn, ed. V. E. Kappeler. Prospect Heights, IL: Waveland.

Knorr Cetina, Karin. 2005. "Complex Global Microstructures: The New Terrorist Societies." *Theory, Culture and Society* 22 (5): 213–34.

Kolvin, I., and T. Fundudis, 1981. "Elective Mute Children: Psychological Development and Background Factors." *Journal of Child Psychology and Psychiatry* 22: 219–32.

Kramer, Rita. 1991. *Ed School Follies: The Miseducation of America's Teachers*. New York: Free Press.

Krislov, Daniel. 2004. "Civil Liberties and the Judiciary in the Aftermath of 9/11." Pp. 134–59 in *The Politics of Terror: The U.S. Response to 9/11*, ed. W. Crotty. Boston: Northeastern University Press.

Kubrin, Charis E. 2005. "Gangstas, Thugs, and Hustlas: Identity and Code of the Street in Rap Music." *Social Problems* 52 (3): 360–78.

Kumpulainen, K., E. Rsnen, H. Raaska, and V. Somppi. 1998. "Selective Mutism among Second-Graders in Elementary School." *European Child and Adolescent Psychiatry* 7: 24–9.

Kutchins, Herb and Stuart A. Kirk. 1997. *Making Us Crazy. DSM: The Psychiatric Bible and the Creation of Mental Disorders.* New York: Free Press.

Lasch, Christopher. 1991. *The True and Only Heaven: Progress and its Critics.* New York: Norton.

Lee, Murray. 2001. "The Genesis of 'Fear of Crime.'" *Theoretical Criminology* 5 (4): 467–85.

L'Engle, Kelly Ladin, Jane D. Brown, and Kristin Kenneavy. 2006. "The Mass Media Are an Important Context for Adolescents' Sexual Behavior." *Journal of Adolescent Health* 38: 186–92.

Levin, Brian. 1999. "Hate Crimes: Worse by Definition." *Journal of Contemporary Criminal Justice* 15 (1): 6–21.

Levin, Jack and Jack McDevitt. 2002. *Hate Crimes Revisited: America's War on Those who Are Different.* Boulder, CO: Westview Press.

Levin, Miriam R. 2000. "Contexts of Control." Pp. 13–39 in *Cultures of Control*, ed. M. R. Levin. Amsterdam: Harwood.

Lianos, Michalis. 2000. "Dangerization and the End of Deviance." *British Journal of Criminology* 40: 261–78.

Liska, Allen E. 1997. "Modeling the Relationships between Macro Forms of Social Control." *Annual Review of Sociology* 23: 39–61.

Lithwick, Dahlia and Julia Turner. 2004. "A Guide to the PATRIOT Act." Pp. 94–103 in *Homeland Security*, ed. N. Smith and L. M. Messina. New York: H. W. Wilson.

Livingston, Jay. 1996. *Crime and Criminology*, 2nd edn. Upper Saddle River, NJ: Prentice-Hall.

Livingston, Ken. 1997. "Ritalin: Miracle Drug or Cop-Out?" *Public Interest* 127: 3–18.

Lloyd, A. H. 1901. "The Organic Theory of Society: Passing of the Contract Theory." *American Journal of Sociology* 6 (5): 577–601.

Lorion, Raymond P. 2001. "Exposure to Urban Violence: Shifting from an Individual to an Ecological Perspective." Pp. 97–113 in *Integrating Behavioral and Social Sciences with Public Health*, ed. N. Schneiderman, M. A. Speers, J. M. Silva, H. Tomes, and J. H. Gentry. Washington, DC: American Psychological Association.

Lutzker, John R. and Jennifer M. Wyatt. 2006. "Introduction." Pp. 3–15 in *Preventing Violence: Research and Evidence-Based Intervention Strategies*, ed. J. R. Lutzker. Washington, DC: American Psychological Association.

Lynch, James P. and William J. Sabol. 2004. "Effects of Incarceration on Informal Social Control in Communities." Pp. 135–64 in *Imprisoning America: The Social Effects of Mass Incarceration*, ed. M. Pattillo, D. Weiman, and B. Western. New York: Russell Sage Foundation.

Lyon, David. 2001. *Surveillance Society: Monitoring Everyday Life.* Buckingham: Open University Press.

Lyon, David. 2003. "Surveillance as Social Sorting: Computer Codes and Mobile Bodies." Pp. 13–30 in *Surveillance as Social Sorting: Privacy, Risk and Digital Discrimination*, ed. D. Lyon. London: Routledge.

Lyon, David. 2004. "Technology vs. 'Terrorism': Circuits of City Surveillance since September 11, 2001." Pp. 297–311 in *Cities, War, and Terrorism: Towards an Urban Geopolitics*, ed. S. Graham. Oxford: Blackwell.

Lyotard, Jean-François. 1984. *The Postmodern Condition: A Report on Knowledge*, trans. G. Bennington and B. Massumi. Minneapolis: University of Minnesota Press.

McDonald, David. 2000. "Violence as a Public Health Issue." *Trends and Issues in Crime and Criminal Justice* 163: 1–6.

Mac Donald, Heather. 2003. *Are Cops Racist?* Chicago: Ivan R. Dee.

MacDonald, John and Robert J. Stokes. 2006. "Race, Social Capital, and Trust in the Police." *Urban Affairs Review* 41 (3): 358–75.

McIntosh, Marjorie Keniston. 1998. *Controlling Misbehavior in England, 1370–1600*. Cambridge: Cambridge University Press.

MacIver, Robert M. and Charles Page. 1949. *Society*. New York: Rinehart.

McMahon, Pamela M. 2000. "The Public Health Approach to the Prevention of Sexual Violence." *Sexual Abuse* 12 (1): 27–36.

Macy, Michael W. 1993. "Backward-Looking Social Control." *American Sociological Review* 58: 819–36.

Maestro, Marcello. 1973. *Cesare Beccaria and the Origins of Penal Reform*. Philadelphia: Temple University Press.

Mamdani, Mahmood. 2004. *Good Muslim, Bad Muslim: America, the Cold War, and the Roots of Terror*. New York: Pantheon Books.

Marks, Carole. 1991. "The Urban Underclass." *Annual Review of Sociology* 17: 445–66.

Marx, Gary T. 1995. "The Engineering of Social Control: The Search for the Silver Bullet." Pp. 225–46 in *Crime and Inequality*, ed. J. Hagan and R. D. Peterson. Stanford, CA: Stanford University Press.

Massey, Douglas S. and Garvey Lundy. 2001. "Use of Black English and Racial Discrimination in Urban Housing Markets: New Methods and Findings." *Urban Affairs Review* 36 (4): 452–69.

Mead, George H. 1925. "The Genesis of the Self and Social Control." *International Journal of Ethics* 35 (3): 251–77.

Meier, Robert F. 1982. "Perspectives on the Concept of Social Control." *Annual Review of Sociology* 8: 35–55.

Meliala, Adrianus. 2001. "The Notion of Sensitivity in Policing." *International Journal of the Sociology of Law* 29: 99–111.

Melossi, Dario. 2004. "Theories of Social Control and the State between American and European Shores." Pp. 32–48 in *The Blackwell Companion to Criminology*, ed. C. Sumner. Oxford: Blackwell.

Menninger, Karl. 1968. *The Crime of Punishment*. New York: Viking.

Mercy, James A., Etienne G. Krug, Linda L. Dahlberg, and Anthony B. Zwi. 2003. "Violence and Health: The United States in a Global Perspective." *American Journal of Public Health* 92 (12): 256–61.

Meyer, D. H. 1976. "The Uniqueness of the American Enlightenment." *American Quarterly* 28 (2): 165–86.

Meyer, Ilan H. and S. Schwartz. 2000. "Social Issues as Public Health: Promise and Peril." *American Journal of Public Health* 90 (8): 1189–91.

Milgram, Stanley. 1963. "Behavioral Study of Obedience." *Journal of Abnormal and Social Psychology* 67: 371–8.

Milgram, Stanley. 1965. "Some Conditions of Obedience and Disobedience to Authority." *Human Relations* 18: 56–76.

Milgram, Stanley. 1974. *Obedience to Authority: An Experimental View*. New York: Harper & Row.

Modell, John and Timothy Haggerty. 1991. "The Social Impact of War." *Annual Review of Sociology* 17: 205–24.

Moldan, Marian B. 2005. "Selective Mutism and Self-Regulation." *Clinical Social Work Journal* 33 (3): 291–307.

Monkonnen, Eric H. 1983. "The Organized Response to Crime in Nineteenth- and Twentieth-Century America." *Journal of Interdisciplinary History* 14 (1): 113–28.

Montgomery, Kathryn. 2000. "Youth and Digital Media: A Policy Research Agenda." *Journal of Adolescent Health* 27 (2): 61–8.

Moskowitz, Eva S. 2001. *In Therapy We Trust: America's Obsession with Self Fulfillment.* Baltimore: Johns Hopkins University Press.

Moynihan, Ray and Alan Cassels. 2005. *Selling Sickness: How the World's Biggest Pharmaceutical Companies are Turning Us All into Patients.* New York: Nation Books.

Moynihan, Ray, Iona Heath, and David Henry. 2002. "Selling Sickness: The Pharmaceutical Industry and Disease Mongering." *British Medical Journal* 324 (13): 886–90.

Müller, Miriam. 2005. "Social Control and the Hue and Cry in Two Fourteenth-Century Villages." *Journal of Medieval History* 31: 29–53.

Musolf, Gil Richard. 2003. "The Chicago School." Pp. 91–117 in *Handbook of Symbolic Interactionism*, ed. L. T. Reynolds and N. J. Herman-Kinney. Lanham, MD: Altamira.

Mythen, Gabe and Sandra Walklate. 2006. "Criminology and Terrorism: Which Thesis? Risk Society or Governmentality?" *British Journal of Criminology* 46: 379–98.

Nadel, S. F. 1953. "Social Control and Self-Regulation." *Social Forces* 31 (3): 265–73.

Nas, Tevfik F., Albert C. Price, and Charles T. Weber. 1986. "A Policy-Oriented Theory of Corruption." *American Political Science Review* 80 (1): 107–19.

Newman, Deborah W. 2003. "September 11: A Societal Reaction Perspective." *Crime, Law and Social Change* 39: 219–31.

Nolan, James L., Jr. 1998. *The Therapeutic State: Justifying Government at Century's End.* New York: New York University Press.

Nolan, James L., Jr. 1999. "Acquiescence or Consensus? Consenting to Therapeutic Pedagogy." Pp. 107–29 in *Counseling and the Therapeutic State*, ed. J. J. Chriss. New York: Aldine de Gruyter.

Nolan, James L., Jr. 2001. *Reinventing Justice: The American Drug Court.* Princeton, NJ: Princeton University Press.

Nolan, James L., Jr. 2003. "Redefining Criminal Courts: Problem-Solving and the Meaning of Justice." *American Criminal Law Review* 40: 1541–65.

Norris, Clive, Nigel Fielding, Charles Kemp, and Jane Fielding. 1992. "Black and Blue: An Analysis of the Influence of Race on Being Stopped by the Police." *British Journal of Sociology* 43 (2): 207–24.

Novak, William J. 1999. "The Legal Origins of the Modern American State." *ABF Working Paper #9925.* Chicago: American Bar Foundation.

Nunn, Sam. 2004. "Thinking the Inevitable: Suicide Attacks in America and the Design of Effective Public Safety Policies." *Journal of Homeland Security and Emergency Management* 1 (4): 1–21.

Nye, F. Ivan. 1958. *Family Relationships and Deviant Behavior.* Westport, CT: Greenwood Press.

Oliverio, Annamarie and Pat Lauderdale. 1996. "Therapeutic States and Attention Deficits: Differential Cross-National Diagnostics and Treatments." *International Journal of Politics, Culture and Society* 10 (2): 355–73.

Pape, Robert A. 2003. "The Strategic Logic of Suicide Terrorism." *American Political Science Review* 97 (3): 343–61.

Parsons, Talcott. 1951. *The Social System.* Glencoe, IL: Free Press.

Parsons, Talcott. 1964. *Social Structure and Personality.* Glencoe, IL: Free Press.

Parsons, Talcott. 1967. "On the Concept of Political Power." Pp. 297–354 in Parsons, *Sociological Theory and Modern Society.* New York: Free Press.

Paternoster, Raymond and Ronet Bachman. 2001. "Control Theories of Crime." Pp. 73–80 in *Explaining Criminals and Crime*, ed. R. Paternoster and R. Bachman. Los Angeles: Roxbury.

Pellicani, Luciano. 2004. "Islamic Terrorism." *Telos* 129: 41–53.

Perry, Barbara. 2001. *In the Name of Hate: Understanding Hate Crimes*. New York: Routledge.

Peterson, Ruth D. and Lauren J. Krivo. 2005. "Macrostructural Analyses of Race, Ethnicity, and Violent Crime: Recent Lessons and New Directions for Research." *Annual Review of Sociology* 31: 331–56.

Phythian, Mark. 2005. "Intelligence, Policy-Making and the 7 July 2005 London Bombings." *Crime, Law and Social Change* 44: 361–85.

Pimsler, Martin. 1977. "Solidarity in the Medieval Village? The Evidence of Personal Pledging at Elton, Huntingdonshire." *Journal of British Studies* 17 (1): 1–11.

Pollack, William S. 2000. *Real Boys' Voices*. New York: Random House.

Portes, Alejandro. 1998. "Social Capital: Its Origins and Applications in Modern Sociology." *Annual Review of Sociology* 24: 1–24.

Postles, David. 1996. "Personal Pledging: Medieval 'Reciprocity' or 'Symbolic Capital'?" *Journal of Interdisciplinary History* 26 (3): 419–35.

Prothrow-Stith, Deborah. 1993. *Deadly Consequences*. New York: Harper Perennial.

Putnam, Robert D. 1995. "Bowling Alone: America's Declining Social Capital." *Journal of Democracy* 6 (1): 65–78.

Putnam, Robert D. 2000. *Bowling Alone: The Collapse and Revival of American Community*. New York: Simon & Schuster.

Rafalovich, Adam. 2005a. "Exploring Clinical Uncertainty in the Diagnosis and Treatment of Attention Deficit Hyperactivity Disorder." *Sociology of Health and Illness* 27 (3): 305–23.

Rafalovich, Adam. 2005b. "Relational Troubles and Semiofficial Suspicion: Educators and the Medicalization of 'Unruly' Children." *Symbolic Interaction* 28 (1): 25–46.

Rafter, Nicole. 2004. "The Unrepentant Horse-Slasher: Moral Insanity and the Origins of Criminological Thought." *Criminology* 42 (4): 979–1008.

Raine, Adrian. 1993. *The Psychopathology of Crime: Criminal Behavior as a Clinical Disorder*. San Diego: Academic Press.

Reid, John Phillip. 1997. *Policing the Elephant: Crime, Punishment, and Social Behavior on the Overland Trail*. San Marino, CA: Huntington Library.

Reiman, Jeffrey. 1996. *... And the Poor Get Prison: Economic Bias in American Criminal Justice*. Boston: Allyn & Bacon.

Reiss, Jr., Albert J. 1951. "Delinquency as the Failure of Personal and Social Controls." *American Sociological Review* 16 (2): 196–207.

Riska, Elianne. 2003. "Gendering the Medicalization Thesis." *Gender Perspectives on Health and Medicine: Key Issues. Advances in Gender Research* 7: 59–97.

Robertson, Phyllis K. 2004. "The Historical Effects of Depathologizing Homosexuality on the Practice of Counseling." *Family Journal* 12 (2): 163–9.

Rose, Dina R. and Todd R. Clear. 1998. "Incarceration, Social Capital, and Crime: Implications for Social Disorganization Theory." *Criminology* 36 (3): 441–79.

Rose, Dina R. and Todd R. Clear. 2004. "Who Doesn't Know Someone in Jail? The Impact of Exposure to Prison on Attitudes toward Formal and Informal Controls." *Prison Journal* 84 (2): 228–47.

Rose, Nikolas. 2000. "Government and Control." *British Journal of Criminology* 40: 321–39.

Rose, Nikolas. 2003. "Neurochemical Selves." *Society* 41 (1): 46–59.

Rosenfeld, Richard. 2004. "Terrorism and Criminology." Pp. 19–32 in *Terrorism and Counter-Terrorism: Criminological Perspectives*, ed. M. Deflem. Amsterdam: Elsevier.

Ross, Edward A. 1896. "Social Control." *American Journal of Sociology* 1 (5): 513–35.

Ross, Edward A. 1901. *Social Control: A Survey of the Foundations of Order*. New York: Macmillan.

Roth, Wendy D. and Jal D. Mehta. 2002. "The *Rashomon* Effect: Combining Positivist and Interpretivist Approaches in the Analysis of Contested Events." *Sociological Methods and Research* 31 (2): 131–73.

Rothman, David J. 2002a [1980]. *Conscience and Convenience: The Asylum and its Alternatives in Progressive America*, rev. edn. Hawthorne, NY: Aldine de Gruyter.

Rothman, David J. 2002b [1970]. *The Discovery of the Asylum*, rev. edn. Hawthorne, NY: Aldine de Gruyter.

Ruonavaara, Hannu. 1997. "Moral Regulation: A Reformulation." *Sociological Theory* 15 (3): 277–93.

Rye, Mark S. and Douglas Ullman. 1999. "The Successful Treatment of Long-Term Selective Mutism: A Case Study." *Journal of Behavior Therapy and Experimental Psychiatry* 30: 313–23.

Sageman, Marc. 2004. *Understanding Terror Networks*. Philadelphia: University of Pennsylvania Press.

Sampson, Robert J. and Dawn J. Bartusch. 1998. "Legal Cynicism and (Subcultural?) Tolerance of Deviance: The Neighborhood Context of Racial Differences." *Law and Society Review* 32 (4): 777–804.

Sampson, Robert J. and John H. Laub. 1993. *Crime in the Making: Pathways and Turning Points through Life*. Cambridge, MA: Harvard University Press.

Sariolghalam, Mahmood. 2003. "Understanding Iran: Getting Past Stereotypes and Mythology." *Washington Quarterly* 26 (4): 69–82.

Scheff, Thomas J. 1966. *Being Mentally Ill: A Sociological Theory*. Chicago: Aldine.

Schissel, Bernard. 1997. "Psychiatric Expansionism and Social Control: The Intersection of Community Care and State Policy." *Social Science Research* 26: 399–418.

Schmertmann, Carl P., Adansi A. Amankwaa, and Robert D. Long. 1998. "Three Strikes and You're Out: Demographic Analysis of Mandatory Prison Sentencing." *Demography* 35 (4): 445–63.

Schneiderman, Lawrence J. 2003. "The (Alternative) Medicalization of Life." *Journal of Law, Medicine and Ethics* 31 (2): 191–8.

Schram, Sanford F. 2000. "In the Clinic: The Medicalization of Welfare." *Social Text* 18 (1): 81–107.

Scott, James C. 1998. *Seeing Like a State: How Certain Schemes to Improve the Human Condition Have Failed*. New Haven, CT: Yale University Press.

Scott, Susie. 2006. "The Medicalisation of Shyness: From Social Misfits to Social Fitness." *Sociology of Health and Illness* 28 (2): 133–53.

Searight, H. Russell and Lesley McLaren. 1998. "Attention-Deficit Hyperactivity Disorder: The Medicalization of Behavior.' *Journal of Clinical Psychology in Medical Settings* 5 (4): 467–95.

Senechal de la Roche, Roberta. 1996. "Collective Violence as Social Control." *Sociological Forum* 11 (1): 97–128.

Shay, Shaul. 2004. *The Shahids: Islam and Suicide Attacks*, trans. R. Lieberman. New Brunswick, NJ: Transaction.

Shelden, Randall G. 2001. *Controlling the Dangerous Classes: A Critical Introduction to the History of Criminal Justice*. Boston: Allyn & Bacon.

Shelden, Randall G. 2004. "The Imprisonment Crisis in America: Introduction." *Review of Policy Research* 21 (1): 5–12.

Shibutani, Tamotsu. 1962. "Reference Groups and Social Control." Pp. 128–47 in *Human Behavior and Social Processes: An Interactionist Approach*, ed. A. M. Rose. Boston: Houghton Mifflin.

Short, John Rennie. 2006. *Urban Theory: A Critical Assessment.* Basingstoke: Palgrave Macmillan.

Siebert, Donald T. 1990. "The Aesthetic Execution of Charles I: Clarendon to Hume." Pp. 7–27 in *Executions and the British Experience from the 17th to the 20th Century: A Collection of Essays,* ed. W. B. Thesing. Jefferson, NC: McFarland.

Silver, Eric and Lisa L. Miller. 2004. "Sources of Informal Social Control in Chicago Neighborhoods." *Criminology* 42 (3): 551–83.

Simmel, Georg. 1950. *The Sociology of Georg Simmel,* trans. and ed. K. H. Wolff. New York: Free Press.

Simon, Jonathan and Malcolm M. Feeley. 2003. "The Form and Limits of the New Penology." Pp. 75–115 in *Punishment and Social Control,* enlarged 2nd edn, ed. T. G. Blomberg and S. Cohen. New York: Aldine de Gruyter.

Simons, Leslie Gordon, Ronald L. Simons, Rand D. Conger, and Gene H. Brody. 2004. "Collective Socialization and Child Conduct Problems: A Multilevel Analysis with an African American Sample." *Youth and Society* 35 (3): 267–92.

Skene, Allyson. 2002. "Rethinking Normativism in Psychiatric Classification." Pp. 114–27 in *Descriptions and Prescriptions: Values, Mental Disorders, and the DSMs,* ed. J. Z. Sadler. Baltimore: Johns Hopkins University Press.

Skodal, Andrew E. (ed.) 1998. *Psychopathology and Violent Crime.* Washington, DC: American Psychiatric Press.

Skolnick, Jerome H. 1966. *Justice without Trial: Law Enforcement in Democratic Society.* New York: Wiley.

Smith, Sandra Susan. 2005. " 'Don't Put my Name on It': Social Capital Activation and Job-Finding Assistance among the Black Urban Poor." *American Journal of Sociology* 111 (1): 1–57.

Somers, A. 1995. "W(h)ither Public Health?" *Public Health Reports* 110: 657–61.

Somers, Margaret R. 2005. "Beware Trojan Horses Bearing Social Capital: How Privatization Turned Solidarity into a Bowling Team." Pp. 233–74 in *The Politics of Method in the Human Sciences,* ed. G. Steinmetz. Durham, NC: Duke University Press.

Spence, Keith. 2005. "World Risk Society and War against Terror." *Political Studies* 53: 284–302.

Squires, Gregory D. and Jan Chadwick. 2006. "Linguistic Profiling: A Continuing Tradition of Discrimination in the Home Insurance Industry?" *Urban Affairs Review* 41 (3): 400–15.

Squires, Peter. 2006. "New Labour and the Politics of Antisocial Behaviour." *Critical Social Policy* 26 (1): 144–68.

Staples, William G. 2000. *Everyday Surveillance: Vigilance and Visibility in Postmodern Life.* Lanham, MD: Rowman & Littlefield.

Starr, Paul. 1982. *The Social Transformation of American Medicine.* New York: Basic Books.

Strong, P. M. 1979. "Sociological Imperialism and the Profession of Medicine: A Critical Examination of the Thesis of Medical Imperialism." *Social Science and Medicine* 13A: 199–215.

Sumner, Colin. 1997. "Social Control: The History and Politics of a Central Concept in Anglo-American Sociology." Pp. 1–33 in *Social Control and Political Order: European Perspectives at the End of the Century,* ed. R. Bergalli and C. Sumner. London: Sage.

Sumner, William Graham. 1906. *Folkways.* Boston: Ginn.

Sutherland, Edwin H. and Donald R. Cressey. 1955. *Principles of Criminology,* 5th edn, Chicago: J. B. Lippincott.

Szasz, Thomas S. 1961. *The Myth of Mental Illness.* New York: Dell.

Szasz, Thomas S. 1963. *Law, Liberty, and Psychiatry.* New York: Collier.

Szasz, Thomas. 2000. "Second Comment on 'Aristotle's Function Argument.'" *Philosophy, Psychiatry, and Psychology* 7 (1): 3–16.

Taylor, Claire. 2001. "The Relationship between Social and Self-Control: Tracing Hirschi's Criminological Career." *Theoretical Criminology* 5 (3): 369–88.

Thomas, Michael J. 2004. "Counteracting Terror: Group Design and Response Modalities." Pp. 91–110 in *Terrorism and Counter-Terrorism: Criminological Perspectives*, ed. M. Deflem. Amsterdam: Elsevier.

Thomson, Irene Taviss. 2005. "The Theory that Won't Die: From Mass Society to the Decline of Social Capital." *Sociological Forum* 20 (3): 421–48.

Toby, Jackson. 1998. "Medicalizing Temptation." *Public Interest* 130: 64–78.

Tonry, Michael. 1996. "Racial Politics, Racial Disparities, and the War on Crime." Pp. 165–86 in *Race, Crime, and Justice*, ed. B. A. Hudson. Brookfield, VT: Dartmouth University Press.

Tonry, Michael. 1999. "Why Are U.S. Incarceration Rates So High?" *Crime and Delinquency* 45 (4): 419–37.

Tonry, Michael and David P. Farrington. 2005. "Punishment and Crime across Space and Time." Pp. 1–39 in *Crime and Punishment in Western Countries, 1980–1999*, ed. M. Tonry and D. P. Farrington. Chicago: University of Chicago Press.

Tsui, Lokman. 2005. "Introduction." *China Information* 19 (2): 181–8.

Tuchman, Gaye. 1996. "Invisible Differences: On the Management of Children in Postindustrial Society." *Sociological Forum* 11 (1): 3–23.

Tucker, James. 1999. "Therapy, Organizations, and the State: A Blackian Perspective." Pp. 73–87 in *Counseling and the Therapeutic State*, ed. J. J. Chriss. New York: Aldine de Gruyter.

Unnever, James D., Francis T. Cullen, and Robert Agnew. 2006. "Why is 'Bad' Parenting Criminogenic? Implications from Rival Theories." *Youth Violence and Juvenile Justice* 4 (1): 3–33.

van Krieken, Robert. 1986. "Social Theory and Child Welfare: Beyond Social Control." *Theory and Society* 15 (3): 401–29.

Wakefield, Jerome C. 2002. "Values and the Validity of Diagnostic Criteria: Disvalued versus Disordered Conditions of Childhood and Adolescence." Pp. 148–64 in *Descriptions and Prescriptions: Values, Mental Disorders, and the DSMs*, ed. J. Z. Sadler. Baltimore: Johns Hopkins University Press.

Walker, Samuel. 1980. *Popular Justice: A History of American Criminal Justice*. New York: Oxford University Press.

Wang, Xia, Thomas G. Blomberg, and Spencer D. Li. 2005. "Comparison of the Educational Deficiencies of Delinquent and Nondelinquent Students." *Evaluation Review* 29 (4): 291–312.

Ward, Lester F. 1883. *Dynamic Sociology*, 2 vols. New York: Appleton.

Ward, Lester F. 1893. *Psychic Factors of Civilization*. Boston: Ginn.

Ward, Lester F. 1903. *Pure Sociology: On the Origins and Spontaneous Development of Society*. New York: Macmillan.

Ward, Lester F. 1906. *Applied Sociology: A Treatise on the Conscious Improvement of Society by Society*. Boston: Ginn.

Ward, Steven C. 2002. *Modernizing the Mind: Psychological Knowledge and the Remaking of Society*. Westport, CT: Praeger.

Warden, G. B. 1978. "Law Reform in England and New England, 1620 to 1660." *William and Mary Quarterly*, 3rd ser., 35 (4): 668–90.

Warner, Margaret. 1984. "Local Control versus National Interest: The Debate over Southern Public Health, 1878–1884." *Journal of Southern History* 50 (3): 407–28.

Weber, Max. 1968. *Economy and Society*, trans. and ed. Guenther Roth and Claus Wittich. New York: Bedminster Press.

Weber, Max. 1978 [1922]. "Excerpts from *Wirtschaft und Gesellschaft*." Pp. 33–42 in *Weber: Selections in Translation*, trans. E. Matthews, ed. W. G. Runciman. Cambridge: Cambridge University Press.

Weigert, Andrew J. 2003. "Terrorism, Identity, and Public Order: A Perspective from Goffman." *Identity* 3 (2): 93–113.

Weisheit, Ralph A. and John M. Klofas. 1998. "The Public Health Approach to Illicit Drugs." *Criminal Justice Review* 23 (2): 197–207.

Weiss, Harald E. and Lesley Williams Reid. 2005. "Low-Quality Employment Concentration and Crime: An Examination of Metropolitan Labor Markets." *Sociological Perspectives* 48 (2): 213–32.

Welch, Michael. 2003. "Ironies of Social Control and the Criminalization of Immigrants." *Crime, Law and Social Change* 39 (4): 319–37.

Welsh, Brandon C. and David P. Farrington. 2004. "Evidence-Based Crime Prevention: The Effectiveness of CCTV." *Crime Prevention and Community Safety* 6 (2): 21–33.

Western, Bruce, Mary Pattillo, and David Weiman. 2004. "Introduction." Pp. 1–18 in *Imprisoning America: The Social Effects of Mass Incarceration*, ed. M. Pattillo, D. Weiman, and B. Western. New York: Russell Sage Foundation.

Wexler, David B. and Bruce J. Winick (eds) 1996. *Law in a Therapeutic Key: Developments in Therapeutic Jurisprudence*. Durham, NC: Carolina Academic Press.

White, Susan. 1998. "Interdiscursivity and Child Welfare: The Ascent and Durability of Psycho-legalism." *Sociological Review* 46: 264–92.

Wiatrowski, Michael D., David B. Griswold, and Mary K. Roberts. 1981. "Social Control Theory and Delinquency." *American Sociological Review* 46 (5): 525–41.

Willert, Jeanette and Richard Willert. 2000. "An Ignored Antidote to School Violence: Classrooms that Reinforce Positive Social Habits." *American Secondary Education* 29 (1): 27–33.

Williams, Christopher R. and Bruce A. Arrigo. 2006. "Introduction: Philosophy, Crime, and Theoretical Criminology." Pp. 1–38 in *Philosophy, Crime, and Criminology*, ed. B. A. Arrigo and C. R. Williams. Urbana: University of Illinois Press.

Williams, Simon J. 2001. "Sociological Imperialism and the Profession of Medicine Revisited: Where Are We Now?" *Sociology of Health and Illness* 23 (2): 135–58.

Wilshire, Bruce W. 1982. *Role Playing and Identity: The Limits of Theatre as Metaphor*. Bloomington: Indiana University Press.

Wilson, James Q. and George L. Kelling. 1982. "Broken Windows." *Atlantic Monthly* 249 (3): 29–38.

Wilson, William Julius. 1987. *The Truly Disadvantaged: The Inner City, the Underclass, and Public Policy*. Chicago: University of Chicago Press.

Wilson, William Julius. 1991. "The Truly Disadvantaged Revisited: A Response to Hochschild and Boxill." *Ethics* 101 (3): 593–609.

Wilson, William Julius and Robert Aponte. 1985. "Urban Poverty." *Annual Review of Sociology* 11: 231–58.

Wingerter, J. Richard. 2003. *Science, Religion, and the Meditative Mind*. Lanham, MD: University Press of America.

Winick, Bruce J. and David B. Wexler (eds) 2003. *Judging in a Therapeutic Key: Therapeutic Jurisprudence and the Courts*. Durham, NC: Carolina Academic Press.

Withrow, Brian L. 2004. "Race-Based Policing: A Descriptive Analysis of the Wichita Stop Study." *Police Practice and Research* 5 (3): 223–40.

Wong, Kam C. 2006. "The USA PATRIOT Act: Some Unanswered Questions." *International Journal of the Sociology of Law* 34: 1–41.

Young, T. R. 1990. *The Drama of Social Life: Essays in Post-Modern Social Psychology.* New Brunswick, NJ: Transaction.

Zaretsky, Eli. 2002. "Trauma and Dereification: September 11 and the Problem of Ontological Security." *Constellations* 9 (1): 98–105.

Zola, Irving K. 1972. "Medicine as an Institution of Social Control." *Sociological Review* 20 (4): 487–504.

Index